MW01096789

Universal Yoga

The Bhagavad Gita for Modern Times

Prem Prakash

Yes International Publishers
Saint Paul, Minnesota

Cover artwork by Lorraine Wells.

For information and permissions address:
Yes International Publishers
1317 Summit Avenue
Saint Paul, MN 55105-2602
www.yespublishers.com
651-645-6808

Library of Congress Cataloging-in-Publication Data

Bhagavadgita. English & Sanskrit.
Universal yoga: the Bhagavad Gita for modern times / Prem Prakash
p. cm.
English and Sanskrit (Sanskrit in roman).
ISBN 978-0-936663-48-7
I. Prem Prakash, 1959-II. Title.
BL 1138.62.E5 2009c
294.5'624--dc22
2009009771

This book is dedicated to
Ma Devi and Swami Jaidev,
spiritual directors of the
Institute of the Himalayan Tradition,
in appreciation of
their work sharing authentic yoga
with the modern world
and their service to their guru,
Sri Swami Rama.

Contents

Introduction

AT THE AGE OF FIFTEEN, I borrowed from my grandmother a copy of *Siddhartha,* the fictional account of a young sage written by Herman Hesse. Reading the novel, I had an epiphany, even though I was not old enough to even know what that term meant. Regardless, I knew I had a powerful experience where I realized clearly that life is a spiritual pilgrimage and that I was going to pursue the spiritual path in search of wisdom.

Seeking to follow up on my revelation, I sought spiritual teachings in the only place I could think to look: in the local phone book! At that time, in the mid-1970s, in the entire Philadelphia area there was just one yoga center. Because the classes were all the way on the other side of town, my parents refused to drive me there in order to investigate this crazy thing called yoga. At that point in American history, virtually no one knew about yoga.

Now, of course, virtually everyone knows about yoga. Unfortunately, a great deal of what they know to be yoga is superficial and silly, for the American marketplace is doing to yoga what it does all too well: yoga is becoming trivialized and commercialized. Movie stars brag about their yoga prowess on television talk shows to enhance their celebrity, people get "buff" by practicing newfangled forms of power yoga, and complimenting someone on having a "yoga butt" has become a pick-up line in singles bars. Yoga is developing an image as just another trend, the latest and greatest for those who know what's in style.

Yoga has become a popular physical activity, like jogging, but yoga is not generally appreciated as a doorway into meditation and spiritual development. Too many teachers in the West have been inadequately trained in the deeper dimensions of what they are teaching. To become a yoga teacher traditionally takes many years of education, practice, and service. Young Westerners who are teaching yoga after participating in brief training program are like medical students who perform surgery after only a few weeks of school. The lack of preparedness frequently results in a misrepresentation of yoga that is as upside down as a headstand.

Yoga has been in this country for only little more than a century. The first of the great Indian yogis to come to America was Swami Vivekananda, India's representative to the World's Parliament of Religions, held in Chicago at the World's Fair of 1893. Considering yogic writings can be dated back 3000 years, with an oral tradition that is much older, yoga in this country is still in its infancy. People like me, who studied with the Indian gurus, are the first Westerners to teach yoga. What we teach, and how we teach, will influence the development of yoga in the West for generations to come. The transmission of yogic teachings from the land of Shiva and Ganesha to the home of Uncle Sam and Mickey Mouse is a historical phenomenon still in the making.

This transfer of yoga is a wonderful opportunity to bring greater health, healing, and a more enlightened consciousness to Western society. To accomplish this, however, requires that we have some understanding of the profundity of the teachings behind the practices. This will enable us to take full advantage of yoga and enjoy its two great rewards: *shanti* (peace) and *shakti* (vitality). If we do not, young aspirants may find phone books filled with yoga centers but they will not find the treasures that authentic yoga has to offer.

This presentation is intended to assist in the transmission of yoga from India to the West. This translation and commentary of the Bhagavad Gita (The Song of the Divine Being) is unique and, I believe, necessary. It is distinctive, written primarily for a Western audience by an American-born yogi-scholar who has immersed himself for the past thirty years in the study of the Bhagavad Gita and the practices prescribed in the text. This translation and commentary are accurate enough to satisfy any scholar and stand firmly in accord with the traditional teachings of the sages of India. At the same time, I feel this presentation is "down to earth" and can convey to the modern Westerner the spiritual fire burning in the Bhagavad Gita, a fire which has warmed yogis for millennia.

There are many translations of the Bhagavad Gita already available, and some of them are quite good. This effort is intended to communicate the Bhagavad Gita in an accurate but accessible manner to today's Western yoga aspirants. Most Westerners who have attempted to explain the Bhagavad Gita simply have not had the scholarly knowledge combined with years of yoga practice necessary to understand yoga philosophy in all its subtle profundity. The results have been readable, but somewhat superficial, explorations.

Only a yogi with years of personal experience can provide an insightful commentary on certain subtle teachings in the text. One example is the subject of meditation (see 5.27–28, 6.10–15). Only by personal realization can one understand the stages of meditative absorption and how this is significant within the greater context of the Bhagavad Gita. This *adhikari* (authority based on experience) becomes increasingly important if the Bhagavad Gita is to be utilized as intended, as a manual of the yoga path. This author has put thirty years of daily yoga and meditation practice into a commentary designed to assist the reader in practically implementing the Bhagavad Gita in daily life.

Finally, until one has spent time with an authentic guru, it is virtually impossible to appreciate the subtle dynamics at work in what makes up the core of the Bhagavad Gita: the dialogue between the student, Arjuna, and the teacher, Krishna. A good guru can guide the student in ways beyond his current understanding; the guru can push emotional buttons and indicate psychological blind spots the student doesn't even know he has.

While Westerners have often fallen short in presenting the Bhagavad Gita, Indian teachers have also been unsuccessful in effectively reaching contemporary Western yoga students, with a few terrific exceptions, such as the work of Sri Swami Rama and Sri Aurobindo. For reasons of nature and of nurture, Indian gurus often do not understand the unique needs of the modern Western yogi. The typical Western aspirant's religious and social background is vastly different from that of the Indian guide. He or she needs yoga philosophy explained in a style and idiom that is sensitive to a personality influenced by cultural forces such as the myth of original sin, democracy, equality between sexes, and MTV. The Bhagavad Gita is a fine wine of philosophy and inspiration, but it now needs to be poured into a new bottle if it is to be imbibed by contemporary yoga practitioners.

One of the principal weaknesses in the Indian presentations of the Bhagavad Gita is an emphasis on a world-denying and body-negative philosophy. This is largely the result of a monastic dominance of yoga during the 400-year occupation of India by first the Moguls and then the British, which fully ended with India's independence in 1947. During this period, the deeper yoga tradition was oppressed throughout the land but was kept alive high in the Himalayan Mountains. As it happened, the main residents of these Himalayan ashrams were celibate men, and their perspective became skewed over the centuries by their isolation from women, children, and a more diverse community. This Bhagavad Gita is part of a movement to re-affirm the original, universal yoga, which honored life in family and society as equally spiritual as monasticism. As we shall see, Krishna teaches that both spirit and flesh are sacred (see 13.19–23, 14.3–4). The ramifications of this vision permeate this work.

The Bhagavad Gita is comprised of 700 verses distributed throughout eighteen chapters. It is the most renowned portion of the Mahabharata, "The Story of the Great Bharata Dynasty," an extensive tale of Indian history, mythology, philosophy, and folklore. The Bhagavad Gita is the core text of the yoga tradition, providing a comprehensive depiction of the spiritual journey from both exoteric and esoteric perspectives. The philosophy taught in the Bhagavad Gita is the backbone of yoga practice and is studied in virtually every yoga community in India. In addition, it is not unreasonable to suggest that all of the world's nearly one billion Hindus, within and outside of India, worship along the lines of its teachings.

The Bhagavad Gita is a text with a variety of interwoven themes revolving around a core philosophy. The essential teaching is that there is one universal, infinite, divine consciousness of which everyone and everything is an expression. Each of the eighteen chapters is a starting point for exploring how one or more themes—including suffering, activity, meditation, duty, and peace—are related to this universal consciousness.

The way to attain this consciousness is through the practice of the universal yoga, as indicated in the title of this book. This is the original, comprehensive yoga of the seers of ancient India. Also called *sanatana dharma* (the eternal way of harmony), it is the tree from which the various specialized branches of yoga have grown (see 4.1–3). The universal yoga is the complete vision of yoga, where all of life is part of the divine picture (see ch. 11).

The universal yoga of the Bhagavad Gita is non-sectarian; there is no dogma to adopt, no sect to join, no god or guru who must be worshipped. There is no theological compulsion; every individual is free to cultivate his or her own notion of divinity (see 9.4–6). It is an inclusive yoga: embracing formal meditation (chapter 6) as well as practices to cultivate wisdom (chapter 4), devotion (chapter 12), and service to others (chapter 3).

Scholarly estimates of the origin of the Bhagavad Gita vary. There is also disagreement as to how much of what we know as the Bhagavad Gita was original material and how much is the result of later compilation. Linguistic analysis has shown there exist significant differences of style and other peculiarities in the text. When we study objective reports on Hindu religion made by those from outside the society—such as the Greeks and Buddhists—we find unbiased accounts revealing that the philosophy of the Bhagavad Gita was developed over the course of centuries. This author concurs with one prominent opinion, which is that the Bhagavad Gita made its literary appearance in the form we now hold approximately 2000–2500 years ago and that there has been no significant change since that time.

Authorship of the Bhagavad Gita is conventionally attributed to Sage Vyasa, a mythical figure who appears throughout Indian history. He is also said to be the author of the Vedas, the Puranas, and other texts which were written over periods of thousands of years. Vyasa, although a proper name, is also a term which means "editor" or "compiler." The yogic understanding of the texts compiled by Vyasa is that an individual may be duly inspired and write with the universal vision of the great yogis. Since yogis are encouraged to avoid fame, the text may be presented under the penname of an illustrious predecessor, such as Sage Vyasa. The orthodox may argue that one Vyasa was indeed the author of the Vedas and associated literature, but we will decline to enter into this dispute as the matter is essentially irrelevant. The Bhagavad Gita is not a text for those obsessed with historical fact; it is for those who wish to follow the path of the yogic sages. It does not matter when, where, or by whom a map was drawn if it provides accurate directions.

The Bhagavad Gita commences on the battlefield of Kurukshetra with an introduction of many significant characters from the Mahabharata. The rest of the text consists primarily of a dialogue between the two principals, Krishna and Arjuna. Arjuna is a member of the Pandava clan, who have been unfairly and unlawfully treated by their cousins, the Kauravas. Krishna is widely known from other contexts as an incarnation of Vishnu, God as Preserver. In the setting of the Bhagavad Gita, however, Krishna is first presented as Arjuna's charioteer and friend. Soon after, Arjuna relates to Krishna as his teacher, then later as a deity.

The interaction of Arjuna and Krishna takes place on the precipice of battle. The conflict between the Pandavas and Kauravas has escalated to war, and both sides are preparing to fight. As Arjuna surveys the situation, he becomes pained by the nature of the conflict and his relationship to many of his enemies. He enters into a deep despair about the hostility around him and life in general. His immediate, personal questions in the early chapters lead to a wide-ranging discussion in which Arjuna desperately seeks for the keys that will open the door to peace and freedom from suffering.

The yogic tradition holds that each of the 700 verses in the Bhagavad Gita is a *mantra* (that which nourishes the mind). One is encouraged, therefore, to approach the text in a contemplative mood. The dialogue between Krishna and Arjuna is to be savored, as it is a reflection of the inner exchange taking place between the individual soul and the infinite consciousness. The sensitive reader can enter directly into this yogic experience through the doorway of the Bhagavad Gita.

We would do well to remember the wisdom of the yogic sages and the brilliance in their style of teaching. The title itself reveals how this text should be conceived: as gita, a "song." Each verse is a note in a subtle and beautiful melody. Not intended for dry intellectual speculation, this tune is intended to inspire one to sing along, to dance along, and to add his voice to the divine chorus.

I began my journey toward yoga by leaving Philadelphia and entering college as a philosophy major, excited to learn the truth from the sages I believed would be my professors. I had imagined something akin to the ashrams of India or Plato's Academy. In my naiveté, I was surprised to find instead a typical, mundane university department. My professors were intelligent, but they were not wise. They knew how to use their minds, but they did not know how to transcend their minds. I eventually dropped out of college and participated in many of the seemingly obligatory rites of those trying to find meaning in the world during those times—I hitchhiked cross-country, experimented with drugs, and danced like crazy to the Grateful Dead.

After reading a number of popular books on yoga, I realized I needed a qualified teacher if I were going to actually penetrate the yogic world. I actively sought teachers who appeared to have integrity, promising if they would take the time to teach me, I would take the time to practice what I learned. I have had the tremendous privilege to study formally with several authentic gurus. In particular, I practiced yoga and meditation under Baba Hari Dass, who gave me permission to teach others. I also learned systems of tantric and vedic worship from Shree Maa and Swami Satyananda Saraswati. Finally, I have also benefited immensely from the inspiration and guidance of Karunamayi Ma and Sri Swami Rama.

It has been clear to me for a long time that I would not renounce the world and live as a monk in India. Instead, I am married and have a son. In 1991, I founded the Green Mountain School of Yoga in Middlebury, Vermont, where I serve as Director, teaching the universal yoga described in this book. I also participate in my community: I attend parent-teacher conferences, pay taxes, and cheer for my favorite football team. I am a strong believer that yoga in the West will be a yoga of those who participate in family life and are active in the world. My path might be described as an "engaged yogi," where I seek for my formal yoga and meditation practices to influence my entire life and benefit my family, community, and the greater world.

I believe the scholar will find this text an accurate translation of the Bhagavad Gita from Sanskrit into English. I hope the casual reader will find this rendering provides a feel for the pulse of Indian poetic philosophy. And I pray the spiritual aspirant will find in these pages a handbook of infinite consciousness.

A Note on Names and References

Throughout the Bhagavad Gita, the names of the characters have symbolic and significant meanings. It is essential to understand the symbolism of the various warriors if the true nature of the conflict on the battlefield of Kurukshetra is to be properly appreciated. As Krishna will teach, Arjuna's real enemies are not his external foes, they are his own detrimental attitudes and behaviors. Arjuna's negative qualities are symbolized by the Kauravas, and his positive traits by the Pandavas.

In this text, the first time an individual is mentioned, his symbolism is followed in parenthesis. For example, "King Dhirtarashtra (Blind Mind)." For ease of reading, subsequent use of a name does not include a description of its symbolism. Names and their symbolism are organized for the reader in Appendix 1.

Chapter 1

Arjuna Vishada Yoga
The Yoga of Arjuna's Despair

Verse 1

dhṛtarāṣṭra uvāca
dharmakṣetre kauravakṣetre samavetā yuyutsavaḥ
māmakāḥ pāṇḍavāś caiva kimakurvata saṁjaya (1)

1. King Dhritarashtra (Blind Mind) said: O Sanjaya (Objectivity), on the *dharmakshetre* (The Divine Arena of Harmony) of Kurukshetra (The Field of Activity), what took place when my people, the Kauravas (Foolish Activities) and the Pandavas (Intelligent Activities) gathered eager for battle?

This first verse does not immediately place us on the battlefield of Kurukshetra with Arjuna and his despair. We instead find King Dhritarashtra asking his minister, Sanjaya, to tell him about the events unfolding on the battlefield. King Dhritarashtra is blind, and Sanjaya has a psychic power by which he can see events at distant places. This scene appears to be like a fairy tale, in which a king asks a magician to serve as his eyes. Symbolically, however, a much more profound story is unfolding.

Each of us, in our unenlightened condition, is spiritually blind like King Dhritarashtra. We need help to perceive accurately the nature of our life and activities. We need the objectivity of Sanjaya, the ability to perceive ourselves and others without the distorting influence of self-centered motivations and projections. When we adopt Sanjaya's objective eyes, we recognize the entire creation is a dharmakshetre, a divine arena of harmony, and our life is a Kurukshetra, a field of activity within that arena.

Verse 2

saṁjaya uvāca
dṛṣṭvā tu pāṇḍavānīkaṁ vyūḍhaṁ duryodhanastadā
ācāryamupasaṅgamya rājā vacanamabravīt (2)

2. Sanjaya said: King Duryodhana (Selfish Desire) gazed upon the Pandavas in battle formation. He then approached his teacher Drona (Habits) and spoke.

King Duryodhana is the leader of the Kauravas, the cruel and devious cousins of the Pandavas. He is their king, as selfish desire is the royal cause of all other ego-centeredness that obstructs spiritual life. King Duryodhana looks out upon his enemies, the Pandavas, the spiritually enhancing qualities, and describes what he views to his teacher, Drona (Habits).

Interestingly, but not surprisingly from a symbolic perspective, Drona is the teacher of both parties in the battle, the Kauravas and the Pandavas. Habits lead to the formations of both positive and negative traits. Habits create and support the formations of *samskaras* (seeds). These seeds sit in an individual's consciousness, usually in the subconscious level, and produce motivations and desires, resulting in positive or negative behaviors. Positive seeds sprout plants of the Pandava variety; negative seeds produce a garden of Kauravas.

Verse 3

paśyaitāṁ pāṇḍuputrāṇāmācārya mahatīṁ camūm
vyūḍhāṁ drupadaputreṇa tava śiṣyeṇa dhīmatā (3)

3. Behold, my teacher, the mighty army of our opposition, the Pandavas, is marshaled in formation by your wise disciple, Dhrishtadyumna (Lucid Intuition), the son of Drupada (Dispassion).

King Duryodhana begins his description of the opposing army by recognizing and, perhaps, unintentionally praising his opponent, Dhrishtadyumna (Lucid Intuition). Intuition is the quality of the psyche which enables an individual to become fully human. Intuition and intellect are the two facets of the *buddhi* (human intelligence). The nature of intelligence is an important topic and will be dealt with more fully later in the text. For now, suffice to say that a person without intuition is only using half their intelligence.

It is worth noting that intuition is identified as the child of dispassion. It is dispassion, the willingness to be honestly objective, that enables one to directly perceive with the faculty of intuition. Without dispassion, it is inevitable that one's perceptions will be clouded by selfishly motivated hopes and fears. Dispassion is not a lack of love or enthusiasm; it is the ability to remain patiently neutral while traversing the pilgrimage of life.

Verses 4–6

atra śūrā maheṣvāsā bhīmārjunasamā yudhi
yuyudhāno virāṭaśca drupadaśca mahārathaḥ (4)

dhṛṣṭaketuścekitānaḥ kāśirājaśca vīryavān
purujit kuntibhojaśca śaibyaśca narapuṅgavaḥ (5)

yudhāmanyuśca vikrānta uttamaujāsca vīryavān
saubhadro draupadeyāśca sarva eva mahārathāḥ (6)

4. Present are dauntless warriors and mighty archers, all skillful in battle, such as Bhima (Steady Breath), Arjuna (Pure Aspiration), Yuyudhana (Spiritual Practices), Virata (Illuminating Meditation), and Drupada aride on his great chariot;

5. Dhrishtaketu (Penetrating Insight), Chekitana (Remembrance of Immortality), the heroic Kashiraja (Noble Radiance), Purujit (One Pointedness), Kuntibhoja (Divine Invocation), and the strong-willed Shaibya (Unselfish Will);

6. The strong Yudhamanyu (Conquering the Mind), the heroic Uttamaujas (Peak Virility), the son of Saubhadra (Splendor), Abhimanya (Mental Focus), and the sons of Draupadi (Divine Energy), all of great chariots.

Additional warriors on the side of the Pandavas are named. Symbolically, these are more of the positive qualities that support intelligent activities and spiritual development.

Verses 7–10

asmākaṁ tu viśiṣṭā ye tānnibodha dvijottama
nāyakā mama sainyasya saṁjñārtham tānbravīmi te (7)

bhavānbhīṣmaśca karṇaśca kṛpaśca samitiṁjayaḥ
aśvatthāmā vikarṇaśca saumadattistathaiva ca (8)

anye ca bahavaḥ śūrā madrthe tyaktajīvitāḥ
nānāśastrapraharaṇāḥ sarve yuddhaviśāradāḥ (9)

aparyāptaṁ tadasmākaṁ balaṁ bhīṣmābhirakṣitam
paryaptaṁ tvidmeteṣāṁ balaṁ bhīmābhirakṣitam (10)

7. Know also, O Drona, Best of the Twice Born, the distinguished leaders of my army. Please acknowledge their names:

8. Yourself, Bhishma (Fear), Karna (Arrogant Individuality), the ever-victorious in conflict Kripa (Giving to Get), Ashvatthaman (Stubbornness), Vikarna (Insincerity), and the son of Somadatta (Poisoned Nectar), Bhurishravas (Negative Patterns).

9. Also present are numerous additional warriors who would lay down their lives for me, armed with a variety of weapons, all skilled in military arts.

10. Our forces led by Bhishma appear unlimited but somehow seem insufficient. Their forces led by Bhima appear limited but somehow seem sufficient.

King Duryodhana presents to Drona the identities of some of the primary soldiers in his army, fighting on behalf of the Kauravas, supporting foolish activities. He refers to Drona as "Best of the Twice Born," the Twice Born being those of the highest social class of the time, the *brahmins* (see 4.13, 18.41–42). For those of limited spirituality, social position determines the status of a person, and there is no better way than flattery to ingratiate oneself to a superior.

He also makes a statement about their degree of commitment, how the soldiers are willing to fight to the death. Certainly foolish activities, under the tutelage of habits, have the same degree of determination and allegiance as do positive traits. In addition, King Duryodhana acknowledges that even though his opponent's army seems smaller and more limited, somehow their power appears greater. This reflects the hard reality that everyone, no matter how immersed in ignorance, recognizes on some deep level the inherent power of goodness over ignorance.

Verses 11–13

ayanyeṣu ca sarveṣu yathābhāgamavasthitāḥ
bhīṣmamevābhirakṣantu bhavantaḥ sarva eva hi (11)

tasya saṁjanayanharṣaṁ Kauravavṛddhaḥ pitāmahaḥ
siṁhanādaṁ vinadyoccaiḥ śaṅkhaṁ dadhmau pratāpavān (12)

tataḥ śaṅkhāśca bheryaśca paṇavānakagomukhaḥ
sahasaivābhyahanyanta sa śabdastumolo 'bhavat (13)

11. All soldiers, attention! Stand guard in your positions in our established formation and protect Bhishma.

12. To cheer Duryodhana, Bhishma, the patriarch of the family, blew his conch shell like a roaring lion.

13. The others joined Bhishma and sounded their conch shells, drums, cymbals, and trumpets in a tumultuous clamor.

Bhishma (Fear) is the leader of the army of foolish activities and must be protected at all costs. The nature of fear, however, is to be afraid, so regardless of the manner in which fear hides behind arrogance and parades in conceit, it is always and in all ways frightened. Fear may blow "like a roaring lion," but it is never more than a frightened kitten.

When the Kauravas strike up their military band, the conches are not melodious; rather they are a cacophony of non-harmonious sounds. Negative forces can never harmonize, even with each other, just as thieves will steal from anyone, even other thieves.

Verses 14–19

tatāḥ śvetairhayairyukte mahati syandane sthitau
mādhavaḥ pāṅḍavaiścaiva divyau śaṅkhau pradadhmatuḥ (14)

pāñcajanyaṁ hṛṣīkeśo devadattam dhanaṁjayaḥ
pauṇḍraṁ dadhmau mahāśaṅkhaṁ bhīmakarmā vṛkodaraḥ (15)

anatavijayaṁ rājā kuntīputro yudhiṣṭhiraḥ
nakulaḥ sahadevaśca sughoṣmaṇipuṣpakau (16)

kāśyaśca parameṣvāsaḥ śikhaṇḍī ca mahārathaḥ
dhṛṣṭadyumno virāṭaśca sātyakiścāparājitaḥ (17)

drupado draupadeyāśca sarvaśaḥ pṛthivīpate
saubhadraścamahābāhuḥ śaṅkhāndadhamuḥ pṛthakpṛthak (18)

sa ghoṣo dhārtarāṣṭrāṇāṁ hṛdayāni vyadārayat
nabhaśca pṛthivīṁ caiva tumulo vyanunādayan (19)

14. On the opposing side, standing in their great chariot yoked to white steeds, Madhava (Krishna as The Sweet One) and Pandava (Arjuna as The Son of Intelligent Activities) simultaneously blew their divine conches.

15. Hrishikesh (Krishna as Master of the Senses), blew his conch, Panchajanya (Cause of the Five Elements); Dhananjaya (Arjuna as Winner of Wealth) blew his conch, Devadatta (Gift of the Gods); and Vikrodara (Bhima as He of Awesome Deeds) blew his great conch, Paundra (Causes Dissolution).

16. King Yudhishthira (Commitment), the son of Queen Kunti (Invocation), blew Anantavijaya (Infinite Victory), Nakula (Without Pain) and Sahadeva (Godlike) blew Sughosha (Clear Sound) and Manipushpaka (Vessel of Jewels), respectively.

17. The excellent archer King of Kashi (Noble Radiance), the great charioteer, Shikhandi (Residing at the Peak), Dhrishtadyumna, Virata, and the undefeatable Satyaki (Truthful Nature),

18. Drupada, the sons of Draupadi, and the mighty-armed son of Saubhadra, Abhimanya, all blew their conches together, O Dhritarashtra, King of the Earth.

19. That explosion of sound reverberated throughout the heavens and earth, piercing the hearts of Dhritarashtra's sons.

The Pandavas blow their conches, releasing a powerful sound wave which reverberated throughout the heavens and earth. The sound of the Kauravas, the limited and transitory power of negativity, is quite impotent and short-lived. This is why we see the instability over time of corrupt people, their societies, and their organizations. The power of positive energy, however, is an immense force which reaches into hearts of beings throughout time and space. Love, being the fullest expression of positive energy, is eternal and omnipresent. This is why love truly holds the key to all power and glory.

This depiction of positive and negative energies is not poetic fancy but a factual description of how energy is transmitted. Love reaches everywhere and is available to any being who opens to its influence. Like a radio signal sent from an infinitely powerful transmitter, love is available to anyone who tunes to the proper channel. Love is an energy which never ceases and never diminishes. All the love in the universe, since the dawn of time, is still active and will forever be so. Any love manifest, be it from from the conches of the Pandavas or the kindness of contemporary aspirants, adds to the immensity of universal love.

Verse 20

atha vyavasthitāndṛṣṭvā dhārtarāṣṭrānkapidhvajaḥ
pravṛtte śastrasaṁpāte dhanurudyamya pāṇḍavaḥ (20)

20. Then, Pandava, under the banner of the monkey Hanuman, on the precipice of battle, took up his bow.

Arjuna's chariot flies the banner of Hanuman, the famous Hindu monkey-god. Hanuman's father is Vayu, the wind god, and his mother, Anjani, is a monkey. As such, Hanuman is half mammal and half divinity, the yogic understanding of a human being. Hanuman is the symbol of the *guru*, the intermediary between humanity and divinity. Like Christ, the guru is the mediator between man and God. The savior as monkey is a wonderful depiction, so evidently symbolic that somber religious dogmatism can rather easily be avoided. It is almost laughable to imagine an inquisition or holy war being fought on behalf of a monkey.

Verses 21–28

hṛṣīkeśaṁ tadā vākyamidamāha mahīpate
senayorubhayormadhye rathaṁ sthāpaya me 'cyuta (21)

yāvadetānnirīkṣe 'haṁ yoddukāmānavasthitān
kairmayā saha yoddhavyamasminraṇasamudyame (22)

yotsyamānānavekṣe 'ham ya ete 'tra samāgatāḥ
dhārtarāṣṭrasya durbuddherryuddhe priyacikīrṣavah (23)

saṁjaya uvāca
evamukto hṛṣīkeśo guḍākeśena bhārata
senayorubhayormadhye sthāpayitvā rathottamam (24)

bhīṣmadroṇapramukhataḥ sarveṣāṁ ca mahīkṣitām
uvāca pārtha paśyaitān samavetānkurūniti (25)

tatrāpaśyatstitānpārthaḥ pitṝnatha pitāmahān
ācāryānmātulānbhrātṝnputrānpautrānsakhīṁstathā (26)

śvasurān suhṛdaścaiva senayorubhayorapi
tānsamīkṣya sa kaunteyaḥ sarvān bandhūnavasthitān (27)

kṛpayā parayāviṣṭo viṣīdannidamabravīt
dṛṣṭvemaṁ svajanaṁ kṛṣṇa yuyutsuṁ samupasthitam (28)

21. Sanjaya conveyed to Dhritarashtra that Arjuna then spoke to Hrishikesh. Arjuna said: O Achuta (Krishna as He Who is Without Lapse), position my chariot in the middle between the opposing armies.

22. In this way I can see who are composed to fight in this epic battle.

23. I wish to look upon those who are eagerly assembled to fight on behalf of the evil-minded son of Dhritarashtra, Duryodhana.

24. Sanjaya said to Bharata (From the Land Dedicated to Light) that Hrishikesh, as requested by Gudakesha (Arjuna as Conqueror of Sleep), drove that fine chariot into the center between the two armies.

25. Facing Bhishma, Drona, and all the other earthly kings, Krishna said: Behold, Partha (Arjuna as Son of Excellent Actions), the Kauravas are gathered here.

26. There, Partha did indeed behold—seeing fathers, grandfathers, teachers, uncles, brothers, sons, grandsons, and also friends.

27. He saw fathers-in-laws, comrades, and relatives in both armies. Kaunteya (Arjuna as Son of Divine Actions), felt himself

28. Invaded by a deep pity. He spoke with sorrow these words: O Krishna, I see before me my very own people, arrayed in formation, ready to fight.

At Arjuna's request, Krishna drives his chariot into the center of the field where the battle is about to begin. Arjuna takes in the panorama of the assembled warriors. He recognizes his familial and social bonds with many of the warriors in both armies. Many of those on opposing sides were blood relatives; they had shared their lives together. The poignancy of the situation and the impending warfare between members of the same family produce in Arjuna a deep sorrow.

Verse 29

sīdanti mama gātrāṇi mukhaṁ pariśuṣyati
vepathuśca śarīre ma romaharṣaśca jāyate (29)

29. My limbs grow weak, my mouth dries up, my body trembles, and my hair stands on end.

In his arising despair and confusion, Arjuna experiences a variety of powerful physical feelings as his emotional pain manifests in his body. Interestingly, Arjuna again undergoes many of these same symptoms later when he has the revelation of seeing the universal form of God (11.14). This demonstrates that the border between spiritual agony and ecstasy is a fine line. Only by passing through the dark night of the soul does one become qualified to enter into divine light. Only an individual sensitive enough to fully feel his pain is capable of experiencing his bliss.

Verses 30–46

gāṇḍīvaṁ sraṁsate hastāttvakcaiva paridahyate
na ca śaknomyavasthātuṁ bhramatīva ca me manaḥ (30)

nimittāni ca paśyāmi viparītāni keśava
na ca śreyo 'nupaśyāmi hatvā svajanamāhave (31)

na kāṅkṣe vijayaṁ kṛṣṇa na ca rājyaṁ sukhāni ca
kiṁ no rājyena govinda kiṁ bhogairjīvitena vā (32)

yeṣāmarthe kāṅkṣitaṁ no rājyaṁ bhogāḥ sukhāni ca
ta ime 'vasthitā yuddhe prāṇāṁstyaktvā dhanāni ca (33)

ācāryāḥ pitaraḥ putrāstathaiva ca pitāmahāḥ
mātulā śvaśurāḥ pautrāḥ śyālā sambandhinastathā (34)

etānna hantumicchāmi ghnato 'pi madhusūdana
api trailokyarājyasya hetoḥ ki/m nu mahīkṛte (35)

nihatya dhārtarāṣṭrānnaḥ kā prītiḥ syājjanārdana
pāpamevāśrayedasmānhatvaitānātatāyinaḥ (36)

tasmānnārha vayaṁ hantuṁ dhārtarāṣṭrān svabāndhavān
svajanaṁ hi kathaṁ hatvā sukhinaḥ syāma mādhava (37)

yadyapyete na paśyanti lobhopahatacetasaḥ
kulakṣayakṛtaṁ doṣaṁ mitradrohe ca pātakam (38)

kathaṁ na jñeyamasmābhiḥ pāpādasmānnivartitum
kulakṣayakṛtaṁ doṣam prapaśyadbhirjanārdana (39)

kulakṣaye praṇaśyanti kuladharmāḥ sanātanāḥ
dharme naṣṭe kulaṁ kṛtsnamadharmo 'bhibhavatyuta (40)

adharmābhibhavātkṛṣṇa praduṣyanti kulastriyaḥ
strīṣu duṣṭāsu vārṣṇeya jāyate varṇasaṅkaraḥ (41)

saṅkaro narakāyaiva kulaghnānāṁ kulasya ca
patanti pitaro hyeṣāṁ luptapiṇḍodakakriyāḥ (42)

doṣairetaiḥ kulaghnānāṁ varṇasaṅkarakārakaiḥ
utsādyante jātidharmāḥ kuladharmāśca śāśvatāḥ (43)

utsannakuladharmāṇāṁ manuṣyāṅāṁ janārdana
karake 'niyataṁ vāso bhavatītyanuśuśruma (44)

aho bata mahatpāpaṁ kartuṁ vyavasitā vayam
yadrājyasukhalobhena hantuṁ svajanamudyatāḥ (45)

yadi māmapratīkāramaśastraṁ śastrapāṇayaḥ
dhārtarāṣṭrā raṇe hanyustanme kṣemataraṁ bhavet (46)

30. My bow, Gandiva (Terrifying Song), slides from my grasp, my skin feels aflame, I am weak-kneed, and my mind is spinning.

31. I see negative omens, O Keshava (Krishna as He with Beautiful Hair), and I cannot envision anything positive that can arise from killing my own family in battle.

32. O Krishna, I am not seeking vain victory, kingdom, or pleasures. For those like us, O Govinda (Krishna as Caretaker of the Senses), what value can be placed on selfish engagements or even our individual lives?

33. The very ones for whom we would procure kingdom, enjoyments, and pleasures are standing here, caring more for battle than their wealth or lives.

34. They are our teachers, fathers, sons, grandfathers, uncles, fathers-in-law, grandsons, brothers-in-law, and other relatives.

35. O Madhusudhana (Krishna as Slayer of Excess), I would never want to kill them, regardless of their attack on me, not for the kingdoms of the three worlds, so much less for an earthly throne.

36. What delight can be ours, O Janardana (Krishna as The Answer to Prayers), for destroying the sons of Dhritarashtra? Sin would be our only accomplishment for slaying these foolish renegades.

37. It simply cannot be proper to slay our kinsmen, the sons of Dhritarashtra. Indeed, how could we ever be happy, O Madhava, if we kill our very own?

38. Even if the others have their intelligence overshadowed by greed and cannot see disaster when families are destroyed, nor crime in treachery to friends,

39. Why should we not display wisdom and turn away from this sin, we who do see wrong in the destruction of the family and social structure, O Janardana?

40. In the destruction of family, immemorial traditions perish, and the loss of these traditions destroys the righteousness of family life.

41. When unrighteousness is prevalent, O Varshneya (Krishna as Scion of Power), women of the family become corrupt. When women become corrupted, social structures become disorganized.

42. This disorganization carries to hell the families themselves and those who bring its destruction. The ancestors fall when deprived of their ritual offerings of food and water.

43. By the misdeeds of the destroyers of family, causing disorganization of social structures, the immemorial traditions of community and family are destroyed.

44. We have heard, O Janardana, that people whose traditions are destroyed end up in hell.

45. Alas! A great sin we commit for striving to kill our own people due to greed for the pleasures of kingdom.

46. It would be better for me if the Sons of Dhritarashtra, weapons in hand, should slay me, unarmed and unresisting, in the battle.

Arjuna provides Krishna with an extensive monologue, describing the horrors of the situation and his reluctance to engage in war. He points out the ethical, social, and personal suffering that will arise from the battle regardless of which side emerges victorious. His perspective is that of any sensitive person confronted with the horror of war, and it is also reflective of the religious traditions of his place and time, with his reference to rituals and offerings to ancestors.

An additional point worth mentioning before Krishna responds, is that Arjuna's concerns turn out to be true. The Mahabharata reveals that after the battle the families and societies were torn asunder, with great cost to the well-being of all. In fact, the surviving Pandavas were so devastated by the effects of the war that they left their homes and families, retreating to the Himalayas to live out their lives in penance.

Verse 47

saṁjaya uvāca
evamuktvārjunaḥ saṁkhye rathopastha upāviśat
visṛjya saśaraṁ cāpaṁ śokasaṁvignamānasaḥ (47)

47. Sanjaya said: Thus having spoken on the field of war, Arjuna sat on the seat of his chariot, casting away his bow and arrows, his mind overwhelmed with despair.

Arjuna has entered the dark night of his soul. His yoga of despair has reached its zenith. His inner power has waned, reflected in his casting aside his weapons. Arjuna is depicted in the Mahabharata as a great warrior, a true hero. Here, on the precipice of battle, he is simply a broken man.

Chapter 2

Samkhya Yoga
The Yoga of Essential Principles

Verses 1–3

saṁjaya uvāca
taṁ tathā kṛpayāviṣṭamaśrupūrṇākulekṣaṇam
viṣīdantamidaṁ vākyamuvāca madhusūdanaḥ (1)

śribhagavānuvāca
kutastvā kaśmalamidaṁ viṣame samupasthitam
anāryajuṣṭamasvargyamakīrtikaramarjuna (2)

klaibyaṁ mā sma gamaḥ pārtha naitattvayyupapadyate
kṣudraṁ hṛdayadaurbalyaṁ tyaktvottiṣṣtha paraṁtapa (3)

1. Sanjaya said: To Arjuna—who was filled with pity, tears filling his eyes, disturbed and despairing—Madhusudhana spoke these words.

2. Shri Bhagavan (Krishna as The Divine Being) said: At this crucial moment, O Arjuna, how does depression arise? So unfitting is this for a nobleman, leading not to heaven but to disgrace.

3. O Partha, surrender not to this mood of impotence; it is not fitting of your true character. Rid yourself of these feeble emotions. Arise, O Parantapa (Arjuna as Destroyer of Foes).

This chapter begins with Krishna's response to Arjuna's painful lament in the previous chapter. Many new students of the Bhagavad Gita find it surprising that Krishna does not seem to respect Arjuna's heartfelt emotions. He doesn't even acknowledge the validity of Arjuna's arguments. In fact, the starting point of his response is a rather severe rebuke to Arjuna's character, calling Arjuna and his feelings unfitting, disgraceful, impotent, and feeble.

When a student first comes to an authentic spiritual teacher, he may expect a gentle and sentimental welcome. He may anticipate an appreciative validation of his sincerity. After all, thinks the Arjuna-like student, one who acknowledges the pain inherent in conflict is certainly noble. The teacher, however, sees through the student's presentation and responds instead to the core issue—the spiritual fact that the student does not know his true Self. As this subject will be discussed in detail, for now let us simply enjoy the drama unfolding as Arjuna reacts to Krishna.

Verses 4–6

arjuna uvāca
kathaṁ bhīṣmamahaṁ saṁkhye droṇaṁ ca madhusūdhana
iṣubhiḥ pratiyotsyāmi pūjārhāvarisūdana (4)

gurūnahatvā hi mahānubhāvān
śreyo bhoktuṁ bhaikṣyamapīha loke
hatvārthakāmāṁstu gurūnihaiva bhuñjīya
bhogān rudhirapradigdhān (5)

na caitadvidmaḥ kataranno garīyo yadvā jayema
yadi vā no jayeyuḥ
yāneva hatvā na jijīviṣāmaste 'vasthitāḥ
pramukhe dhārtarāṣṭrāḥ (6)

4. Arjuna said: How could I, O Madhusudhana, engage in armed combat with Bhishma and Drona, both worthy of adoration, O Arisudana (Krishna as Slayer of Enemies)?

5. It would be better for me to desist from slaying my teachers and live in this world on beggar's fare. Even though these teachers have become fortune hunters, to kill them would leave blood stains on every aspect of my life.

6. Nor is it apparent which is the advantageous outcome, that we win or that they are victorious over us. Killing the Sons of Dhritarashtra would leave us with no desire to live.

Arjuna continues his argument against fighting. As we listen to Arjuna, we are struck with the seeming reasonableness of his position. Arjuna is an emotional man at this point, and he seems grounded in a reasonable empathy and concerned spirituality. He does not seek for worldly gain and only wants to avoid unnecessary fighting. He is even willing to sacrifice his life by not fighting, if that would be the proper thing.

The enlightened ones, however, have eyes which see and ears which hear. Even though Arjuna's speech is filled with lofty sentiments, Krishna will soon reveal how Arjuna is still essentially selfish. Arjuna's real reluctance is uncovered when we remember his cousins symbolically represent his closely-held negative qualities. The individual at this stage of development has begun to glimpse that many of his previous influences have become detrimental to his spiritual growth. Yet he remains attached to his selfish habits, feeling that to eliminate them would mean the end of much that gives his life meaning and fulfillment.

Verse 7

kārpaṇyadoṣopahatasvabhāvaḥ pṛcchāmi tvāṁ dharmasaṁmūḍhacetāḥ
yacchreyaḥ syānniścitaṁ brūhi tanme
śiṣyaste 'haṁ śādhi māṁ tvāṁ prapannam (7)

7. I am being attacked by some weakness in my emotions. My mind is confused about proper conduct. I ask you, tell me what is clearly the best course of action. I submit myself as your disciple. Please instruct me as I have come to you for refuge.

Arjuna, in an apparently humble manner, acknowledges his confusion, pain, and lack of understanding. He seems to recognize that he needs the aid of one wiser than himself. He identifies Krishna as his guru and claims to offer himself in discipleship.

Verses 8–9

na hi prapaśyāmi mamāpanudyādyacchokamucchoṣaṇamindriyāṇām
avāpya bhūmāvasapatnamṛddhaṁ rājyaṁ surāṇāmapi cādhipayatam (8)

saṁjaya uvāca
evamuktvā hṛṣīkeśaṁ guḍākeśaḥ paraṁtapaḥ
no yotsya iti govindamuktvā tūṣṇīṁ babhūva ha (9)

8. I have no vision as to what will shatter this distress which saps the strength of my senses, not even if I were to obtain a vast kingdom of earthly wealth or lordship over the gods.

9. Sanjaya said: Having thus spoken to Hrishikesh, the one known as Gudakesha and Parantapa said to Govinda: "I will not fight," and fell into silence.

Before Krishna even has a chance to respond to his new self-proclaimed disciple, Arjuna is again pressing his case. Even though Arjuna recognizes he lacks vision as to the proper course, and even though he has identified himself as Krishna's disciple, he does not even wait for his teacher to respond. Arjuna insists upon reaching his own decision and concludes with his own course of action—to lay down his arms and refuse to engage.

Verse 10

tamuvāca hṛṣīkeśaḥ prahasanniva bhārata
senayorubhayormadhye viṣīdantamidaṁ vacaḥ (10)

10. O Bharata, Hrishikesh, with a gentle smile, spoke to him who stood between the two armies, stuck in despair.

The term *prahasan* (gentle smile) conveys a deep poignancy on the part of Krishna. He loves Arjuna dearly and wants only the best for his friend. Krishna has heard Arjuna's sensitive and painful cries of confusion. He would do anything he can to help his companion, but he sees Arjuna is describing a problem which does not exist. Arjuna is defining his situation based on a misunderstanding of who he is.

This misunderstanding of one's basic spiritual identity is called *avidya* (primal ignorance) in the yogic tradition. An individual personality has forgotten his real nature as consciousness, a soul one with all souls and the supreme soul, God. Arjuna is like a fish in the ocean crying because there is no water. Krishna will not try to correct the illusory problem of no water; he will awaken Arjuna to the fact that he is surrounded, on all sides and in every way, by the ocean of consciousness.

Verse 11

śribhagavānuvāca
aśocyānanvaśocastvam prajñāvādāṁśca bhāṣase
gatāsūnagatāsūṁśca nānuśocanti paṇḍitāḥ (11)

11. Shri Bhagavan said: You say you feel sorrow for those for whom there should be no sorrow, believing your words are wise. The wise are not disturbed by death nor by life.

There is a peace which surpasseth understanding, only experienced by the wise. The hallmark of this peace is a graceful acceptance of all of life. This acceptance includes all and everything: pains and pleasures, happiness and sadness, as well as sickness and death. The wise, in this peaceful acceptance, do not experience the sorrow demonstrated by Arjuna.

Arjuna is attempting to describe his personal problems on a spiritual level, where they do not apply. Arjuna's avidya is distorting his ability to properly perceive himself, others, and the entire situation before him. Like a man wearing tinted glasses, Arjuna's world may appear dark and dismal, but that does not make it so.

Verse 12

na tvevāhaṁ jātu nāsaṁ na tvaṁ neme janādhipāḥ
na caiva na bhaviṣyāmaḥ sarve vayamataḥ param (12)

12. Never did I not exist, nor you, nor these leaders of men; neither shall any of us ever cease to live.

At this early stage of the student's spiritual education, the teacher starts with the primary lesson of the immortality of consciousness. This consciousness is initially understood by the aspirant to be individualized, as he believes himself to be an individual person. As we will see throughout the text, however, all individuality originates, exists, and again merges back into one Infinite Consciousness like waves on an ocean.

Verse 13

dehino 'sminyathā dehe kaumāraṁ yauvanaṁ jarā
tathā dehāntaraprāptirdhīrastatra na muhyati (13)

13. As the embodied one passes through childhood, youth, and old-age, so does he likewise pass on to another body. The wise are not confused by this.

The soul is eternal while the body is transient. The soul is the conscious principle which enlivens the body. The body passes through phases, rising and falling through youth and old age. For the truly wise, the end of the body and the acceptance of a new body is like the changing of clothing. For the common person, death is viewed as a terrible, traumatic event. For the sage, the end of one life and the beginning of another is as simple as changing from one's pajamas into clean clothes at the beginning of a new day. Certainly this level of consciousness is exalted and, as Arjuna will soon protest, hardly accessible at the beginning stages of spiritual development.

Verses 14–15

tataḥ śvetairhayairyukte mahati syandane sthitau
mādhavaḥ pāṅḍavaścaiva divyau śaṅkhau pradadhmatuḥ (14)

pāñcajanyaṁ hṛṣīkeśo devadattaṁ dhanaṁjayaḥ
pauṇḍraṁ dadhmau mahāśaṇkhaṁ bhīmakarmā vṛkodaraḥ (15)

14. O Kaunteya, sense-contacts produce the transitory arising and passing of experiences such as cold and heat, happiness and sadness, and so forth. Bear them with endurance.

15. The wise one is not swayed by these, O Purusharshabha (Arjuna as Great Being); his mind is balanced during times of happiness and sadness. He becomes eligible for the nectar of immortality.

The soul is pure consciousness, unaffected by the travails of changes and challenges of incarnation. The being who has not attained this consciousness, however, experiences himself as an individual body-mind complex. As such, what happens to the body and what passes through the mind is felt to be his identity. The stimulus of the world produces effects which are impermanent, like passing storms. These storms are to be recognized as transitive phenomena which do not alter the eternal nature of the soul. During a thunderstorm a human being may wear a raincoat, but that does not make him a raincoat-being.

Verses 16–17

nāsato vidyate bhāvo nābhāvo vidyate sataḥ
ubhayorapi dṛṣṭo 'ntastvanayostattvadarśibhiḥ (16)

avināśi tu tadviddhi yena sarvamidaṁ tatam
vināśamavyayasyāsya na kaścitkartumarhati (17)

16. What is unreal does not exist. What is real cannot cease to exist. This dual realization is the vision of the seers of essential truth.

17. Know as indestructible That by which everything is manifested and pervaded. No one has the power to destroy That which is ever-existing.

The yogic vision holds that reality has three characteristics—*satyam* (it is eternally real), *shivam* (it is inherently beneficent), and *sundaram* (it is beautiful). The individual who perceives the universe in this way is in reality. The individual who perceives in a way which is not in conformity with reality is, therefore, perceiving an unreal situation.

All existence arises from an eternal ocean of reality. All beings, all forms, are waves on this ocean. The waves arise, exist for a period of time, and then submerge again back into the ocean. The ocean is the cause and the wave is the effect. The ocean is the source of power; the wave is the result of the expression of its source.

From the yogic vision of *advaita* (non-duality) there is no difference between ocean and wave. Wave is simply a concept; it is actually the ocean itself. Wave is a way of describing activity of the ocean, but waves have no independent reality. Ocean can be said to exist without waves, but waves cannot exist without the substratum of the ocean. Krishna approaches this dialogue from the non-dual perspective; he knows himself as the ocean of consciousness. Arjuna has identified himself as a wave, separate from the ocean, and is thus confused.

Verses 18–19

antavanta ime dehā nityasyoktāḥ śarīriṇaḥ
anāśino 'prameyasya tasmādyudhyasva bhārata (18)

ya ena ṁ vetti hantāraṁ yaścainaṁ manyate hatam
ubhau tau na vijānīto nāyaṁ hanti na hanyate (19)

18. One can certainly say that these bodies will eventually end, but the consciousness physically cloaked remains eternal, indestructible, and limitless. Therefore, venture into battle, O Bharata.

19. He who thinks there can be killing, and he who thinks there exists a killer, both know not the truth. There exists no killer nor being killed.

Of course, points out Krishna, bodies live and die. Of this there can be no argument. The lesson he is teaching Arjuna is that there exists a consciousness which does not die. This consciousness is not vulnerable to the calamities of existence, such as death. It is the witness to the passage of birth, life, and death. It is immune to being disturbed by events which seem so significant within the passage of time.

Arjuna's reluctance to enter into the battle of Kurukshetra is a problem shared by all. Everyone in the unenlightened condition is reluctant to enter into the fray of incarnation. Life is a messy process, filled with complexity and paradox. We seek for some safe haven to which we can run when faced with our personal battles.

Krishna is leading Arjuna to a recognition that his avoidance is a subtle reinforcement of his avidya, spiritual ignorance. If Arjuna's fear was valid, he should indeed try to find a refuge from the turmoil. His confusion and anxiety, however, are based on identifying himself as a human being with attachments to his body/mind and social relationships. Krishna is helping Arjuna awaken from this limited identity and realize himself as a consciousness which is unperturbed by false limiting ideas, such as death.

Once again, it is valuable to have compassion for Arjuna and his predicament. To overcome the fear of death, as well as the fear of living life fully, is no small matter. Even though Arjuna is presented the truth which will set him free, it is difficult for him to overcome long-standing conditioning and firmly entrenched ideas. Isn't this the state of every aspirant?

Verse 20

na jāyate mriyate vā kadacinnāyaṁ bhūtvā bhavitā vā na bhūyaḥ
ajo nityaḥ śaśvato 'yaṁ purāṇo na hanyate hanyamāne śarīre (20)

20. There is no birth and there is no death, nor is there manifestation and then cessation. There exists a birthless, eternal, ever-existing Ancient One not killed when the body is killed.

Birth and death, existence and dissolution, and all phenomena of change are the result of the activity of nature. The nature of Mother Nature is change. The structure of creation and the manner of nature's processes will be discussed in more detail later in the text. The teaching at this point is the differentiation between that which changes and the unchanging, perennial consciousness.

Arjuna does not realize himself as part of the eternal consciousness; he identifies himself with his body/mind complex, which is part of nature. As such, he perceives himself as subject to change, death, and the vicissitudes of life. Arjuna is looking outward to the world to understand himself and his problems. Krishna is pointing Arjuna inward, toward the core of his being, to the one consciousness which is the eternal stage on which nature dances.

Verse 21

vedāvināśinaṁ nityaṁ ya enamajamavyayam
kathaṁ sa puruṣaḥ pārtha kaṁ ghātayati hanti kam (21)

21. O Partha, for one who knows the indestructible, eternal, unborn, ever-existing, could he really believe he could slay or be killed?

We can hear Krishna's sweet voice, his face gleaming with the gentle smile mentioned in verse 10, delicately chiding Arjuna. For Krishna, the notion that death can befall the eternal is humorous. How can the eternal become transient? How can the unchangeable suffer change? How can the infinite be limited? What silly ideas. Like an adult who must convince a child the monsters in his dream are imaginary, the teacher must awaken the student to a perception beyond mortal illusions. The problem does not exist in reality but is in the belief system of the aspirant.

Verse 22

vāsāṁsi jīrṅāni yathā vihāya navāni gṛhṇāti naro ' parāṇi
tathā śarīrāṇi vihāya jīrṇānyanyāni saṁyāti navāni dehī (22)

22. As one casts off worn-out clothing and accepts others that are new, so does the embodied one lay aside worn-out bodies and take on new ones.

Let us envision the expression on Arjuna's face. Krishna has informed him that his anxiety and fears are meaningless, his concerns are not real, and he doesn't even know himself. Certainly Arjuna must be puzzled. All of us budding Arjunas identify ourselves with our bodies and, thus confused, believe that what befalls the body has bearing and importance.

The student asks the teacher for guidance, and the teacher responds with the truth, but the student does not yet have ears to hear. So, out of love, the teacher tries to reach the student on a level the student can understand. Instead of continuing to speak of one infinite, eternal consciousness, Krishna tries in this verse to use an analogy that Arjuna can understand.

Verses 23–24

nainaṁ chindanti śastrāṇi nainaṁ dahati pāvakaḥ
na cainaṁ kledayantyāpo na śoṣayati mārutaḥ (23)

acchedo 'yamadāhyo 'yamakledyo 'śoṣya eva ca
nityaḥ sarvagataḥ sthāṇuracalo 'yaṁ sanātanaḥ (24)

23. This cannot be cut by weapons, fire does not burn it, waters do not drown it, wind does not wither it.

24. It cannot be cut into pieces, it will not burn, it cannot get wet, and it does not wither. It is eternal, all-pervading, the foundation, immovable. It is always and forever.

Krishna refers to the means of destruction of the four primal *bhutas* (elements), which are the basis of all of nature's forms. These are not elements in the Western sense, as they are not physical in any way, even on a subatomic level. The bhutas are subtle energies which manifest as physical structures.

The four bhutas are: earth, water, fire, and air. The earth element creates solids, the water element creates liquids, the fire element creates heat and light, and the air element creates gaseous substances. The body is comprised of these four elements and is liable to being cut, burnt, and wet and to withering. The mind is considered the fifth bhuta, and beyond the elements is the Self, immune to all of these ravages. (See 7.4–6, 13.5–6.)

It is worthwhile for the reader to understand the title of this chapter, Samkhya Yoga, the Yoga of the Essential Principles. Traditional Samkhya philosophy is based on the teachings of the ancient sage Kapila. The principal teaching of Samkhya is that there exists a mutually relating dualism consisting of consciousness, called *purusha*, and nature, called *prakriti* (see chapter 13 for a detailed presentation of Samkhya).

At this stage of Arjuna's development, however, it is not necessary or even valuable for him to enter into deep philosophical contemplation. What is of immediate concern is that he be able to differentiate the two Essential Principles: himself as consciousness, purusha, and how this is separate from the transitive phenomenon of his body and environment, prakriti.

Verse 25

avyakto 'yamacinto 'yamavikāryo 'yamucyate
tasmādevaṁ viditvainaṁ nānuśocitumarhasi (25)

25. It is spoken of as unmanifest, inconceivable, and unchanging. Knowing it as such, there is no reason for your depression.

This is Krishna's final word in this section regarding the nature of consciousness. In the context of Arjuna's teaching, Krishna states there is no cause for depression as nothing that takes place in the battle will change pure consciousness. For Arjuna to realize the truth of this teaching he will have to raise his consciousness beyond identification with his body/mind complex and know himself as consciousness.

Verses 26–28

atha cainaṁ nityajātaṁ vā manyase mṛtam
tathāpi tvaṁ mahābāho naivaṁ śocitumarhasi (26)

jātasya hi dhruvo mṛtyurdhruvaṁ janma mṛtasya ca
tasmādaparihārye 'rthe tvaṁ śocitumarhasi (27)

avyaktādīni bhūtāni vyaktamadhyāni bhārata
avyaktanidhanānyeva tatra kā paridevanā (28)

26. Even if you believe it to be perpetually taking birth and dying, O Mahabaho (Arjuna as Mighty-Armed), you have no reason for depression.

27. For everyone born, death is certain. Likewise, from this perspective, birth is certain for those who have died. Since this is inevitable, you have no reason for depression.

28. Beings are manifest as a middle state between an unmanifest origin and unmanifest ending. What here is lamentable?

Krishna again descends from his lofty heights to spoon-feed Arjuna on a level that may be effective. Krishna tells Arjuna that even if he were to identify himself as an individual, perhaps as an individual soul who inhabits a particular body/mind complex, change is still inevitable. From the vision of Krishna, the reality of change is nothing to be upset about. It is only Arjuna's clinging to the impermanent that is causing his suffering.

Verse 29

āścaryavatpaśyati kaścidenamāścaryavadvadati tathaiva cānyaḥ
āścaryavacainamanyaḥ śṛṇoti śrutvāpyenaṁ veda na caiva kaścit (29)

29. One person will look upon this in wonderment, another will speak about this in wonderment, and another will listen to this in wonderment. But, even after hearing, no one can fully comprehend this.

This teaching about the reality of consciousness is wonderful in the truest sense of the word—it fills one with wonder. One gasps in awe at the glory and splendor of the divine universe, filled with light, filled with love. Such a spectacle of beauty, grace, and harmony! This vision is granted to those who can accept a peace which surpasses understanding. It is a vision that is dark to the mind but light to the heart. The mind, with its limited concerns and anxieties, must be transcended. The soul, the wave that is the expression of the ocean, must stand on its own, without mental supports, to enjoy the vision of Krishna.

Verse 30

dehī nityamavadhyo 'yaṁ dehe sarvasya bhārata
tasmātsarvāṇi bhūtāni na tvaṁ śocitumarhasi (30)

30. There is a dweller in the body of all, O Bharata, who is eternally invulnerable. You therefore have no sound reason to grieve for anyone.

That there is no cause for grief may be the most radical statement possible. The entire world believes that suffering is real. Every religion, every psychology, every political system, even the common materialist believes his suffering to be real, legitimate, and based on some truth about the nature of the world and his place in it. Krishna does not attempt to dissect Arjuna's problem, because his problem is based on an illusion. Arjuna believes himself to be something he is not, and all his problems arise from this faulty premise.

Krishna attempts to rouse Arjuna from the slumber of avidya, spiritual ignorance, so Arjuna can realize there is no need to suffer. Krishna exhorts Arjuna to break his allegiance to limited beliefs. There is no need to live like a vulture on the carrion of limiting ideas when one can fly free like an eagle in the spiritual sky.

Verses 31–33

svadharmamapi cāvekṣya na vikampitumarhasi
dharmyāddhi yuddhācchreyo 'nyatkṣatriyasya na vidyate (31)

yadṛcchayā copapannaṁ svargadvāramapāvṛtam
sukhinaḥ kṣatriyāḥ pārtha labhate yuddhamīdṛśam (32)

atha cettvamimaṁ dharmyaṁ saṁgrāmaṁ na kariṣyasi
tataḥ svadharmaṁ kīrtiṁ ca hitvā pāpamavāpsyasi (33)

31. Furthermore, taking into account the essential nature of your particular personality, there should be no vacillation. For a noble warrior such as yourself, there is nothing more meritorious than a war based on the need to protect society.

32. Noble warriors have cause for happiness, O Partha, when such a battle arises unsought. It is an open door to the heavenly worlds.

33. If, however, you refrain from engaging in this battle necessary for the protection of your society, you will be in conflict with your own inner direction and integrity. You will become confused and misdirected due to self-centeredness.

The grace and patience of an authentic spiritual teacher is unlimited. The teacher will never cease in his efforts to awaken the disciple. There is no limit to the work of the guru, neither in time invested nor in degree of compassion. We see this here as Krishna again attempts to meet Arjuna at his own level. Arjuna has a particular temperament which he must express or else feel psychologically frustrated. So Krishna encourages Arjuna to respect his own constitution and avoid the debilitating despair that keeps him from fulfilling his personal potential and responsibility to society.

Every human being has a particular *dharma*, which in this context refers to a social duty. Everyone has a role to play in humanity's movement on the cosmic stage. To link our personal dharma with the divine dharma is to form a yoga, or union. This verse symbolically represents the encouragement of God (Krishna) for the individual soul (Arjuna) to fulfill his life's purpose (dharma) in the unique role of his lifetime (Kurukshetra).

Verses 34–37

akīrtiṁ cāpi bhūtani kathayiṣyanti te 'vyayām
sambhāvitasya cākīrtirmaraṇādati ricyate (34)

bhayādraṇāduparataṁ maṁsyante tvāṁ mahārathāḥ
yeṣāṁ ca tvaṁ bahumato bhūtvā yāsyasi lāghavam (35)

avācyavādāṁśca bahūnvadiṣyanti tavāhitāḥ
nindatastava sāmarthyaṁ tato duḥkhataraṁ nu kim (36)

hato vā prāpsyasi svargaṁ jitvā vā bhokṣyase mahīm
tasmāduttiṣṭha kaunteya yuddhāya kṛtaniścayaḥ (37)

34. Throughout creation you will forever be spoken of as a disgrace. To one accustomed to honor, this disgrace is worse than death.

35. The great charioteers will believe you quit the battle due to fear; those who held you in high esteem will deride you.

36. Your enemies will curse you, ridiculing your masculine potency. Is there a pain deeper than this?

37. Death during battle will bring you into heaven; victory in battle will bring you the splendors of this earth. Arise, then, O Kaunteya. Be resolute to fight!

Krishna tosses his fishing line into the pond of Arjuna's social identity and pride in order to evaluate to what extent Arjuna is actually receptive to spiritual teachings. The teacher needs to determine if the student is proud of social position, fearful of losing reputation, or influenced by relative religious values of heavens and hells. If the student is not weakened by these superficial concerns, the teacher can proceed to help.

Verse 38

sukhaduḥkhe same kṛtvā lābhālābhau jayājayau
tato yuddhāya yujyasva naivaṁ pāpamavāpsyasi (38)

38. Be balanced internally in both pleasure and pain, gain and loss, victory and defeat. Go forth boldly into battle and you will avoid confusion and misdirection.

Krishna is exhorting Arjuna to put aside his personal worries and enthusiastically participate in the course of his life. God encourages the soul to fully embrace life and its experiences. With a focus on inner peace, one is to enter into the battlefield of the world. With an inner balance, one can fully participate in all the ventures of earthly life without succumbing to confusion.

Verse 39

eṣā te 'bhihitā sāṁkhye buddharyoge tvimāṁ śṛṇu
buddhyā yukto yayā pārtha karmabandhaṁ prahāsyasi (39)

39. This is the teaching of Samkhya philosophy, The Yoga of Essential Principles. Hear now of the complementary teaching of Karma Yoga, The Yoga of Selfless Action, by which you will attain intuitive vision, O Partha, and cast aside the bondage of karmic law.

Krishna has presented the essence of Samkhya in a fashion related to Arjuna's situation. He highlighted the difference between recognizing oneself as consciousness, purusha, or misidentifying oneself with nature's phenomena, prakriti. Now the discussion changes from the subject of consciousness to that of activity. Here begins an introductory teaching on karma yoga, which will be more fully developed in the next chapter and continue to be an important theme throughout the text.

Verse 40

nehābhikramanāśo 'sti pratyavāyo na vidyate
svalpamapyasya dharmasya trāyate mahato bhayāt (40)

40. On this path no effort is wasted nor do obstacles prevail. Even a little of this noble path saves one from the great fear.

Krishna begins his teaching on the subject of activity by offering these encouraging words to Arjuna. In the course of spiritual development there will be periods of accomplishment and periods of discouragement. The path is not straight; it is a spiral that curves upwards from one's current level to unexplored planes of consciousness above.

Whatever steps one takes on this spiral path are not wasted. One never descends once attaining a certain stage. There may be setbacks, but there is no real decline in consciousness. Like money earned and placed in a savings account, it is forever held in the name of the depositor. One may ignore the money, even forget it belongs to him, but it still remains in his ownership.

Verse 41

vyavasāyātmikā buddhirekeha nurunandana
bahuśākhā hyanantāśca buddhayo 'vyavasāyinām (41)

41. On this path, O Kurunandana (Arjuna as Delight of the Kurus), the firm focus of the intuitive vision is one-pointed. The vision of someone without firm focus is scattered in a multitude of directions.

In this universe of infinite possibilities, there exist infinite avenues of interest. The mind can focus on any of an unlimited number of different subjects. Traveling the spiritual path is really as simple as focusing on those aspects of life which exist on the path—such as beauty, love, harmony, wisdom, and compassion. It is a matter of training the mind to focus and disciplining attention toward the spiritual goal.

Verses 42–44

yāmimāṁ puṣpitāṁ vācaṁ pravadantyavipaścitaḥ
vedavādaratāḥ pārtha nānyadastīti vādinaḥ (42)

kāmātmānaḥ svargaparā janmakarmaphalapradām
kriyāviśeṣabahulāṁ bhogaiśvaryagatiṁ prati (43)

bhogaiśvaryaprasaktānāṁ tayāpahṛtacetasām
vyavasāyātmikā buddhiḥ samādhau na vidhīyate (44)

42. O Partha, the foolish who utter flowery speech and cling to the letter of the law deny there exists an authentic path of transcendence.

43. Their very Self seems laced with selfish desire, and they hold their personal ideal of heaven as the loftiest goal. They participate in complex activities, seeking selfish enjoyment and personal power. Know that their types of actions result in rebirth.

44. Those whose awareness is preoccupied with enjoyments and power will not have the firm intuitive wisdom needed to guide them to divine consciousness.

One of the gravest dangers to the sincere spiritual aspirant is that posed by organized religion. Human beings are social animals, and it is extremely difficult to break mammalian conditioning. There exist tremendous biological and social forces that work to keep an aspirant within the confines of comfortable collective beliefs, such as religious codes. It is a rare soul who is willing to confront the loneliness required of authentic spiritual practice.

The reason organized religion is a threat to spiritual growth is that it is such a seductive forgery. It is tempting to want to belong to a group, particularly if that group claims its leader is an exalted being or holds a set of teachings which are considered absolutely true for all humanity. A false security is attained when one feels himself to have a set of clearly defined answers to life's challenges, and to believe that an all-powerful savior is protecting and guiding one's life. Authentic spiritual life is a much more refined and subtle path.

This false hope of finding the divine consciousness in external teachers and sects is why Krishna is so adamant with Arjuna. Arjuna is trying to reach a compromise with those very forces which seek to keep him within the parameters of social stability. No compromise is possible here. Arjuna must grow beyond his background, beyond his religion, even beyond his humanity. Krishna informs Arjuna that he must kill his family members, even his gurus, if he wishes to reach his own Self.

This killing is, of course, symbolic. Nevertheless, it is certainly an extremely powerful metaphor for the complete extinguishment of limiting factors in the life of an aspirant. There comes a stage in one's development when no negotiation with limiting forces is possible; the only choice is victory or defeat. One must rouse his full courage, raise high his inner weapons, and destroy any and all forces which seek to keep him from fulfilling his potential.

Verses 45–46

traiguṇyaviṣayā vedā nistraigunyo bhavārjuna
nardvandvo nityasattvastho niryogakṣema ātmavān (45)

yāvānartha udapāne sarvataḥ saṁplutodake
tāvānsarveṣu vedeṣu brāhmaṇasya vijānataḥ (46)

45. The subject matter of conventional religious teachings is all within the three qualities of nature. O Arjuna, become inwardly free of these, become free of duality, become stable in purity without concern for what you may acquire or possess. Be your Self.

46. As a pond is of small value when water is flooded everywhere, such is the value of conventional religious teachings for the sage of inner wisdom.

The matter of the three qualities of nature is a very important part of the teachings in the Bhagavad Gita. Chapter 14 and much of chapter 18 are devoted to this subject. The meaning at this point is in reference to conventional religious organizations and their pursuit of personal rewards. Whether these rewards are of worldly power or gain, or even if they are heavenly rewards, they are still limited and self-centered. The Bhagavad Gita seeks to bring an aspirant to the exalted status of a *rishi* (seer) based on his own personal realization.

A story may help illustrate this section of five verses (42–46).

Once, God and the Devil were walking along. God bent over and picked up a beautiful, shining gem. It glowed in radiance on God's upraised palm.

"What is that?" questioned the Devil.

God answered, "This is the truth."

"Oh," said the Devil, snatching it from God's hand. "Give it to me. I'll organize it for you."

Verses 47–48

karmaṇyevādhikāraste mā phaleṣu kadācana
mā karmaphalaheturbhūrmā te saṅgo 'stvakarmaṇi (47)

yogasthaḥ kuru karmāṇi saṅgaṁ tyaktvā dhanaṁjaya
siddhyasiddhyoḥ samo bhūtvā samatvaṁ yoga ucyate (48)

47. Your right is to action alone; results are not your entitlement. Seek not results as your motivation, but neither cling to an attitude of inactivity.

48. Firm in your yoga, do your work, O Dhananjaya. Release clinging and hold your mind unconcerned with success or failure. This balanced calm is yoga.

Here is a concise definition of karma yoga, the yoga of selfless activity. As the question of proper action is near the root of Arjuna's dilemma, understanding activity becomes one of the crucial themes of the Bhagavad Gita. The essential teaching is that activity should be considered sufficient unto itself. One is to act appropriately in the world, fulfilling responsibilities without personal attachment.

The bank teller takes care to account for the money that passes through his hands without imagining the cash belongs to him. Similarly, the yogi may posses wealth of any degree, but he simply does not become attached to it nor use it for selfish purposes.

There are several classic definitions of yoga. One of the most well known is given by Patanjali in his Yoga Sutras: *yogash chitta vritti nirodha* (yoga is the stilling of mental agitation). This is the experience of yoga in meditation. Here, Krishna gives the first of three definitions of yoga given in the Bhagavad Gita: *samatvam yoga* (yoga is balanced calm). The other definitions of yoga are presented in 2.50, where we learn that "yoga is skillful action," and in 6.23, yoga is "disconnection from causes of suffering."

It may be helpful for Westerners to contemplate the profound implications of these definitions of yoga. Much of the teaching of yoga in the West at this point in time is based on the practice of *asanas* (physical postures) in order to obtain bodily health and attractiveness. Certainly health and vitality are valuable benefits, but from the perspective of this authentic yoga a strong body is valuable only to the extent that it is stable in meditation and useful as a vehicle of service to others.

Verses 49–50

dūrena hyavaraṁ karma buddhiyogāddhanaṁjaya
buddhau śaraṇamanviccha kṛpaṇāḥ phalahetavaḥ (49)

buddhiyukto jahātīha ubhe sukṛtaduṣkṛte
tasmādyogāya yujyasva yogaḥ karmasu kauśalam (50)

49. To act for oneself is the mark of an inferior person, O Dhananjaya. Follow this path of intuitive, selfless action. Those who pursue the fruit of their actions are not yet on the path of grace.

50. One who has harmonized his intelligence with the Divine Will relinquishes duality even while in this world of duality. Make this yoga your goal. Yoga is skillful action.

Two important terms are used in these verses. The first is *buddhi*, in both verses 49 and 50, which represents the mind infused with spiritual intuition. The second term is *phalahetavah*, in verse 49, which literally means "desirous of fruits." This refers to those who are motivated in their actions by the hope of personal reward. Both of these terms will be repeatedly used throughout the text.

Buddhi is the function of the mind which is capable of understanding spiritual teachings. It is intuition, the ability to know directly that which cannot be known by the senses or cognitive mind. Buddhi reflects the light of the soul. It is capable of making accessible to the mind those insights and perceptions which lay in spheres above its immediate domain. The cognitive aspect of mind, called *manas*, is basically an extensive computer. It processes the input received from the senses while interacting with the external world and then coordinates these into a composite depiction of the world. It is sometimes referred to in yoga as the eleventh sense, since its function is related entirely to the external world.

In verse 50 we also have Krishna's second definition of yoga, *yogah karmasu kaushalam* (yoga is skillful action). This skill is the ability to act with efficiency. One is able to focus and not waste time and energy on mental preoccupations.

This may sound like a simple definition for a subject as profound as yoga. Yes, the definition is simple, but that does not mean it is easy. To be skillful and efficient means to organize one's life in such a way that one's energy is not frittered away on superficials but is fully utilized for spiritual growth and service. This involves a lifestyle which revolves around internal development and external service. The specifics of this lifestyle will vary based on an aspirant's skills and life circumstances, but it always involves a sacrifice of one's personal agenda for the purpose of serving the greater good.

Verse 51

karmajaṁ buddhiyuktā hi phalaṁ tyaktvā manīṣiṇaḥ
janmabandhavinirmuktāḥ padaṁ gacchantyanāmayam (51)

51. Wise are those who have harmonized their intuition with the Divine Will. Releasing clinging to the fruits of their actions, they become free of the bonds of birth and death, reaching the state beyond sorrow.

Just as the cognitive mind must be educated and developed if it is to be a useful tool, likewise with the intuition. Intuition must be harmonized with the influences radiated from spheres of consciousness habitated by the soul. With training and practice, these divine influences are accessible and recognizable to the buddhi.

Verses 52–53

yadā te mohakalilaṁ buddhirvyatitariṣyati
tadā gantāsi nirvedaṁ śrotavyasya śrutasya ca (52)

śrutivipratipannāte yadā sthāsyati niścalā
samādhāvacalā buddhistadā yogamavāpsyasi (53)

52. When your intuition crosses the turbulent sea of confusion and delusion, you will be unfazed by any previous or future conventional religious teaching.

53. When your intuitive perception is not bewildered by conventional religious teachings, you will stand unshaken and stable in divine consciousness, attaining yogic insight.

Krishna has asked Arjuna to kill his external teachers in order that his internal teacher may live. Arjuna is used to receiving teachings from teachers, scriptures, and social devices. Krishna is now encouraging him to go inward, into the intuitive wisdom of his heart, and discover the eternal fount from which all wisdom arises. As the disciple develops his own buddhi, he possesses a touchstone by which he can measure the teachings presented in the marketplace of ideas. The student develops his own *adhikari* (authority) from the inner path of yoga.

Verse 54

arjuna uvāca
sthitaprajñasya kā bhāṣā samādhisthasya keśava
sthitadhīḥ kiṁ prabhāṣeta kimāsīta vrajeta kim (54)

54. Arjuna said: O Keshava, can you describe the nature of one who holds this transcendent wisdom, who is in divine consciousness? How does such a one speak, how does he sit, how does he move?

Arjuna must certainly be amazed at Krishna's depiction of life immersed in spiritual wisdom. How wonderful it sounds. But can such a state of consciousness actually be possible? If so, what would it be like? How can the student, still lost in confusion, even recognize a person at this level of consciousness?

Verses 55–58

śribhagavānuvāca
prajahāti yadā kāmānsarvānpārtha manogatān
ātmanyevātmanā tuṣṭaḥ sthitaprajñastadocyate (55)

duḥkheṣvanudvignamanāḥ sukheṣu vigataspṛhaḥ
vītarāgabhayakrodhaḥ sthitadhīrmunirucyate (56)

yaḥ sarvatrānabhisnehastattatprāpya śubhāśubham
nābhinandati na dveṣṭi tasya prajñā pratiṣṭhitā (57)

yadā saṁharate cāyaṁ kūrmo 'ṅgānīva sarvaśaḥ
indriyāṇīndriyārthebhyastasya prajñā pratiṣṭhitā (58)

55. Sri Bhagavan said: His transcendent wisdom is stable when he can cast aside the mind's selfish desires, O Partha, and when his Self sits in its own Self-contentment.

56. Call him a sage whose mind is untroubled during periods of unhappiness and who is free of attachment during periods of happiness. He has released selfish desires, fear, and anger.

57. Firmly established in transcendent wisdom is the one whose caring is impartial and who neither rejoices before what is considered desirable nor disdains what is deemed undesirable.

58. Firmly established in this transcendent wisdom is one who can withdraw the senses from their objects of perception as a tortoise can withdraw its limbs.

Krishna describes for Arjuna the quality of a person who has stabilized his consciousness in transcendent wisdom. These qualities all revolve around an inner stability, an autonomy based on spiritual realization. The forces of biological impulse and social conditioning no longer overwhelm such a one. His contentment is found regardless of circumstances. A friend to all, whether recognized as such or not, he abides in the cave of his heart, the *hridayam.* Visitors are welcome to visit him at his abode, but he will not leave his inner seat, as nothing in the world profits him if it means leaving his soul's home.

Verses 59–61

viṣayā vinivartante nirāhārasya dehinaḥ
rasavarjaṁ raso 'pyasya paraṁ dṛṣṭvā nivartate (59)

yatato hyapi kaunteya puruṣaya vipaścitaḥ
indriyāṇi pramāthīni haranti prasabhaṁ manaḥ (60)

tāni sarvāṇi saṁyamya yukta āsīta matparaḥ
vaśe hi yasyendriyāṇi tasya prajñā pratiṣṭhitā (61)

59. Sense pleasures may cease to attract while one is abstaining, but the taste for the pleasure still remains. Even this taste ceases, though, when one has the supreme vision.

60. Even though one may strive toward the goal and practice discernment, O Kaunteya, his turbulent senses will occasionally still forcefully disrupt his mind.

61. Bringing the senses under control, the yogi should remain steadfast in seeking Me. One of transcendent wisdom is he whose senses are under control.

Krishna makes a distinction between the person of accomplishment and the one still striving. During the stage of spiritual practice, an aspirant will find himself enjoying periods of peace and contentment, particularly during solitary meditation. He may find it surprising, then, when he returns to the world of activities and relationships and falls back upon old conditioned attitudes.

The aspirant will find himself troubled at these disruptions to his peace. This is dismay is wonderful; the discomfort will goad him onward. While he works to control the turbulent senses and unruly mind, he can hold before him the polestar of these teachings and follow the compass of steadfast seeking towards the Self.

This is the first verse in which Krishna speaks in the first person, which will be repeated throughout the text. Here, Krishna encourages Arjuna to seek "me." Who is this "me?" Why should Arjuna seek Krishna when Krishna is standing right in front of him?

It must be remembered that every character in the Bhagavad Gita is an aspect of one's own consciousness. Arjuna is the individual spiritual aspirant, identified with his body and mind, searching for answers and clarity. Krishna is the sage, having identified with the pure consciousness of the One Self, knowing the answers and abiding in clarity.

Most students read the Bhagavad Gita and, naturally enough, identify with Arjuna. It is helpful to also read the Bhagavad Gita from Krishna's perspective. When Krishna refers to "me," it is with the sense of pure awareness, the pure feeling of "I am," the transcendent consciousness shared by all sentient beings. Krishna knows himself as this consciousness, and he seeks to bring his friend into the *ananda* (bliss) of this consciousness.

When Jesus said, "No one comes to the Father but through me," he was referring to the same "me," the same Self, the same consciousness spoken of by Krishna. If we do not acknowledge the unity of divine consciousness shared by all beings, we descend into the multiplistic, hierarchical, conventional religions of which Krishna has previously cautioned Arjuna.

Verses 62–63

dhyāyato viṣayānpuṁsaḥ saṅgasteṣūpajāyate
saṅgātsaṁjāyate kāmaḥ kāmātkrodho 'bhijāyate (62)

krodhādbhavati sammohaḥ sammohātsmṛtivibhramaḥ
smṛtibhraṁśādbuddhināśo buddhināśatpraṇaśyati (63)

62. When one dwells on sense pleasures, attachment forms in the mind. From attachment arises desire, and from unfulfilled desire springs anger.

63. From anger arises a confusion which causes one to forget the spiritual goal. This loss is the destruction of true intelligence, and with this loss of intelligence one is as good as dead.

Humanity shares a particular psychological process that is universal, regardless of time or culture. This process has been explained by the great seers of the yogic tradition as the path to peace or to suffering. The path of peace and Self realization involves controlling the mind and senses and relinquishing egoic-selfishness. The path of suffering begins with the seed of selfish desire and ends in a state of spiritual death.

Only the greatest yogis are entirely free of anger, so it is no surprise when ordinary people find themselves under the influence of this emotion. The path to freedom from anger is to accept responsibility and avoid blaming external forces. This empowers the individual as it places the possibility of control within one's own mind, rather than outside oneself.

The root of anger is always selfish desire. The mind believes, "Someone does not act in a way pleasing to me, and I have been denied what I desire." The conclusion of this line of thought runs through confusion, continues through destruction of intelligence, and dead-ends in a state of spiritual demise.

Verses 64–65

rāgadveṣaviyuktaistu viṣayānindriyaiścaran
ātmavaśyairvidheyātmā prasādamadhigacchati (64)

prasāde sarvaduḥkhānāṁ hānirasyopajāyate
prasannacetaso hyāśu buddhiḥ paryavatiṣṭhate (65)

64. One of disciplined mind, who can live in the world with his senses integrated with the Self, free from attraction and repulsion, attains spiritual tranquility.

65. This tranquility brings with it an end to all suffering. One's intelligence becomes established in the peace of his own Self.

If one's consciousness is focused on trying to get things from the world, one is on a path to frustration and unhappiness as there is always more to get. If one is focused on giving to the world, one is on a path to peace and joy as there is always more to give. The mind and body, with the attendant senses, are considered spiritually integrated when they serve spirit by serving others. The body and mind are vehicles through which spirit incarnates and brings its gifts to the world of objects and relationships.

Verses 66–67

nāsti buddhirayuktasya na cāyuktasya bhāvanā
na cābhāvayataḥ śantiraśāntasya kutaḥ sukham (66)

indriyāṅāṁ hi caratāṁ yanmano 'nu vidhīyate
tadasya harati prajñaṁ vāyurnāvamivāmbhasi (67)

66. For the unintegrated, there is no light of spiritual intelligence nor focused direction. Without properly directed attention one can find no peace. Without peace, how can there be happiness?

67. As a ship on the sea is carried away by the wind, so transcendental wisdom is carried away when the mind is tossed by the restless senses.

Through spiritual practice, such as meditation, one comes to recognize that thoughts are like winds which blow the ship of consciousness in various directions. One is to take responsibility for his thoughts in the same way that he takes responsibility for his actions. Thoughts of wisdom and compassion bring about a peaceful sea on which the ship of consciousness can steer to lands of spiritual joy and exploration. Selfish thoughts produce tumultuous storms which dash the ship of awareness into barren lands of hurry, worry, fear, and self-doubt. Neither God nor guru can steer the ship of mind. It is the aspirant alone who must claim his own power and learn how to operate the vehicles of thought.

Verse 68

tasmādyasya mahābāho nigṛhītāni sarvaśaḥ
indriyāṇīndriyārthebhyastasya prajñā pratiṣṭhitā (68)

68. Therefore, O Mahabaho, the one of transcendental wisdom keeps his senses independent of their objects.

In Patanjali's Yoga Sutras, the classic text on the stages of meditation, eight levels of practice are described. The first four levels are based on external controls—behavioral control (*yamas* and *niyamas*), physical control (*asanas*), and subtle-energy control (*pranayama*). This verse makes reference to the fifth level, called *pratyahara*, which is the ability to keep the mind and senses calm regardless of external involvement. Pratyahara is the passage between the external stages and the purely internal stages of meditation.

Verse 69

yā niśā sarvabhūtānāṁ tasyāṁ jāgarti saṁyamī
yasyāṁ jāgrati bhūtāni sā niśā paśyato muneḥ (69)

69. In the night of worldly life, the self-mastering sage is awake. What the world calls the light of day is night to the sage of spiritual vision.

From the spiritual perspective, those who are suffering from the illness of egoic worldly life are truly sick. Yet the worldly often view themselves as well, and they see the sages as suffering from some mental quirk by which they are not attracted to the glitz and glamour of the world. Referring back to verses 64–65, we can define the sages as those who find happiness in giving and the worldly as those who unsuccessfully pursue happiness by getting. These two paths start from different premises, and they produce diametrically opposed results. Everyone is required to make the choice for himself as to which path is worth travelling.

Verses 70–72

āpūryamāṇamacalapratiṣṭhaṁ samudramāpaḥ praviśanti yadvat
tadvatkāmā yaṁ praviśanti sarve sa śāntimāpnoti na kāmakāmī (70)

vihāya kāmānyaḥ sarvānpumāṁścarati niḥspṛhaḥ
nirmamo nirahaṅkāraḥ sa śāntimadhigacchati (71)

eṣā brāhmī sthitiḥ pārtha naināṁ prāpya vimuhyati
sthitvāsyāmantakāle 'pi brahmanirvāṇamṛcchati (72)

70. One knows peace who absorbs selfish desires, as the motionless sea is filled but unmoved by inflowing waters. Peace is not for one who embraces his selfishness.

71. One attains peace who abandons selfish desires and acts unmotivated by greed, obsessiveness, or egotism.

72. This is the state of Infinite Consciousness, O Partha, on reaching which one is never again bewildered, and at the time of death one may become absorbed in the Infinite Consciousness.

Verse 72 introduces one of the most important terms in the text. This is *Brahman*, which we are translating as "Infinite Consciousness." Infinite is this Consciousness because there is nothing that does not exist within its scope. All limited individual consciousnesses, all objects, all time and space continuums, are manifestations of this Consciousness. It is the one mind in which all forms are its thoughts. It is what might rightly be called by the Western term, God, yet it is more than any notion of God which can be conceived by the human mind.

Brahman comes from the root *bri,* to grow. Brahman is infinitely growing, eternally expressing the divine state. Brahman cannot be fathomed by the mind, but it can be experienced by the yogi. Brahman will be explored in more detail later in the text; for now we will simply state that Brahman is the Infinite Consciousness of which the yogi experiences himself to be a part and from which the egoic individual feels himself to be apart.

Chapter 3

Karma Yoga
The Yoga of Selfless Action

Verses 1–2

arjuna uvāca
jyāyasī cetkarmaṇaste matā buddhirjanārdana
tatkiṁ karmaṇi ghore māṁ niyojayasi keśava (1)

vyāmiśreṇeva vākyena buddhiṁ mohayasīva me
tadekaṁ vada niścitya yena śreyo 'hamāpnuyām (2)

1. Arjuna then said: O Janardana, you seem to propose that insight is superior to action. Why then, O Keshava, do you urge me to act in this brutal way?

2. My intelligence is bewildered by your seemingly conflicting teachings. Decisively, clearly, tell me the one guiding principle by which I can attain the highest good.

Arjuna is confused. Krishna has spoken to him eloquently about identifying himself with consciousness and not his body/mind complex. Krishna has also spoken about harmonizing his physical and mental vehicles with his soul in order for activity to be an expression of spiritual reality. Arjuna still has trouble understanding why he should act, particularly in this case when the activity of battle is so dramatic. He was under the impression that insight alone is the goal of spiritual development. He does not yet understand that insight naturally expresses itself in action.

Verse 3

śrībhagavānuvāca
loke 'smindvividhā niṣṭhā purā proktā mayānagha
jñānayogena sāṁkhyānāṁ karmayogena yoginām (3)

3. Shri Bhagavan said: O Anagha (Arjuna as Innocent One), in this world there are two paths that I have taught—the path of insight into the essential principles for yogis of a contemplative nature and the path of activity for more active yogis.

How patient is the teacher with his student. Krishna already told Arjuna (2.39) that activity is complementary to insight. Here he acknowledges that based on their personality, some yogis will find one aspect of the path more attractive. As we will see, insight and activity are mutually supportive yogas. The inner development that results in insight produces beneficial activity, and activity clarifies and enhances insight.

Verses 4–5

na karmaṇāmanārambhānnaiṣkarmyaṁ puruṣo 'śnute
na ca saṁnyasanādeva siddhiṁ samadhigacchati (4)

na hi kaścitkṣaṇamapi jātu tiṣṭhatyakarmakṛt
kāryate hyavaśaḥ karma sarvaḥ prakṛtijairguṇaiḥ (5)

4. Not by refraining from activity does one become free of the demands of activity, nor by mere renunciation does one attain to perfection.

5. No one remains inactive for even a moment. Everyone is constantly propelled to act by nature's ceaseless drive.

Renunciation plays a major role in the spiritual traditions of many cultures. In some Indian sects, renunciation is considered to mean refraining from all activity, or at least refraining from involvement in the world to the greatest possible extent. It is believed that the fewer the social responsibilities, the greater the renunciation. This is the basis for the lifestyle of many of the *sadhus* in India, the homeless, wandering yogis.

From the perspective of the Bhagavad Gita, renunciation is not refraining from activity but relinquishing selfishly motivated acts and desires for reward. This is a more holistic orientation than that of the homeless or monastic traditions. Activity, as Arjuna will learn, is sacred when it arises from a spiritual impulse and is directed toward service to others.

No one can remain inactive for even a moment because the nature of Nature is change. When one sits in meditation he can perceive that there is no complete stillness. Even if the mind becomes calm, respiration and circulation continue to take place, and there exists a subtle movement in the body as the muscles keep the meditator upright. The goal of meditation, therefore, is not some imaginary perfect stillness which does not exist. The goal is a balanced stillness in which peace can arise.

Verses 6–7

karmendriyāṇi saṁyamya ya āste manasā smaran
indriyārthānvimūḍhātmā mithyācāraḥ sa ucyate (6)

yastvindriyāṇi manasā niyamyārabhate 'rjuna
karmendriyaiḥ karmayogamasktaḥ sa viśiṣyate (7)

6. One who restrains his behavior but still mentally longs for pleasures is still deluded and in conflict.

7. But one whose senses are controlled as a result of mental discipline, O Arjuna, is superior as he can engage himself in activity without attachment.

Control of behavior is not sufficient to bring about peace. The control must be internalized. Like a child educated to behave properly by caring parents, the young disciple must learn to integrate mature spiritual values and not simply mimic his elders.

Verses 8–9

niyataṁ kuru karma tvaṁ karma jyāyo hyakarmaṇaḥ
śarīrayātrāpi ca te na prasiddhyedakarmaṇaḥ (8)

yajñārthātkarmaṇo 'nyatra loko 'yaṁ karmabandhanaḥ
tadarthaṁ karma kaunteya muktasaṅgaḥ samācara (9)

8. Perform the duties that naturally arise in your life, as this is far better than inaction. Even staying alive in your body cannot take place without activity.

9. Except for work done as a divine offering, all activity in this realm brings karmic bondage. Therefore, O Kaunteya, do your work as a divine offering and become free of attachments.

Every person has a unique dharma, his own role to play in the world. In the vast machinery of the universe, every individual is an intricate piece without which the whole cannot reach its optimum. This work is to be undertaken as a divine offering. The goal of spirituality is not to be free of activity; it is to become free of attachment.

Verses 10–13

sahayajñāḥ prajāḥ sṛṣṭvā purovāca prajāpatiḥ
anena prasaviṣyadhvameṣa vo 'stviṣṭakāmaduk (10)

devānbhāvayatānena te devā bhāvayantu vaḥ
parasparaṁ bhāvayantaḥ śreyaḥ paramavāpsyatha (11)

iṣṭānbhogānhi vo devā dāsyante yajñabhāvitāḥ
tairdattānapradāyaibhyo yo bhuṅkte stena eva saḥ (12)

yajñaśiṣṭāśinaḥ santo mucyante sarvakilbiṣaiḥ
bhuñjate te tvaghaṁ pāpā ye pacantyātmakāraṇāt (13)

10. In primeval times Prajapati, the Lord of All Beings, created humanity along with divine offerings. He pronounced, "By divine offerings will you manifest and enjoy the beautiful milk of your creative impulses."

11. In this way, through divine offerings, enter into creative partnership with the higher beings and assist in the manifestation of the universe. By supporting each other, the supreme benevolence will be attained.

12. Your selfless acts generate contact with the higher beings who can help support your life. Receive their gifts and reciprocate through continued selflessness. Only a thief takes without giving in return.

13. People with positive qualities enjoy their rightful share of bounty

attained by selflessness and are released from imprisoning flaws. Those selfish ones who care only for their own welfare partake of poison.

Humanity is not alone in the universe as the sole conscious species. On the scale of spiritual evolution, in the development of consciousness, there exist beings of lower and higher stages. Plants and animals are lower beings, in the sense that they operate primarily on an instinctive level. Humanity has developed the higher faculty of intellect, so it is further along in spiritual evolution. The *devas*, the beings who live on higher realms, have developed the still higher faculty of intuition so they are even more spiritually advanced.

The universe is a cooperative venture. All beings share the same dharma of *yajna*, making divine offerings. These offerings are twofold: first, to learn from those more advanced than themselves and enter into a creative partnership with them and second, to serve those less developed. The dharma of human beings is to learn from the devas and to serve animals and plants. We fulfill this by practicing spiritual disciplines and ethical living and caring for the earth and the environment. (See also 4.12.)

Verses 14–16

annādbhavanti bhūtani parjanyādannasaṁbhavaḥ
yajñābhavati parjanyo yajñaḥ karmasamudbhavaḥ (14)

karma brahmodbhavaṁ viddhi brahmākṣarasamudbhavam
tasmātsarvagataṁ brahma nityaṁ yajñe pratiṣṭhitam (15)

evaṁ pravartitaṁ cakraṁ nānuvartayatīha yaḥ
aghāyurindriyāramo moghaṁ pārtha sa jīvati (16)

14. Food is the source of living creatures, and rain brings food into existence. From selflessness rain falls, and selflessness is expressed by actions.

15. Appreciate how the source of all action is in the Creator, and the Creator springs from the imperishable ground of being. The Creator, who encompasses all, is eternally expressed by selfless activity.

16. One who does not serve the world by assisting in the rotation of the cosmic wheel has a dreadful nature, O Partha. He enjoys superficial happiness and lives in vain.

The rotation of the wheel of life is a sacred venture in which all beings can contribute. From the motionless, eternal ground of being arises Brahma, the Creator. Brahma creates by selflessly expressing his divine nature. All and everything, therefore, is an expression of divine being.

Humanity participates in the divinity of creation by simulating Brahma's primal selfless action. In our own small spheres of life, we are to manifest divinity by selflessly offering ourselves in service and creative expression. People do not act in a vacuum, as we saw in verses 10–13. Our actions intercourse with beings of different levels of consciousness who reside on different planes of being.

Our actions also have an environmental impact. Our selflessness brings us into harmony with nature and, in alliance with the devas, we co-create our world. The reference to selflessness bringing rain can be understood as a poetic expression, but it would be an error to underestimate the extent to which humanity impacts environmental phenomena. Long before ecology and environmentalism became sciences, the yogic sages perceived how humanity must harmonize with nature if it wishes to survive and prosper.

Verses 17–19

yastvātmaratireva syādātmatṛptaśca mānavaḥ
ātmanyeva ca saṁtuṣṭastasya kāryaṁ na vidyate (17)

naiva tasya kṛtenārtho nākṛteneha kaścana
na cāsya sarvabhūteṣu kaścidarthavyapāśrayaḥ (18)

tasmādasaktaḥ satataṁ kāryaṁ karma samācara
asakto hyācarankarma paramāpnoti pūruṣaḥ (19)

17. For one who finds delight in the Self, satisfaction in the Self, contentment in the Self, there exist no obligations to be fulfilled.

18. He has no desires to be fulfilled by performing or refraining from action. He is autonomous in his relationships.

19. Therefore, perform your naturally occurring responsibilities without attachment. You will attain to the supreme state if you act without attachment.

A person who finds satisfaction within will not be compelled to use others in an attempt to fulfill a perceived inner emptiness. There will be no manipulation or seduction, no addictions or co-dependent relationships. Love arises when there is freedom from selfishness.

The nature of love is to express itself, to constantly expand its current parameters. Thus, activity naturally occurs as an expression of love. In fact, love will inspire activity with a spontaneous kindness and joy. The yogi who knows the Self does not act like a tiresome "do-gooder." He is more like a dancer, gaily making his way across the dance floor of the universe, engaging happily with those who can hear God's tunes and encouraging the shy ones to enter the dance.

Verses 20–21

karmaṇaiva hi saṁsiddhimāsthitā janakādayaḥ
lokasaṁgrahamevāpi saṁpaśyankartumarhasi (20)

yadyadācarati śreṣṭhastattadevetaro janaḥ
sa yatpramāṇaṁ kurute lokastadanuvartate (21)

20. King Janaka and others attained perfection by the path of action. Act like these great souls, maintaining the vision of world harmony.

21. In whatever way a great person behaves, the common people follow his example. Whatever standard he sets is followed by the world.

What passes for love in the world frequently ends in disappointment because it was tinged from the beginning with subconscious needs and impulses. The great sages live in the world to serve. They have found the secret that happiness is produced by loving others and helping enrich their lives. Their love does not fade away.

The general public today marvels at movie stars, sports stars, political stars, and other celebrities who parade on the world stage. But these people are not stars in the sense that they have no inner illumination. Their glow, their glamour, is the result of superficial projections onto them by their admirers. When the public becomes bored and seeks for the next big thrill, these celebrities find their popularity fades, and they become relegated to "has-been" status. They are treated like old news, and their inner poverty and darkness is often exposed.

The sages, the great men and women of the world, are the true stars. Their illumination is real, arising from their inner majesty. They glow as celestial beings in the spiritual sky. In a healthy society, the yogis are the role models, admired and emulated by adults and youth alike. One touchstone for measuring the health of a culture is to examine the nature of individuals who are considered successful.

Verses 22–25

na me pārthāsti kartavyaṁ triṣu lokeṣu kiṁcana
nānavāptamavāptavyaṁ varta eva ca karmaṇi (22)

yadi hyahaṁ na varteyaṁ jātu karmaṇyatandritaḥ
mama vartmānuvartante manuṣyāḥ pārtha sarvaśaḥ (23)

utsīdeyurime lokā na kuryāṁ karma cedaham
saṅkarasya ca kartā syāmupahanyāmimāḥ (24)

saktaḥ karmaṇyavidvāṁso yathā kurvanti bhārata
kuryādvidvāṁstathāsaktaścikīrṣurlokasaṁgraham (25)

22. As for me, O Partha, there is no work in the three worlds to be accomplished nor anything yet for me to obtain; yet I still persist with activity.

23. If I were not tirelessly serving, O Partha, others would follow my example.

24. If I ever cease to serve, the worlds would fall in ruin. I would be the cause of grave confusion and the demise of humanity.

25. While the ignorant may perform their work with attachment, the wise should also act, O Bharata, but without attachment, simply for the support of world harmony.

Krishna is considered to be an avatar of Vishnu, the god who nurtures balance. Like all enlightened sages, he has no personal purpose to accomplish in this world as he already sits atop the spiritual summit. There is nothing to be gained by such beings; they are whole and complete within themselves. They appear on the earth only to serve others.

Those in the unenlightened state of avidya, primal ignorance, believe the goal of life is to find a way to secure the maximum amount of pleasure while incurring the smallest degree of pain. The great beings, however, find their fulfillment and delight in helping others.

Aspirants on the spiritual path can follow the lead of the sages by organizing their lives to contribute the greatest degree of benefit to their families and communities. An aspirant is a sage in training; a saint is just a fool who never gave up.

Verses 26–29

na buddhibhedaṁ janayedajñānāṁ karmasaṅginām
joṣayetsarvakarmāṇi vidvānyuktaḥ samācaran (26)

prakṛteḥ kriyamāṇāni guṇaiḥ karmāṇi sarvaśaḥ
ahaṅkāravimūḍhātmā kartāhamiti manyate (27)

tattvavittu mahābāho guṇakarmavibhāgayoḥ
guṇā guṇeṣu vartanti iti matvā na sajjate (28)

prakṛterguṇasaṁmūḍhāḥ sajjante guṇakarmasu
tānakṛtsnavido mandānkṛtsnavinna vicālayet (29)

26. The wise should not unsettle the minds of the ignorant who act with attachment. Working in a spirit of yoga, be an inspiration to others.

27. All actions are performed by the attributes of nature. He who is deluded by the ego believes himself to be an independent actor.

28. One who knows the essential principles of nature and how they are formulated as attributes and activities, O Mahabaho, perceives how the attributes as senses are drawn to the attributes as objects, and he remains unaffected.

29. Those who are confused and allured by the attributes of nature get attached to their worldly manifestations. These people have a partial vision, but their minds should not be unsettled by those of a whole vision.

Verses 26 and 29 caution the spiritual aspirant against unsettling the mind of those still oppressed by ignorance. This is a warning against any sort of proselytizing or marketing of spirituality. The yogi should not aggressively publicize himself or his path. His character and lifestyle will magnetically attract those who may learn from him. Paramahamsa Ramakrishna said about the manner in which the sage and student come together, "When the flower blooms, the bees come uninvited."

Verses 27 and 28, sandwiched between instruction to the sage, introduce the manner in which the world is perceived. Let us examine in a general way how perception takes place and how this may generate a feeling of egoism and isolation.

The objective world is an expression of prakriti, primal nature. Prakriti is comprised of three *gunas* (qualities). These are *rajas* (activating), *sattva* (balancing), and *tamas* (inertia). The three qualities produce nature's phenomena of, respectively, creation, preservation, and destruction. In terms of perception, sattva creates the senses called *jnanendriyas*, which receive information from the world—eyes, ears, nose, mouth, and skin. Rajas creates the senses called *karmendriyas*, by which one acts in the world—arms, legs, mouth, anus, and genitals. Tamas creates the *tanmatras*, the perceivable sensations of the world—that which is seen, heard, tasted, smelled, and touched.

Interaction between an individual and the world takes place in the following way. The receiving senses perceive undefined vibrations of energy from the external world. Each sense brings its information to the manas, cognitive mind. The mind takes this information and utilizes it to form a comprehensive picture of the outside world, complete with sounds, tastes, smells, and so on. Based on the image of the world created by the mind, behavior will be motivated and expressed through the senses of activity. (See 13.5–6 for a detailed examination of perception.)

The description above is cursory, but it provides for an understanding of what is meant by the phrase "partial vision" in verse 29. The one with partial vision feels himself an isolated island of perception amid a vast world over which he has little control. He does not appreciate how the world he perceives is formed in his own mind and how much his desires influence his perception. The sage realizes his mind is in a partnership with the external world; he knows he is responsible for his perceptions and activities.

Verse 30

mayi sarvāṇi karmāṇi saṁyasyādhyātmacetsā
nirāśīrnirmamo bhūtvā yudhyasva vigatajvaraḥ (30)

30. Renouncing all your selfish actions for me, abiding in Self-awareness, free from personal expectations and possessiveness, go forward and fight with a spirit free of mental fever.

Krishna encourages Arjuna to fight in the proper state of mind. There are two components of this encouragement. One is to be in the proper state of mind. This is a distillation of the instruction Krishna has been giving Arjuna. He wants his student to be in a balanced, selfless state so his understanding will be great and his activity will be beneficent.

The second component is that Arjuna go and fight. Nowhere does Krishna encourage Arjuna to hesitate or retreat. He is constantly pushing Arjuna forward, into the battle, into his life, into his spiritual growth. One of my gurus, Neem Karoli Baba, was famous for telling his devotees to "*jao,*" a Hindi word which literally means "go" or "go away." Even if someone had traveled thousands of miles to see him, Baba would welcome them with some food and tea and then offer his jao.

Baba's jao, however, was not meant to mean "leave me." It was the same "go forward" that Krishna gave Arjuna. The sages say, "Go into your life, go live your passions and dreams, go ahead and make mistakes, go and don't be afraid." They don't want us forever sitting at their feet. They want us in the world, with our families, in our communities, on the world's battlefields, engaging in life for the purpose of service. The blessing of the sage is always: "Go, don't hold back, don't be attached. Go—with my love always with you."

Verse 31

ye me matamidaṁ nityamanutiṣṭhanti mānavāḥ
śraddhāvanto'nasūyanto mucyante te'pi karmabhiḥ (31)

31. Those who have faith and avoid negative thinking and who sincerely follow this teaching of mine become free of karmic imprisonment.

Karma is the law of cause and effect. Benefic actions produce an energy which at a later time will result in the fulfillment of desires. Selfish actions produce an energy which later brings about the frustration of desires or unwanted experiences.

The fulfillment or frustration of desires, however, is not the goal of the spiritual aspirant. For him, all karma is bondage. Negative karma binds with iron chains; positive karma with chains of gold. Karma is imprisoning because the yogi seeks to be unbound from any mechanistic phenomenon of causal law. He wants to be liberated from being forced into any experience, enjoyable or not. He wants to be free to soar in the heaven of his own inner joy and free to descend to the hard ground to serve others. Karma can provide rewards and punishment; it cannot provide freedom.

Verse 32

ye tvetadabhyasūyanto nānutiṣṭhanti me matam
sarvajñānavimūḍhāṁstānviddhi naṣṭānacetsaḥ (32)

32. Those who disregard my teaching and do not tread the spiritual path are blind to life's wisdom. They wander lost and desolate.

A ship without a compass is certain to get lost in the darkness of night and turmoil of storms. Any captain who would set sail without a compass is a fool. Yet all too many people wander this world without any clear direction, without any sense of purpose or certainty that their life has meaning. The yogi has one goal—spiritual growth. With this goal as his polestar, he is able to enter every situation and find its meaning. When the goal is growth, everything is a lesson. For the aspirant, therefore, there are no great successes nor grand tragedies as everything is ultimately useful for personal development.

Verse 33

sadṛśaṁ ceṣṭate svasyāḥ prakṛterjñānavānapi
prakṛtiṁ yānti bhūtāni nigrahaḥ kiṁ kariṣyati (33)

33. As the one of wisdom acts according to his nature, so do all beings follow their natural path. What purpose can aggressive restraint accomplish?

Behavior cannot completely be controlled by discipline and willpower. Behavior is the result of mental phenomena, such as desires, that arise from states of one's consciousness. One can control behavior through restraint, but the energy and motivation which precipitate behavior will, sooner or later, find expression.

Consciousness is the determiner of behavior. For meaningful behavioral change, consciousness must be changed. An individual will not be able to renounce something, no matter how harmful, as long as he believes it has meaning and value. This is why people are so reluctant to give up bad habits even when they recognize the harm befalling them.

To change behavior, the mental phenomena of desires, motivations, and habits must be redirected. When energy is channeled into spiritual pursuits, negative habits will be seen in a clear light, and they will naturally be released in the same way that someone would naturally drop foul garbage. Destructive tendencies need not be forcibly renounced; they will naturally fall away as one progresses on the spiritual path. The proper attitude for this procedure is not to seek to master negativities; rather, it is to seek to master love.

Verse 34

indriyasyendriyasyārthe rāgadveṣau vyavasthitau
tayorna vaśamāgacchettau hyasya paripanthinau (34)

34. Lurking within every attachment is attraction or repulsion expressed by one of the senses. Avoid the influence of this duality, for these are the energies of distraction.

The yogic tradition holds that every human being has a fullness within that is the source of love, joy, and peace. Called by different names, this source is one's true spiritual Self, unscathed by the tribulations and hassles of life. Most people find it incredible that their deepest identity is loving and peaceful, as we are more apt to experience ourselves as angry and stressed. The yogis acknowledge our present suffering but state that it is simply a superficial experience that arises due to a series of five psychological dynamics which are called *kleshas* (obstructions).

The first klesha is avidya, which refers to a primal ignorance. This is the dynamic by which the individual forgets his intrinsic fullness. Avidya is the result of the power of *maya*, the divine illusion (see 7.14). By the force of avidya, a feeling of emptiness arises as one forgets his spiritual identity. As a response to the pain of this forgetfulness, the second klesha, *asmita*, then occurs. Asmita is the creation of, and attachment to, a limited identity based on biological and social conditioning.

Under the influence of asmita, an individual identifies himself with a set of definitions which narrow his ability to understand himself and relate to others. This is generally what we would call "ego," the feeling of being an isolated individual in an enormous world filled with those different from oneself. Asmita also generates a dualism which produces the third and fourth kleshas—*raga* and *dvesha*, obsessive attraction and violent repulsion, which are referenced in this verse.

Under raga and dvesha, we seek for external objects and relationships which we incorrectly believe can fill the inner void, and we attempt to repel experiences and people who we believe can disrupt our lives. The end result of this process is the fifth klesha—*abhinivesha*, fear of change, especially the fear of death. This fear permeates our lives as we are afraid to let go of whatever security we feel we have. Abhinivesha produces an anxiety that things can always get worse, so cling tight to whatever little, tentative happiness you may chance to find!

Verse 35

śreyānsvadharmo viguṇaḥ paradharmātsvanuṣṭhitāt
svadharme nidhanaṁ śreyaḥ paradharmo bhayāvahaḥ (35)

35. Far better is it for imperfection in one's own path than accomplishment in what is not his true calling. Better to die following one's own calling than to live with the peril inherent in imitating another.

What a beautiful teaching to remain true to oneself. Arjuna held in his mind several false notions about spirituality, including the idea that renunciation meant refraining from the battle before him. He believed in a hierarchy of spiritual values based on form rather than content. Krishna here encourages his student to stay true to his own path, the path that is for his steps alone. By following the dictates of one's own intuition, each of us can grow into the spiritual adept we long to be.

Verses 36–39

arjuna uvāca
atha kena prayukto 'yaṁ pāpaṁ carati pūruṣaḥ
anicchannapi vārṣṇeya balādiva niyojitaḥ (36)

śrībhagavānuvāca
kāma eṣa krodhaḥ eṣa rajoguṇasamudbhavaḥ
mahāśano mahāpāpmā viddhyenamiha vairiṇam (37)

dhūmenāvriyate vahniryathādarśo malena ca
yatholbenāvṛto garbhastathā tenedamāvṛtam (38)

āvṛtaṁ jñānametena jñānino nityavairiṇā
kāmarūpeṇa kaunteya duṣpūreṇānalena ca (39)

36. Arjuna said: What is it, O Varshneya, that appears to compel one to wrongdoing as if by force, seemingly against his own will?

37. Shri Bhagavan said: It is selfish desire and foolish anger, arising from nature's quality of activation. This is the enemy here, all devouring and supremely destructive.

38. As a fire is covered by smoke, as a mirror by dust, as an embryo by the womb, so is the aspirant enveloped by these enemies.

39. Wisdom is enveloped, O Kaunteya, by this never-resting foe of the wise—the insatiable fire of selfish desire.

In Western religious traditions, there is often posited to be a malevolent force that manipulates the flesh, placing it in opposition to spirit. Personified as the devil, this force is believed to be at war with God, possessing strength powerful enough to overwhelm innocent people.

In these and the following verses, we have a more sophisticated description of the forces involved in distracting humanity from the spiritual path. These forces are not evil; rather, they spring from the same ground of nature as produces all of creation. We may remember, from the discussion of verses 26–29 in this chapter, that nature's energy is comprised of three gunas, or qualities. Rajas guna is the energy of creation, constantly agitating the existing status quo to bring about further creation. When this energy predominates in the human mind, especially when it overpowers sattva guna, balance, it manifests as selfish desire and foolish anger.

Since activation is part of eternal nature, it is never resting and never-ending. The aspirant who attempts to squelch nature will never succeed, as nature's power is divine and greater than man. This is why repressed monastics so often fail in their goal. The spiritual path is not an attempt to eliminate nature's energy; it is rather learning how to live in harmony with nature. In this harmony, there is no distorted perception of nature as evil, or of nature and spirit in conflict.

Verses 40–41

indriyāṇi mano buddhiraśyādhiṣṭhānamucyate
etairvimohayatyeṣa jñānamāvṛtya dehinam (40)

tasmāttvamindriyāṇyādau niyamya bharatarṣabha
pāpmānaṁ prajahi hyenaṁ jñānavijñānāśanam (41)

40. The senses, the cognitive mind, and the intelligence are said to be the seat of selfish desire. Veiling wisdom through these vehicles bewilders the embodied soul.

41. Therefore, O Bharatarshabha (Arjuna as Best of the Bharatas), control the initial promptings of the senses and slay this self-centeredness which destroys both wisdom and knowledge.

The *atman* (the soul) is never actually affected by ignorance. The atman is a wave on the ocean of Infinite Consciousness and, as such, can never be separated from that Consciousness. Through relationship with the body/mind complex, however, the soul apparently becomes bewildered about its true nature.

By controlling the first promptings of selfishness, the tendency toward bewilderment can be sublimated. It is like pulling a small plant from the ground. If one waits for the plant to grow into a giant tree, the task of its removal becomes much more difficult.

Verses 42–43

indriyāṇi parāṇyāhurindriyebhyaḥ paraṁ manaḥ
manasastu parā buddhiryo buddheḥ paratastu saḥ (42)

evaṁ buddheḥ paraṁ buddhvā saṁstabhyātmānamātmanā
jahi śatruṁ mahābāho kāmarūpaṁ durāsadam (43)

42. Superior to objects are the senses, superior to the senses is the cognitive mind, superior to the cognitive mind is the intelligence, superior to the intelligence is He.

43. Thus, awaken to Him who is beyond even the intelligence by steadying the lower self by your Self, and destroy, O Mahabaho, your most challenging enemy in the form of selfish desire.

There exists a hierarchy in the body/mind complex in relation to the soul. This is based on the degree to which the soul can directly relate to a given vehicle. Just as the general of an army will speak directly to a high ranking officer, who then ensures orders are passed down through the ranks, so the soul affects intelligence, which then coordinates the operations of the cognitive mind and senses.

The great sages are those who have formed a yoga, a union, by which intelligence has harmonized body and mind with the soul. In this elevated state selfish desire fully ceases. Then the soul, Arjuna, emerges victorious over his inner enemy of selfishness.

Chapter 4

Jnana Yoga
The Yoga of Wisdom

Verses 1–3

śribhagavānuvāca
imaṁ vivasvate yogaṁ proktavānahamavyayam
vivasvānmanave prāha manurikṣvākave 'bravīt (1)

evaṁ paramparāprāptamimaṁ rājaṣayo viduḥ
sa kāleneha mahatā yogo naṣṭaḥ paraṁtapa (2)

sa evāyaṁ mayā te 'dya yogaḥ proktaḥ purātanaḥ
bhakto 'si me sakhā ceti rahasyaṁ hyetaduttamam (3)

1. Shri Bhagavan said: This perennial wisdom I taught to Vivasvan (The Sun God), Vivasvan taught it to Manu (The Primal Man), and Manu taught it to Ikshvaku (The First King).

2. Thus it continued to be handed down through a lineage of royal sages until it was lost to the world through the passage of time, O Parantapa.

3. This same ancient yoga, the highest of secrets, I today declare to you, for you are my devotee and my friend.

The spiritual tradition of the Indian people is today called "Hinduism," although this is a misnomer. Hindu is a name that was applied to the ancient peoples of India living in the Indus River valley by those coming to their lands for trade or conquest. The philosophy of life lived by these people is rightly called *sanatana dharma.* Sanatana means "eternal," and dharma, in this context, means "the way of harmony." The traditional spirituality of India, reflected in the Bhagavad Gita, is the sanatana dharma, "the eternal way of harmony."

Krishna informs Arjuna that his teaching is expressive of the sanatana dharma. It is not a new teaching presented to mankind for the first time. It is not a new revelation, as the eternal way has always been present with humanity. Different times and cultures may require a slightly different presentation of this perennial philosophy, but the essential teachings and principles remain the same.

As sanatana dharma has always existed, there is no original founder. There is no one superior book, no religious leader for all, no rites and rituals meant for everyone, no dogmas for all to observe. The sages of India and all other lands form one great spiritual family. Their desire is to help struggling, suffering humanity unite in divine consciousness. This is the teaching Krishna is presenting to Arjuna, and he wants to ensure that his student understands the universality of the spiritual path.

Verses 4–5

arjuna uvāva
aparaṁ bhavato janma paraṁ janma vivasvataḥ
kathametadvijānīyāṁ tvamādau proktāvaniti (4)

śribhagavānuvāca
bahūni me vyatītāni janmāni tava cārjuna
tānyahaṁ veda sarvāṇi na tvaṁ vettha paraṁtapa (5)

4. Arjuna said: Later is your birth than that of Vivasvan. How am I to understand you were the one who beget this teaching to him?

5. Shri Bhagavan said: Many are my previous births, as are yours also, O Arjuna. I am aware of them all, but you know them not, O Parantapa.

Arjuna's identity is attached to his current body/mind complex. He fails to remember any of his previous lives. Krishna is reminding Arjuna of the extensive history of the soul's pilgrimage. The soul travels through creation for vast periods of time. The Buddha said this can be likened to the time it takes for a mountain that is one mile high, one mile wide, and one mile long, to be worn away by a bird carrying a silk scarf in its mouth and passing the scarf on the mountain peak once every hundred years.

Verse 6

ajo 'pi sannavyayātmā bhūtānāmīśvaro 'pi san
prakṛtiṁ svāmadhiṣṭhāya saṁbhavāmyātmamāyayā (6)

6. Although I am unborn and my Self is ever-existing, and although I am the Lord of all that exists, I invest myself with my own natural potency, and I come into manifestation via the play of my self-limitation.

The essential nature of the Self of all beings is independent and autonomous. It comes into manifestation by voluntarily embracing its own energy of limitation. All individual souls share the Self, and all experience the limitation of the divine consciousness. The Lord, however, is considered a unique individuated soul, called Bhagavan, Ishvara, Paramatma, and other names in the yogic literature.

The Lord is the aspect of the Self which accepts the limiting potency as a play. He is never fully bound because he knows life is simply a gesture of love on the stage of consciousness. The experiences the individual souls suffer and dread, such as sickness and death, are like all other aspects of a profound drama, to be watched and appreciated. As a good theatrical production requires many different situations and subplots, so the grand play of creation requires souls to play their part, whether they find it pleasing or not. In fact, the purpose of the play is not to please Arjuna, the individual soul; it is to please the Lord, Krishna.

Verses 7–9

yadā yadā hi dharmasya glānirbhavati bhārata
abhuytthānamadharmasya tadātmānaṁ sṛjāmyaham (7)

paritrāṇāya sādhūnāṁ vināśāya ca duṣkṛtām
dharmasaṁsthāpanārthāya saṁbhavāmi yuge yuge (8)

janma karma ca me divyamevaṁ yo vetti tattvataḥ
tyaktvā dehaṁ punarjanma naiti māmeti so 'rjuna (9)

7. Whenever there is a decline of righteousness and harmony, O Bharata, and unrighteousness and imbalance rise, then I come forth into manifestation.

8. For the protection of the good and destruction of the cruel and for the establishment of righteousness and harmony, I come into the world age after age.

9. One who understands the essential nature of my divine birth and activities is not subject to another birth but comes to my state when leaving this body, O Arjuna.

These verses describe the advent of an *avatar* (incarnation of the Lord). It is said that the Lord, the individual soul who is not actually limited through manifestation, descends to this world and works to restore righteousness and harmony. Regardless of the philosophy of the Lord's descent as avatar, let us remember the Bhagavad Gita is a yogic text, grounded in the highest principles of sanatana dharma, the eternal path of harmony. From this perspective, we must meditate on these verses from the highest level of consciousness if we are to properly understand the teaching. From this perspective, we must see how each individual plays a role similar to the avatar. Every spiritual aspirant should challenge himself to determine to what extent he is fulfilling the purpose of his own incarnation.

To what extent is one honoring the divinity within and serving the world by helping the righteous and bringing balance? When one fails to accomplish his task, he lives in the confusion of Arjuna. As one rises in divine service, consciousness becomes absorbed into the Lord, into Krishna, and one becomes His vehicle. When this absorption is complete, no precise individuated identity exists. The drop of water has entered the ocean, though it is equally true the ocean has entered the drop. With this accomplishment, appearance in creation is no longer driven by the karma of desire, but by the longing to love and serve.

Verses 10–11

vītarāgabhayakrodhā manmayā māmupāśritāḥ
bahavo jñānatapasā pūtā madbhāvamāgatāḥ (10)

ye yathā māṁ prapadyante tāṁstathaiva bhajānyaham
mama vartmānuvartante manuṣyāḥ pārtha sarvaśaḥ (11)

10. Emancipated from selfish attachment, from fear and anger, absorbed in me, taking refuge in me, many have become purified by illuminating wisdom practices and have entered into my state of being.

11. As I am approached, so do I accept each aspirant. Everyone, everywhere, is on the path to Me, O Partha.

The universal yoga presented in the Bhagavad Gita is not a sectarian teaching meant for the few. It is a presentation of the perennial philosophy for all humanity. All great wisdom texts serve the same universal spiritual tradition. Everyone is already on the spiritual path, though there certainly exist among people different degrees of awakening. Stephen Gaskin once said that there is only one church and that your membership button is your belly button!

Verse 11 teaches that God can be approached in innumerable ways. Every aspirant is free to understand God based on his level of development. Limitless are the forms of God imagined by men, while God remains beyond all forms and imaginations. Limitless are the paths to God created by the sages, while God remains beyond all paths and traditions. This universality ensures that true spirituality is open-minded, without prejudice or dogmatism.

The universal path, in whatever presentation, regardless of external appearance, will have certain characteristics. The aspirant will be called upon to develop the consciousness described in verse 10. He will be required to illuminate his being through *sadhana* (spiritual practice), and he will need to offer his selfish ego into the fire of selfless service.

Verse 12

kāṅkṣantaḥ karmaṇāṁ siddhiṁ yajanta iha devatāḥ
kṣipram hi mānuṣe loke siddhirbhavati karmajā (12)

12. Those who are desirous of worldly rewards make religious offerings to the various higher beings, expressions of partial divinity. Through this path, one can quickly gain worldly rewards.

The ancient sages of all the world's spiritual traditions recognized the existence of beings on more subtle planes of reality. Called *devas* here, meaning "shining ones," or "angels" in the Western traditions, the labels refer to the same class of beings. These higher souls interact with our world and work to provide people with the health and prosperity needed to live full, productive lives. By cultivating a relationship with these beings, a person is able to procure for himself gain in this material world. (See 3.10-13).

The Bhagavad Gita acknowledges that material benefit can be acquired through propitiation of the devas, but this is not considered the highest spiritual goal. The highest goal is to realize the one Self shared by all—man, animal, plant, bird, and angel alike. The angels, like men, are mortal. Although time in the heavenly realms is immense by human standards, the devas themselves will one day leave their higher world after reaping the fruit of their positive karma. At that time they will need to be reborn as human beings to continue their spiritual development.

As we have seen in the two previous sets of verses, compulsory rebirth is evidence of unripe spiritual growth and proof that the conclusion of spiritual growth has not yet taken place. The goal of spirituality is the completion of the spiritual curriculum of creation, the eradication of all selfishness and absorption into the one divine Self.

Verse 13

cāturvarṇyaṁ mayā sṛṣṭaṁ guṇakarmavibhāgaśaḥ
tasya kartāramapi māṁ viddhyakartāramavyayam (13)

13. The fourfold societal order was created by me based on the natural qualities of human nature and social functions. Though I am the creator of this system, I remain thoroughly transcendent, without any action or change.

The traditional Indian system of social organization is called *varnashram dharma.* This is based on the duties performed according to the system of four *varnas* (social divisions) and four *ashrams* (stages in life). The four ashrams deal with individual duties related to the four traditional periods of life: *brahmachari* (student), *grihastha* (family life), *vanaprastha* (retirement), and *sannyasa* (renunciate). This verse deals specifically with the four varnas, the collective social structure organized into four divisions—*brahmins* (spiritual teachers), *kshyatrias* (leaders in government and the military), *vaishyas* (business class), and *shudras* (manual laborers).

In the India of Krishna's time, all classes were considered vital for the social body. The brahmins were the head (wise mind); the kshatriyas, the strong back (leadership); the vaishyas, the belly (providing prosperity); and the shudras, the arms (heavy lifting). Within the four varnas, every person was employed in their natural and proper niche. All divisions of labor were honored equally, and everyone enjoyed a relatively similar quality of life.

Besides supporting the natural social divisions, Krishna also makes the point that the Self, the pure "I," is transcendent to any social identification. While the aspirant may be involved in any profession or social activity, he is still to retain a transcendent attitude of pure spiritual identity. Any man or woman can attain Self-realization and engage in selfless service regardless of the formal nature of their status and employment. (See 18.41–44 for additional discussion on varnashrama dharma.)

Verses 14–15

na māṁ karmāṇi limpanti na me karmaphale spṛhā
iti māṁ yo 'bhijānāti karmabhirna sa badhyate (14)

evaṁ jñātvā kṛtaṁ karma pūrvairapi mumukṣubhiḥ
kuru karmaiva tasmāttvaṁ pūrvaiḥ pūrvataraṁ kṛtam (15)

14. Activity does not impact my being, nor am I desirous of gain. One who knows me thus is not bound by the karma of activity.

15. In this attitude of wisdom, work was accomplished by the ancient sages as they sought liberation. So should you behave as did your spiritual elders in their times.

The aspirant who undertakes the universal yoga is not breaking new ground. He or she is part of an illustrious lineage of aspirants throughout world history who sought liberation. They shared in common the willingness to transcend selfish desires and act only for the purpose of service. In this way they became free of karmic bondage, free of limiting identity, free to enjoy being alive.

Verses 16–18

kiṁ karma kimakarmeti kavayo 'pyatra mohitāḥ
tatte karma pravakṣyāmi yajjñatvā mokṣyase 'śubhāt (16)

karmaṇo hyapi boddhavyaṁ boddhavyaṁ ca vikarmaṇaḥ
akarmaṇaśca boddhavyaṁ gahanā karmaṇo gatiḥ (17)

karmaṇyakarma yaḥ paśyedakarmaṇi ca karma yaḥ
sa buddhimānmanuṣyeṣu sa yuktaḥ kṛtsnakarmakṛt (18)

16. What is action? What is inaction? These are questions which perplex even the most intelligent. I will teach you what is the essence of action, understanding which you will be released from your distress.

17. One must deeply understand the essence of action, the essence of wrong action, and the essence of inaction. Difficult to understand is this teaching about action and its ramifications.

18. One who can perceive activity in seeming inaction and inactivity during action has developed his intuitive vision beyond that of the common person. Such a one is a yogi and fulfills his karmic duties while in this higher consciousness.

The Bhagavad Gita begins with Arjuna's confusion about the proper course of action. Krishna entered into dialogue with him and has now captured his attention enough that the initial question can be reviewed. Should Arjuna fight? Should he refrain from fighting? Is his fighting right or wrong? These are the issues at stake.

Krishna acknowledges these questions are profound and difficult to understand. The ordinary person does not even raise such questions because he fails to appreciate this line of inquiry will reveal his freedom from his distress. The common person does not have the intuitive vision to see anything other than the conventional categories of action/inaction and right/wrong.

The sage, through meditation, develops his intuitive vision and is able to perceive that the question of action is a spiritual question. Action is to be undertaken when it is beneficial in dharmic terms, when it is of service to the greater good. Action is refrained from when it is not spiritually beneficial, and this includes honoring that a wholesome act may simply not be one's personal duty but better left for another.

Activity takes place in inactivity when the yogi rests within, allowing nature to manifest her power and create the best possible means of accomplishing her divine objectives. This may result in his being engaged in a task or not. The yogi wonders in gentle amazement at the ways in which nature moves him. He becomes a spiritual dancer, spontaneously active, moving to a subtle celestial song heard only by the accomplished.

Verses 19–23

yasya sarve samārambhāḥ kāmasaṅkalpavarjitāḥ
jñānāgnidagdhakarmāṇaṁ tamāhuḥ paṇḍitaṁ budhāḥ (19)

tyaktvā karmaphalāsaṅgaṁ nityatṛpto nirāśrayaḥ
karmaṇyabhipravṛtto 'pi naiva kiñcitkaroti saḥ (20)

nirāśīryatacittātmā tyaktasarvaparigrahaḥ
śārīraṁ kevalaṁ karma kurvannāpnoti kilbiṣam (21)

yadṛcchālābhasaṁtuṣṭo dvandvātīto vimatsaraḥ
samaḥ siddhāvasiddhau ca kṛtvāpi na nibadhyate (22)

gatasaṅgasya muktasya jñānāvasthitacetasaḥ
yajñāyācarataḥ karma samagraṁ pravilīyate (23)

19. The one whose motivations are free from the impulse of selfish desire and whose actions are burned to ash in the fire of wisdom is called wise by the learned.

20. Having cast aside concern with rewards from his work, ever content, emotionally independent, such a one does nothing even while engaged in activity.

21. Without selfish concerns, his personal consciousness aligned with his Self, free of possessiveness, utilizing his body to fulfill his karmic responsibilities, he commits no foolish errors.

22. Satisfied with whatever naturally comes to him, rising above duality, free of jealousy, and content in success or failure, he acts but he is not bound.

23. Such a one is liberated from selfish attachments, his consciousness is grounded in wisdom, and he engages in actions as a divine offering. The effects of his activities dissolve.

The yogi whose life is lived on behalf of the divine consciousness sees all as sacred. The mind-created division between world and spirit disappears. He realizes that all activity can be a spiritual practice. Not just formal rites and rituals, but even the most mundane activities of daily life can be infused with love and passion, transforming them into divine offerings of great majesty. Work is worship, play is worship, chopping wood and carrying water is worship.

With this attitude, activity is given to God without expectation for reward or recognition. Easily, gracefully, actions are undertaken because they are felt to be joyful. Duties and responsibilities are the bane of the mundane thinker, but they are transformed in the heart of the yogi. Swami Satyananda Saraswati said of duties that they are to be dropped in a spirit of renunciation, then picked back up as privileges.

Verse 24

brahmārpaṇaṁ brahma havirbrahmāgnau brahmaṇā hutam
brahmaiva tena gantavyaṁ brahmakarmasamādhinā (24)

24. The Infinite Consciousness is in the act of offering, the Infinite Consciousness is the article offered, and the Infinite Consciousness is the one making the offering into the fire of Infinite Consciousness. One who realizes the true relationship of Infinite Consciousness and activity enters into Infinite Consciousness.

This is a well-known verse in the Bhagavad Gita and is cited in many different contexts, including commonly being used as a prayer before eating. The wheel of life is the manifestation of Brahman, Infinite Consciousness. It revolves as creation, preservation, and destruction. While the wheel of immanent Brahman eternally turns, Brahman also remains eternally transcendent. The relationship of the immanent and transcendent characteristics of Brahman is discussed in 8.3.

Verses 25–33

daivamevāpare yajñaṁ yoginaḥ paryupāsate
brahmāgnāvapare yajñaṁ yajñenaivopajuhvati (25)

śrotrādīnīndriyāṇyanye saṁyamāgniṣu juhvati
śabdādīnviṣayānanya indriyāgniṣu juhvati (26)

sarvāṇīndriyakarmāṇi prāṇakarmāṇi cāpare
ātmasaṁyamayogāgnau juhvati jñānadīpite (27)

dravyayajñāstapoyajñā yogayajñāstathāpare
svādhyāyajñānayajñāśca yatayaḥ saṁśitavratāḥ (28)

apāne juhvati prāṇaṁ prāne 'pānaṁ tathāpare
prāṇāpānagatī ruddhvā prāṇāyāmaparāyaṇāḥ (29)

apare niyatāhārāḥ prāṇānprāṇeṣu juhvati
sarve 'pyete yajñavido yajñakṣapitakalmaṣāḥ (30)

yajñaśiṣṭāmṛtabhujo yānti brahma sanātanam
nāyaṁ loko 'styayajñasya kuto 'nyaḥ kurusattama (31)

evaṁ bahuvidhā yajñā vittā brahmaṇo mukhe
karmajānviddhi tānsarvānevaṁ jñātvā vimokṣyase (32)

śreyāndravyamayādyajñājjñānayajñaḥ paraṁtapa
sarvaṁ karmakhilaṁ pārtha jñāne parisamāpyate (33)

25. Some yogis make their offerings to the gods, the higher beings, while other yogis make their offering into the fire of Infinite Consciousness.

26. Some yogis offer hearing and other senses into the fire of restraint; others offer sound and other sensory experiences into the fire of the senses.

27. Some offer all the activities of their senses and their life energy into the fire of the yoga of self-control, kindled by wisdom.

28. Some offer as a sacrifice their material goods, others offer their austerities, and others offer their yogic practices. Some make the offering through their study of wisdom and Self-contemplation; others strive through the observance of vows.

29. Others offer their outgoing breath into their incoming breath and the incoming breath into the outgoing breath. Controlling the flow of the breath, they seek to discipline their life energy.

30. Others restrict their diet, making an offering by refocusing their life energy back into itself. All of these yogis appreciate the nature of selfless offerings, and through their offerings their obstructions are eliminated.

31. Those who subsist on the nectar remaining after their offering attain to the eternal Infinite Consciousness. Neither this world nor any other is enjoyed by one who makes no offering, O Kurusattama (Arjuna as Truest of Kauravas).

32. Thus, there are many means of making offerings to be laid before Infinite Consciousness. Recognize how they all arise from activity, and then, by understanding the relationship of selfless offerings and activity, you will gain liberation.

33. Superior to any offering of material wealth is the offering of one's wisdom, O Parantapa. All actions, O Partha, culminate in wisdom.

This is a significant, but in no means complete list, of different means by which a yogi can make a personal offering in order to approach Infinite Consciousness. In verse 25, we are reminded that some make offerings to the gods, an offering that will bring material rewards but incomplete spiritual results (see 4.12). Verse 33 states the greatest offering is the one in which the yogi offers the totality of himself and his understanding.

Between these two verses is a variety of physical and mental approaches to subjugate selfish impulses and elevate noble motivations. The particular emphasis of the individual yogi will be based on his constitution and intuition and the guidance of his teacher. Regardless of specific practice, however, as verse 32 teaches, all means of spiritual development are considered worthy and respectable.

Verse 34

tadviddhi praṇipātena paripraśnena sevayā
upadekṣyanti te jñānaṁ jñāninastattvadarśinaḥ (34)

34. Learn by humbly approaching the wise ones. Earnestly inquire of them and serve them well. They will instruct you in the vision of the essence.

The yogic tradition is an initiatory tradition. The aspirant must, at some point in his development, become a disciple of a guru, take initiation, and practice under the guidance of the teacher. The egoic impulse is simply too powerful for an individual to be able to root out its subtle influences on his own. There are rare instances where someone has achieved enlightenment without a living guru, but one who considers himself worthy of such an exception is deluded by his own pride. For those who believe a teacher is unnecessary, there is a lively axiom: "One who is his own guru has a fool for a disciple."

The relationship with a teacher, however, must be properly understood. For instance, the Bhagavad Gita consists of 700 verses, yet only this single verse discusses the need for a teacher. The teacher plays an important, pivotal role in the disciple's development, but the aspiring yogi is still responsible for his own advancement. My yoga guru, Baba Hari Dass, was fond of stating, "I can cook for you, but I cannot eat for you."

It is also important for the aspirant to recognize that it is not necessary for his guru to be fully enlightened. The guru need only be enlightened enough to help the aspirant progress to the next stage of his growth. The fantasy of every beginning yogi needing a "perfect master" has led to many misunderstandings regarding the role of the guru and that of the disciple. The guru's job is to point to the path and to provide directions for its traversing. The job of the disciple is to walk in the indicated direction. Concern with the spiritual status of one's guru leaves one prone to a cult of personality. The spiritual marketplace is littered with the debris of disappointment as former "true believers" discover their supposed omniscient and omnipotent gurus were actually fallible men and women.

The task of the guru is enormous. His sole goal is to assist the disciple in transcending limiting personality obstructions. This is a thankless task, one which can only be performed by a being whose love for others is so deep that they can continue their service in the face of phony worship and unfair criticism. One becomes a guru when his enlightenment is deep enough that his only desire is a spontaneous arising in his heart to help bring others to the same freedom he enjoys, without expecting appreciation or recognition.

Verses 35–39

yajjñātvā na punarmohamevaṁ yāsyasi pāṇḍava
yena bhūtānyaśeṣeṇa drakṣyasyātmanyatho mayi (35)

api cedasi pāpebhyaḥ sarvebhyaḥ pāpakṛttamaḥ
sarvaṁ jñānaplavenaiva vṛjinaṁ saṁtariṣyasi (36)

yathaidhāṁsi samiddho 'gnirbhasmasātkurute 'rjuna
jñānāgniḥ sarvakarmāṇi bhasmasātkurute tathā (37)

na hi jñānena sadṛśam pavitramiha vidyate
tatsvayaṁ yogasaṁsiddhaḥ kālenātmani vindati (38)

śraddhāvāṁllabhate jñānaṁ tatparaḥ saṁyatendriyaḥ
jñānaṁ labdhvā parāṁ śāntimacireṇādhigacchati (39)

35. Knowing this, O Partha, you will no longer be swayed by delusion. You will be able to see all beings in the Self and thus in me.

36. Even if you are the most ignorant among the ignorant, the raft of this wisdom will enable you to cross over the vast sea of inequity.

37. Just as a fire ablaze reduces its fuel to ashes, O Arjuna, so does the fire of wisdom reduce to ashes the karma of activity.

38. There is nothing whatsoever as purifying as this wisdom. Through its application a yogi becomes fully accomplished, discovering this same wisdom in his Self.

39. Disciplining the senses, one of faith arrives at this wisdom by holding that as his supreme goal. On attaining wisdom, the state of supreme peace quickly arises.

The power of *jnana* (spiritual wisdom) is immense. Its ability to transform even the most ignorant is akin to a light being brought into a dark room. It does not matter how dark the room is, nor how long it has been dark; once the light appears, the room is illuminated.

The light of wisdom is the means for developing human character. Discipline in behavior can be helpful, but prior to a transformation in consciousness it is difficult for behavior to remain consistent. Like a man who has approached the mirage closely and can now perceive no water actually exists, one whose consciousness is infused with jnana is able to correctly perceive the nature of objects and relationships. Without the actual, personal, direct experience of knowing the mirage was an illusion, the individual will find it impossible to break his belief in the false source of water. This is why firsthand experience is given so much importance in the yogic tradition. The words of the sages and scriptures are to be respected, but only immediate experience will bring the aspirant into realization.

Verses 40–42

ajñaścāśraddadhānaśca saṁśayātmā vinaśyati
nāyaṁ loko 'sti na paro na sukhaṁ saṁśayātmanaḥ (40)

yogasaṁnyastakarmāṇaṁ jñānasaṁchinnasaṁśayam
ātmavantaṁ na karmāṇi nibadhnanti dhanaṁjaya (41)

tasmādajñānasaṁbhūtaṁ hṛtstaṁ jñānāsinātmanaḥ
chittvainaṁ saṁśayaṁ yogamātiṣṭhottiṣṭha bhārata (42)

40. One who has no wisdom, who holds no faith, and who doubts the reality of the Self is virtually destroyed. There can be no happiness in this world nor even in the higher realms for one trapped by doubt.

41. One who utilizes this yoga of renouncing the results and rewards of activity, who by wisdom destroys false doubts, and who is Self-determined may be active without producing bondage, O Dhananjaya.

42. Therefore, with the sword of Self-wisdom cut asunder this doubt born of ignorance. Dwell in your heart; stand strong and firm in yoga. Arise, O Bharata!

Krishna cheers Arjuna to overcome the hurdle of his doubt and to venture forth. The doubt he refers to is not the reasonable questioning of the sincere aspirant. This should be apparent in this Bhagavad Gita, as the entire text is but a response of Krishna to Arjuna's questions and doubts. Doubt that arises from the student's intelligence and integrity is an asset that should be honored by the student and respected by the teacher.

The type of doubt Krishna wants Arjuna to overcome is the doubt which paralyzes. It often manifests as questions for which no answer will ever suffice. The yogic tradition is not concerned with blind faith or comfortable theology; its focus is on helping the aspirant attain success in life by fulfilling his potential. Doubt which is used as a defense against actually taking steps to improve one's life is what Krishna wants Arjuna to cut asunder. The inner guru, Krishna, is encouraging every soul, "Arise, aspirant, go forth and achieve success."

Chapter 5

Karma Sannyasa Yoga
The Yoga of Renouncing Binding Action

Verses 1–3

arjuna uvāva
saṁnyāsaṁ karmaṇāṁ kṛṣṇa punaryogaṁ ca śaṁsasi
yacchreya etayorekaṁ tanme brūhi suniścitam (1)

śrībhagavānuvāca
saṁnyāsaḥ karmayogaśca niḥśreyasakarāvubhau
tayostu karmasaṁnyāsātkarmayogo viśiṣyate (2)

jñeyaḥ sa nityasaṁnyāsī yo na dveṣṭhi na kāṅkṣati
nirdvandvo hi mahābāho sukhaṁ bandhātpramucyate (3)

1. Arjuna said: You praise the renunciation of activity, O Krishna, and also perform the yoga of selfless action. Tell me decidedly which of these two is spiritually more beneficial?

2. Shri Bhagavan replied: Both renunciation and selfless action share the same goal of spiritual development. Of the two, however, selfless action is superior to merely renouncing activity.

3. The ultimate example of renunciation is he who is not moved by selfish desire or repulsion and is free from dualistic conflicts. O Mahabaho, such a one finds happiness in his release from the bondage of karma.

Arjuna is still confused about proper action because his mind is used to thinking in a dualistic manner. He has trouble understanding how what seem like opposites are poles of a non-dual harmony. With greater attention he would have understood that the teaching presented by Krishna was an interweaving of action and renunciation. Arjuna, however, cannot yet perceive their proper relationship.

Krishna teaches repeatedly throughout this Bhagavad Gita that renunciation is an internal matter and that selfless service is to be undertaken. To simply refuse to participate in life is not the spiritual objective. The goal is to renounce selfish action, engaging in activity beneficial to the greater good without expectation of personal reward or recognition.

Verses 4–6

saṁkhyayogau pṛthagbālāḥ pravadanti na paṇḍitāḥ
ekamapyāsthitaḥ samyagubhayorvindate phalam (4)

yatsāṁkhyaiḥ prāpyate sthānaṁ tadyogairapi gamyate
ekaṁ sāṁkhyaṁ ca yogaṁ ca yaḥ paśyati (5)

saṁnyāsastu mahābāho duḥkhamāptumayogataḥ
yogayukto munirbrahma nacireṇādhigacchati (6)

4. Only the spiritually immature say the path of insight into the essential principles and the path of selfless action are distinct, not those who are wise. One well-established in either of these paths will enjoy the rewards of both.

5. The spiritual state attained by those on the path of insight is reached also by those on the path of selfless action. Who sees insight and selfless action is one who truly sees.

6. Renunciation without yoga, O Mahabaho, is full of pain. With yoga, the sage quickly attains Infinite Consciousness.

In Arjuna's mind, and perhaps in the minds of many aspirants, the path of insight leading to detachment and the path of activity leading to service are seen as mutually exclusive. This view is described by Krishna as being spiritually immature and lacking understanding. Insight and activity, renunciation and service, are two wings on the bird of spiritual progress. Insight into the interrelationship of all living beings leads to a desire to perform service. Service supports the insight of the universal community. This creates a positive spiral of growth. An aspirant may, based on personal constitution, rely more favorably on one aspect of the path than the other. Nonetheless, he will eventually discover that insight and activity are both necessary in the universal yoga.

Egoic renunciation is impossible without selfless activity. The attempt by an aspirant to overcome egoic attachment by removing himself from others only deepens the feelings of isolation and separateness that are at the root of the fear-based ego. All spiritual activity is for the purpose of relieving the suffering of all sentient beings.

Verse 7

yogayukto viśuddhātmā vijitātmā jitendriyaḥ
sarvabhūtāmabhūtātmā kurvannapi na lipyate (7)

7. One who is practiced in the yoga of activity, who is pure in the Self, who is mastered by the Self, and who has conquered his senses feels his Self as the Self of all beings. Although he is outwardly active, he accrues no karma.

This verse describes the relationship of selfless activity, Self-realization, and the transcendence of karma. Acts performed by an accomplished sage are like the person himself: pure, mastered, and self-conquered. His experience of activity, as we shall see in the following set of verses, is that he is not an independent actor but a vehicle through which divine action takes place.

Verses 8–13

naiva kiṁcitkaromīti yukto manyeta tattvavit
paśyañśṛṇvanspṛśañjighrannaśnangacchansvapañśvasan (8)

pralapanvisṛjangṛhṇannunmiṣannimiṣannapi
indriyāṇīndriyārtheṣu vartanta iti dhārayan (9)

brahmaṇyādhāya karmāṇi saṅgaṁ tyaktvā karoti yaḥ
lipyate na sa pāpena padmapatramivāmbhasā (10)

kāyena manasā buddhyā kevalairindriyairapi
yoginaḥ karma kurvanti saṅgaṁ tyaktvātmaśuddhaye (11)

yuktaḥ karmaphalaṁ tyaktvā śāntimāpnoti naiṣṭhikīm
ayuktaḥ kāmakāreṇa phale sakto nibadhyate (12)

sarvakarmāṇi manasā saṁnyasyāste sukhaṁ vaśī
navadvāre pure dehī naiva kurvanna kārayan (13)

8. The yogi who understands the essence of reality thinks, "I do nothing at all." In sight, hearing, touch, smell, taste, when walking, sleeping, breathing,

9. In speaking, in releasing or grasping, when opening or closing the eyes, he knows it is only the operation of the senses in relationship to their corresponding objects of perception.

10. The one who can work in a spirit of detachment, leaving his activities to Infinite Consciousness, is untouched by negative consequences as the lotus petals are untouched by water.

11. The yogi's sense of activity is to engage the body, mind, intellect, and senses without attachment for the purpose of self-purification.

12. The yogi abandons attachment to the fruits of work—results and rewards—and attains a firmly grounded peace. One who acts without a spirit of yoga is invariably propelled by selfish desire and attachment to results and rewards. Thus, he is bound by karma.

13. The embodied one who has control of his impulses and is mentally free of compulsive behavior dwells at ease in "the city of nine gates" (the body), neither seeking nor causing activities.

The accomplished yogi lives in a state of spontaneity and a feeling of flowing with life. He does not experience himself as an actor, but a vehicle through which actions take place. Like a musical instrument played by a master musician, the yogi feels himself the instrument of the divine. He feels the song course through him, knowing he is not the source.

This spirit of detachment is not the removal of care or concern shown by the narcissist. Detachment is a quiet inner calm that makes it possible for the yogi to respond, rather than react, to what takes place in his life. Since his actions are not motivated by selfish desires, he is free to act, or not act, in a manner intended to benefit the greater community.

In verse 10, for instance, the yogi's consciousness is described as "untouched by negative consequences." This does not mean negative experiences may not befall the yogi during the course of his life. All human beings are vulnerable to sickness, poverty, mistreatment, and so forth. "Untouched" means, rather, that his peace remains undisturbed regardless of these experiences.

The "city of nine gates" mentioned in verse 13 is the body and the manner in which the senses serve as "gates" through which the external world makes its impressions. The main teaching of this verse is that an embodied being can dwell in peace during incarnation in the body.

The peace of God and His kingdom are not attained by death, but by becoming mentally free of compulsive behavior. One who has attained to this kingdom is known as a *jivanmukti* (liberated while still embodied). The nature of a jivanmukti is discussed in more detail in verses 19–26.

Verses 14–17

na kartṛtvaṁ na karmāṇi lokasya sṛjati prabhuḥ
na karmaphalasaṁyogaṁ svabhāvastu pravartate (14)

nādatte kasyacitāpaṁ na caiva sukṛtaṁ vibhuḥ
ajñānenāvṛtaṁ jñānaṁ tena muhyanti jantavaḥ (15)

jñānena tu tadajñānaṁ yeṣāṁ nāśitamātmanaḥ
teṣāmādityavajjñānaṁ prakāśayati tatparam (16)

tadbuddhayastadātmānastanniṣṭhāstatparāyaṇāḥ
gacchantyapunarāvṛttiṁ jñānanirdhūtakalmaṣāḥ (17)

14. The Lord does not generate the idea of personal agency or the motivation for worldly activity, nor does he regulate the karmic law of causes and effects. These originate in the essential impulse of human nature.

15. The All-Pervading One takes no account of what might be positive or negative activities. When wisdom is veiled, ignorance arises, and beings in this ignorance act from delusion.

16. The Self radiates like the sun of the Supreme in those whose ignorance has been destroyed by wisdom.

17. Those who contemplate the Essence of All, identifying their Self with that Essence, having this Essence as their singular goal, the Essence being the sole object of their devotion have their impurities cleansed by wisdom and are no longer compelled to rebirth.

Several terms are used synonymously in this group of verses. Prabhu, Lord; Vibhu, All-Pervading One; Atma, Self; and Tat, Essence of All. These are different expressions of the Infinite Consciousness which Sri Krishna wants Arjuna to enjoy. Arjuna experiences himself as a limited individual, captive within a body and mind, bound by time and space, vulnerable to a powerful external universe which can overwhelm him at anytime.

The path from Arjuna's mind to Krishna's consciousness begins by taking responsibility for one's state of mind and its repercussions. As these verses point out, God is not the cause of pain-producing activity. Rather, selfishness and its resulting pain arise from the darkness of ignorance within a person's mind. The Divine is the sun which shines upon the darkness, dissolving its reality. The person immersed in ignorance, however, prefers to remain indoors, frightened, hiding from the light, seeking the temporary pleasures and pain that take place in the darkness of limited understanding.

Verse 18

vidyāvinayasaṁpanne brāhmaṇe gavi hastini
śuni caiva śvapāke ca paṇḍitāḥ samadarśinaḥ (18)

18. Sages behold with equality of vision a learned and gentle religious person, a cow, an elephant, a dog, or an outcast.

This is a beautiful summary of how a sage sees that everything in creation plays an equally important part. All creatures are one family under the umbrella of divine consciousness. The sage beholds all as inherently equal, but this does not disqualify him from recognizing differences that exist on the material plane. Though the religious person and the dog may be equal from a spiritual standpoint, it would be sensible to expect that only one of them would enjoy gnawing on an old bone.

Verses 19–26

ihaiva tairjataḥ sargo yeṣāṁ sāmye sthitaṁ manaḥ
nirdoṣaṁ hi samaṁ brahma tasmād brahmaṇi te sthitāḥ (19)

na prahṛṣyetpriyaṁ prāpya nodvijetprāpya cāpriyam
sthirabuddhirasaṁmūḍho brahmavid brahmaṇi sthitaḥ (20)

bāhyasparśeṣvasaktātmā vindatyātmani yatsukham
sa brahmayoga yuktātmā sukhamakṣayamaśnute (21)

ye hi saṁsparśajā bhogā duḥkhayonaya eva te
ādyantavantaḥ kaunteya na teṣu ramate budhaḥ (22)

śaknotīhaiva yaḥ soḍhuṁ prākśarīravimokṣaṇāt
kāmakrodhodbhavaṁ vegaṁ sa yuktaḥ sa sukhī naraḥ (23)

yo 'ntaḥsukho 'ntarārāmastathāntarjyotireva yaḥ
so yogī brahmanirvāṇaṁ brahmabhūto 'dhigacchati (24)

labhante brahmanirvāṇamṛṣayaḥ kṣīṇakalmaṣāḥ
chinnadvaidhā yatātmānaḥ sarvabhūtahite ratāḥ (25)

kāmakrodhaviyuktānāṁ yatīnāṁ yatacetasām
abhito brahmanirvāṇaṁ vartate viditātmanām (26)

19. Even while embodied, one can become established in Infinite Consciousness by bringing the mind into equilibrium. Infinite Consciousness is free from selfish flaws and is perfectly balanced.

20. One of firm intelligence, who is not bewildered, does not revel on obtaining what is pleasing nor become upset when faced with the displeasing—he is a knower of Infinite Consciousness and is established in this Consciousness.

21. When one is no longer attached to external experiences, he finds the happiness he sought within his own Self. He remains in yoga, a union of his Self and Infinite Consciousness, enjoying never-ending happiness.

22. The superficial enjoyments born of external stimuli are only the wombs of sorrow. They have a beginning and an end, O Kaunteya; no wise person finds them delightful.

23. One who is able to desist from the impulsive rush of selfish desire and anger before the time of death is a yogi and a truly happy person.

24. The one who finds happiness within, delight within, and the inner light is a yogi who enters Infinite Consciousness and becomes absorbed in Infinite Consciousness.

25. Those sages who have attained this absorption into Infinite Consciousness are those whose foolishness is depleted, whose sense of separation

has been sundered, who are Self directed, and who relate to all beings with kindness.

26. Those who have detached from selfish desire and anger, who are self-controlled, and whose individual consciousness is harmonized know the Self and are quickly absorbed into Infinite Consciousness.

This set of eight verses describes in more detail the state of consciousness of the jivanmukti, the one liberated while still embodied. We can see again the main theme that Krishna reiterates to Arjuna: the path to Infinite Consciousness is the relinquishment of selfishness and external supports. This path is one of increasing service to others and the establishment of a divine autonomy within. Krishna presents a teaching of great simplicity, which conveys vast implications as it has the potency to revolutionize the life of an aspirant.

Verses 27–28

sparśānkṛtvā bahirbāhyāṁścakṣuścaivāntare bhruvoḥ
prāṇāpānau samau kṛtvā nāsābhyantaracāriṇau (27)

yatendriyamanobuddhirmunirmokṣaparāyaṇaḥ
vigatecchābhayakrodho yaḥ sadā mukta eva saḥ (28)

27. Detaching from superficial contacts and fixing the gaze between the eyebrows, balancing the inward flowing and outward flowing energies of the breath,

28. With senses, relational mind, and intellect controlled; the one of silence is wholly intent on liberation, without selfish will, fear, or anger. Such a one is ever free.

Let us remember the Bhagavad Gita is a textbook of the universal yoga which includes all branches of this art and science. Thus far Krishna has discussed several aspects of yoga, focusing primarily on wisdom, detachment, and selfless service. Here, in anticipation of chapter 6, the process of meditation is introduced.

In his Yoga Sutras, the great sage Patanjali described yoga as *ashtanga yoga* (eight-limbed yoga). He named it thus because the rungs on the ladder of ascent in his system number eight. These are as follows:

Yama (To Limit) – Ethical Restraints
Niyama (Without Limit) – Ethical Behaviors
Asana (Seat) – Stabilizing the Physical Posture
Pranayama (Regulation of Life Force) – Stabilizing the Breath
Pratyahara (Internalizing the Mind) – Bringing it to Subjective Awareness
Dharana (Contemplation) – Focusing the Mind
Dhyana (Meditation) – Holding the Mind Steady
Samadhi (Union) – Abiding In the Self

The process of scaling the summit of yoga will now briefly be described. The yogi begins with yama and niyama, regulating his ethical life in order that he develops a calm mind, free of selfishness, anxieties, and neurosis. He then learns in asana how to sit in a meditation posture. To be able to sit still for extended periods of time is the purpose of asana practice. True asana practice has little to do with what is taught in the West as yoga, with its emphasis on making the body attractive and sexy. By practicing certain pranayama exercises, learned from an experienced guru, his breath becomes steady and rhythmic. The breath and mind are intimately connected, and stabilization of the breath contributes immensely to the quieting of the mind.

With pratyahara, the yogi begins the actual inward journey. This is the stage at which the aspirant turns his mind towards its source, focusing on his mediation rather than sensory stimuli. At this stage the mind is still tumultuous, and the yogi must struggle. In dharana, the yogi develops a certain degree of concentration, and the mind is increasingly held stable, though lapses in meditation still occur. In dhyana, the yogi is able to hold his mind in meditation. It becomes still like a candle that does not flicker. Finally, in samadhi the mind becomes absorbed in the Self, which is its source.

Verse 29

bhoktāraṁ yajñatapasāṁ sarvalokamaheśvaram
suhṛdaṁ sarvabhūtānāṁ jñātvā māṁ śāntimṛcchati (29)

29. One comes to peace who knows me as the enjoyer of sacred offerings and spiritual austerities, the great Lord of all the world, and the friend of all beings.

When the yogi realizes his Self in samadhi, he realizes there exists only one Self in all beings. Every sentient creature lives, moves, and has its being in the Self. Called "God" in the West, this Divine Being is the compassionate friend of all. This was the source of the clarion call that inspired the aspirant inward. All spiritual activities, all offerings and sacrifices, all prayers, were directed towards this One. This realization is the source of the deep peace enjoyed by the accomplished yogi.

Chapter 6

Dhyana Yoga
The Yoga of Meditation

Verses 1–4

śrībhagavānuvāca
anāśritaḥ karmaphalaṁ kāryaṁ karma kroti yaḥ
sa saṁnyāsī ca yogī ca na niragnirna cākriyaḥ (1)

yaṁ saṁnyāsamiti prāhuryogaṁ taṁ viddhi pāṇḍava
na hyasaṁnyastasaṅkalpo yogī bhavati kaścana (2)

āruruksormuneryogaṁ karma kāraṇamucyate
yogārūḍhasya tasyaiva śamaḥ kāraṇamucyate (3)

yadā hi nendriyārtheṣu na karmasvanuṣajjate
sarvasaṅkalpasaṁnyāsī yogārūḍhastadocyate (4)

1. Shri Bhagavan said: The one who engages in appropriate activity without seeking rewards is the true renunciate and yogi, not the one who lights no fires and abandons activity.

2. Know that what people identify as renunciation, O Pandava, is the same as yoga. One who does not renounce his selfishness can never truly become a yogi.

3. Selfless activity is the means to become a yogi of inner silence. Once one has attained yoga, contentment becomes the means.

4. When one is free of attachment to external objects and preferred activities and has renounced selfish intentions, such a one has ascended to yoga.

Krishna repeats his teaching that renunciation does not mean the relinquishment of activity, but the renunciation of selfish motives and desires for personal reward. This is the real renunciation, which is identical with karma yoga. Krishna goes on to identify karma yoga as the path to inner quietude. This is because the agitated mind, always pursuing pleasure and avoiding pain, comes to rest as service to others becomes the guiding principle.

Once this inner quiet is attained, karma yoga has served its purpose. The yogi will still serve others, but now it is entirely the result of spontaneous compassion. No longer need he engage in service for the purpose of purifying his own mind. Now that his mind is purified, he can begin in earnest the path of meditation based on contentment, the subject of this chapter.

Verses 5–6

uddharedātmanātmānaṁ nātmānamavasādayet
ātmaiva hyātmano bandhurātmaiva ripurātmanaḥ (5)

bandhurātmātmanastasya yenātmaivātmanā jitaḥ
anātmanastu śatrutve vartetātmaiva śatruvat (6)

5. Let one uplift his Self by the Self, as the Self should not be disrespected. The Self is one's own best friend or worst enemy.

6. For the one who is in harmony with his own Self, the Self appears as a friend. For the one not in harmony with his Self, he feels in conflict, as if the Self were an enemy.

The atman, the Self, what might be called "soul" in the West, has developed a confusion about its identity. Through the primal ignorance known as avidya, "lack of wisdom," the atman has come to identify with the vehicles which make incarnation possible. The atman confuses itself with the body/mind complex and comes to feel it is mortal, vulnerable, oppressed. This is the confusion which gripped Arjuna at the very beginning of the Bhagavad Gita.

The pure consciousness of the Self impresses its energy on the ocean of the mind, which causes ripples to appear. These ripples are the various thoughts which, taken as a collective, form the personality, the sense of being an isolated individual. Ignorance is the idea that somehow these waves are separate from the ocean. Fear arises when the personality becomes frightened of absorption into the ocean.

One who feels himself in harmony with the foundation of his existence is like the wave which knows it belongs to the ocean, arises as an expression of the majesty of the ocean, and will eventually return into the ocean in a homecoming celebration. Such a soul feels connected with his own Self and in harmony with others and their mutual divine source. One who identifies himself as a individual wave feels lonely, frightened, and isolated from other waves. He fails to understand his true nature and his inherent relationship to all life.

Verses 7–9

jitātmanaḥ praśāntasya paramātmā samāhitaḥ
śitoṣṇasukhaduḥkheṣu tathā mānāpamānayoḥ (7)

jñānavijñānatṛptātmā kūṭastho vijitendriyaḥ
yukta ityucyate yogī samaloṣṭāśmakāñcanaḥ (8)

suhṛnmitrāryudāsīnamadhyasthadveṣyabandhuṣu
sādhuṣvapi ca pāpeṣu samabuddhirviśiṣyate (9)

7. When the Self rests in peace, the Supreme Self is revealed. Contentment then exists even during the experience of dualities, such as heat-cold, happiness-unhappiness, honor-dishonor.

8. The yogi is firm in yoga when his Self is satisfied with spiritual wisdom and knowledge of creation. His consciousness is spiritually stable, and he has conquered the impulse to seek external happiness. For such a one, a lump of earth, a stone, and a piece of gold are the same.

9. Excellent is such a one—able to maintain even-mindedness toward those who praise him, toward friend and enemy, the indifferent and non-responsive, those who hate him and his family, even between saint and sinner.

The one who realizes the indivisibility of the wave and the ocean enjoys the relationship of the Self, atman, and Supreme Self, *Paramatma*. The wave and ocean are one, yet in some significant way they are different, and this is why the sport of surfing can exist. The paramatma-ocean expresses its creative potency as the atma, and the atma-wave revels in being able to enjoy a relationship with its source. The One manifests as many in order to enjoy loving relationships.

One of the foremost characteristics of a yogi who has achieved this realization is that he becomes even-minded before the dualities of the manifest world. His peace is stable and independent. Changes occur—the body lives and dies, wealth and beauty appear and pass, friends and enemies exchange roles—while the yogi remains a calm enjoyer of the divine play.

Verses 10–15

yogī yuñjīta satatamātmānaṁ rahasisthitaḥ
ekākī yatacittātmā nirāśīraparigrahaḥ (10)

śacau deśe pratiṣṭhāpya sthiramāsanamātmanaḥ
nātyucchritaṁ nātinīcaṁ cailājinakuśottaram (11)

tatraikāgraṁ manaḥ kṛtvā yatacittendriyakriyaḥ
upaviśyāsane yuñjyādyogamātmaviśuddhaye (12)

samaṁ kāyaśirogrīvaṁ dhārayannacalaṁ sthiraḥ
saṁprekṣya nāsikāgraṁ svaṁ diśaścānavalokayan (13)

praśāntātmā vigatabhīrbrahmacārivrate sthitaḥ
manaḥ saṁyamya maccitto yukta āsīta matparaḥ (14)

yuñjannevaṁ sadātmānaṁ yogī niyatamānasaḥ
śāntiṁ nirvāṇaparamāṁ matsaṁsthāmadhigacchati (15)

10. The yogi should constantly direct his awareness towards his Self, creating an autonomous inner peace. With his individual consciousness in harmony with his Self, he should be without greed for success or experience.

11. Placing his body in a stable meditation posture, in an environment of purity, with an attitude neither pompous nor deprecated, covered with a cloth, deer skin, and grass,

12. Having made his mind one-pointed, with individual consciousness and external impulses quieted, he should sit in yogic meditation for Self purification.

13. With body, neck, and head aligned, eyes focused at the base of the nose with an undistracted gaze,

14. At peace in the Self, fearless, firm in the vow to advance toward God, with cognitive mind quieted, contemplating the sense of "me"—I am—let him strive to unite with the Supreme Goal.

15. The yogi who harmonizes with his Self and subdues unnecessary activity in the cognitive mind enters into a deep peace. He attains the supreme absorption of his consciousness.

In his Yoga Sutras, Patanjali identifies the culminating state of yoga as *chittah vritti nirodha* (the stilling of mental agitations). He describes this as dwelling in the *svarupa* (one's real form). (See 5.27–28.) When the individual mind becomes still, the yogi transcends identification with the form of the body and realizes the Self. The yogi is no longer drowned in the turbulence of his thoughts, but recognizes his own true nature as consciousness independent of the mind/body complex.

These verses give a broad presentation of the general principals of meditation practice. Each aspirant, however, is free to practice any method of meditation as he is guided by his guru and intuition. All paths of meditation ascend to the same mountaintop.

In verse 15 above and in 2.72, the Bhagavad Gita uses the term *nirvana* (absorption) as a synonym for samadhi. This is significant because nirvana is a term used almost exclusively by Buddhists, while samadhi is the term generally used by Hindus. The Bhagavad Gita reevaluates many terms and practices in the light of the universal yoga and demonstrates how all spiritual traditions share a common understanding.

It may be argued that these two terms refer to different experiences. This argument, however, is not shared by those yogis, regardless of traditional affiliation, who have actually stilled their minds and enjoyed absorption into the Self. There are several stages to this absorption described in different ways in various texts, but the Bhagavad Gita is not interested in enhancing sectarian differences in matters of relative unimportance. Its goal is to support the aspirant in developing wisdom, regardless of the language he uses to express himself.

Great sages such as Paramahamsa Ramakrishna give testimony to the universal nature of spiritual reality. Ramakrishna was a Bengali sage who lived from 1836–1888. During his lifetime he practiced many spiritual disciplines under several different gurus. Because of his great ardor, he achieved success in all of his yearnings and enjoyed personal revelations of various Hindu gods and goddesses, Jesus, and Allah and the highest samadhi. He personally recounts how he reached the culmination of each tradition he studied and how each practice in which he engaged led him to the same spiritual reality. The life of Ramakrishna is a living testimony to the universal path presented in the Bhagavad Gita.

Verses 16–17

nātyaśnatastu yogo-sti na caikāntamanaśnataḥ
na cāti svapnaśīlasya jāgrato naiva cārjuna (16)

yuktāhāravihārasya yuktaceṣṭasya karmasu
yuktasvapnāvabodhasya yogo bhavati duḥkhahā (17)

16. Yoga is not for one who eats too much or too little, nor, O Arjuna, for one who sleeps too much or too little.

17. Yoga destroys the suffering of one who is balanced in his worldly habits and recreation, who is moderately active, and who regulates his sleep routine.

It may seem like a simple matter to find a balance in the apparently mundane matters of daily life, such as eating, sleeping, and recreation. But finding this balance is a subtle process, very much part of the path of yoga. The aspirant must learn to find the middle path between the extremes of too much and too little, between aggression and passivity. Developing a balanced lifestyle involves comprehensively regulating one's life and energy.

Verses 18–20

yadā viniyatam cittamātmanyevāvatiṣṭhate
niḥspṛhaḥ sarvakāmebhyo yukta ityucyate tadā (18)

yathā dīpo nivātastho neṅgate sopamā smṛtā
yogino yatacittasya yuñjato yogamātmanaḥ (19)

yatroparamate cittaṁ niruddhaṁ yogasevayā
yatra caivātmanātmānaṁ paśyannātmani tuṣyati (20)

18. When the individual consciousness becomes settled in the Self, free of egoic desires, it is said to be in yogic consciousness.

19. An unflickering lamp in a windless place is an illustration of the mind of the yogi. He has brought his individual consciousness under control and in union with his Self.

20. When individual consciousness becomes tranquil and constrained through the dedicated practice of yoga, the Self beholds the Self as the Self and enjoys its own innate satisfaction.

Through the practice of yoga, the aspirant transforms his consciousness so that he is no longer confused about his true identity. The sense of being a mortal, frail, bewildered human being gives way to a consciousness of being the immortal Self. Awareness of the body and mind continue, but there is no longer a feeling of deep attachment and concern. The body/mind complex is like a suit of clothes being worn for a period of time. Regardless of the quality of the clothing, it is still just a temporary covering which will one day be relinquished.

The yogi who has stilled his mind is no longer subject to the turmoil of mental and emotional agitation. He discovers within the satisfaction and security he previously sought in external objects and relationships. To realize one's own Self as the source of peace, joy, and light is the accomplishment of the yogi. To abide in this state of consciousness is a very exalted state. Krishna lives in this consciousness, and he knows Arjuna does not. His words are encouragement for his disciple and friend, pointing to the lofty goal that he will one day reach if he follows the path of yoga.

Verses 21–22

sukhamātyantikaṁ yattabuddhi grāhyamatīndriyam
vetti yatra na caivāyaṁ sthitaścalati tattvataḥ (21)

yaṁ labdhvā cāparaṁ lābhaṁ manyate nādhikaṁ tataḥ
yasminsthito na duḥkhena guruṇāpi vicālyate (22)

21. In this state, one realizes a happiness beyond the farthest reaches of the senses and the intelligence, and there is no longer any decline in consciousness.

22. On gaining this state one thinks there is no greater gain to be had. Its establishment makes one immune to even the greatest sorrow.

Every sentient being wants to be happy. This search for happiness is the root of all motivations. People pursue pleasure and avoid pain because they want to live with the highest degree of happiness. Individuals define pleasure and pain for themselves, based on the development of their mind and emotions, and then they work to achieve these goals. This is essentially the history of humanity.

From the sage's perspective, people are not wrong to seek happiness, they are simply seeking it in areas where it cannot be found. The common person seeks happiness in experience of the senses, primarily food, sex, and money. The more intellectually developed person seeks happiness in the realm of ideas and their implementation, such as in academics, science, and politics. The happiness sought by the soul, however, cannot be found in the body or mind. Lasting happiness can only be found in spiritual accomplishment. When this truth is accepted, great hardships and suffering can be avoided because one stops wandering into byways of sorrow and instead becomes efficient in the pursuit of happiness by practicing spiritual disciplines.

Verses 23–26

taṁ vidyādduḥkhasaṁyogaviyogaṁ yogasaṁjñitam
sa niścayena yoktavyo yogo-nirviṇṇacetasā (23)

saṅkalpaprabhavānkāmāṁstyaktvā sarvānaśeṣataḥ
manasaivendriyagrāmaṁ viniyama samantataḥ (24)

śanaiḥ śanairuparamedbuddhyā dhṛtigṛhītayā
ātmasaṁsthaṁ manaḥ kṛtvā na kiṁcidapi cintayet (25)

yato yato niścarati manaścañcalamasthiram
tatastato niyamyaitadātmanyeva vaśaṁ nayet (26)

23. Yoga can be defined as a disconnection from the causes of suffering. This yoga should be practiced with determination and unswerving dedication.

24. Completely renounce all selfish desires arising from egoic determinations, and utilize the cognitive mind to restrain the entire spectrum of external seeking.

25. Slowly, patiently, one can quiet agitation by applying the power of intelligence to bring the cognitive mind into stillness and harmony with the Self.

26. As the mind wanders again and again, so it should, again and again, be brought back to the Self.

Here is our third definition of yoga: "disconnection from the causes of suffering." (See also 2.48, 2.50.) In addition to a definition, the aspirant is told there is a path that requires determination and dedication. The path is indeed a path. It is to be walked; it cannot be run. The development of spiritual maturity is an organic process and, like all of nature's processes, moves slowly. To hurry on the spiritual path, to seek shortcuts, is futile and the sign of greed. Achieving spiritual illumination will take patience, repeated application of spiritual disciplines, and a continuing inspiration of spiritual resolve.

The path itself involves progressing inwardly to increasingly subtle spheres of consciousness. The manas, the cognitive mind, and the *indriyas* (the outward-seeking senses) are restrained by the buddhi, the intuitive intelligence. The work of the buddhi produces contact with atma, the true Self. Eventually the intellect, which contains the seed of individuality, flings itself into the flame of the Self as a divine offering. The fulfillment of the development of all individual capabilities is to offer them in service to the divine. This was the gesture of Jesus on the cross, Buddhi under the bodhi tree, and countless other aspirants who offered their individual self to the one Self shared by all.

Verses 27–28

praśāntamanasaṁ hyenaṁ yoginaṁ sukhamuttamam
upaiti śāntarajasaṁ brahmabhūtamakalmaṣam (27)

yuñjannevaṁ sadātmānaṁ yogī vigatakalmaṣaḥ
sukhena brahmasaṁsparśamatyantaṁ sukhamaśnute (28)

27. A yogi who has calmed the mind and pacified selfish passion comes to supreme happiness in the stainless Infinite Consciousness.

28. The yogi who is constantly in harmony with the Self, free of impurities, effortlessly experiences the ultimate happiness of communion with Infinite Consciousness.

The state of samadhi requires the mind to be a stainless mirror capable of reflecting purely that which is placed in front of it. When the mind has no external seeking, it produces no distorting influence. When not engaged in the external world, the mind is absorbed into the Self, resting in peace and happiness.

This very exalted state, described in verse 27, is achieved by successful yogis during meditation. Yet there is an even higher state, described in verse 28, of the rare yogi who can maintain this state constantly, even while active. He is in *sahaja samadhi* (the natural samadhi), enjoying the ultimate happiness of communion with Infinite Consciousness while in meditation and while active in the world.

Krishna dangles before Arjuna the carrot of attainment to inspire his disciple onward. As we shall soon see, Arjuna is overwhelmed by the depiction Krishna gives of the samadhi state. He can hardly envision it as a possible achievement.

Verses 29–32

sarvabhūtasthamātmānaṁ sarvabhūtāni cātmani
īkṣate yogayuktātmā sarvatra samadarśanaḥ (29)

yo māṁ paśyati sarvatra sarvaṁ ca mayi paśyati
tasyāhaṁ na praṇaśyāmi sa ca me na praṇaśyati (30)

sarvabhūtasthitaṁ yo māṁ bhajatyekatvamāsthitaḥ
sarvathā vartamāno 'pi sa yogī mayi vartate (31)

ātmaupamyena sarvatra samaṁ paśyati yo 'rjuna
sukhaṁ vā yadi vā duḥkhaṁ sa yogī paramo mataḥ (32)

29. One whose Self is united in yoga sees the Self as abiding in all beings and all beings in the Self. Such is the vision of Divine Equality.

30. He who sees me—The Self—everywhere and sees everything in me, never does he feel he and I could be lost to each other.

31. The yogi who honors me as the Self residing in all beings is firmly established in unity. He abides in me regardless of how active he may be.

32. A supreme yogi is one, O Arjuna, who sees everything equally as an expression of his own Self, regardless if it be tinged with happiness or sorrow.

The Self is pure consciousness, the essence of the "I" feeling. This consciousness manifests as both the insentient matter of the universe as well as the sentient beings within creation. This is the macrocosmic creation, which is duplicated in a microcosmic manner within a human being.

In a human being, the Self manifests as a divine energy which begins its descent into the body at the top of the skull. At the crown of the head, this divine force rests in a potential state, poetically depicted as Shiva, God eternally immersed in the stillness of meditation. When the energy becomes active and descends into the body, it is poetically depicted as Shakti, the Goddess who is eternally active in the dance of creation, preservation, and destruction. Shakti is also called prakriti and is discussed later in the text (7.4–6, 13.3–6).

The descent of Shakti, cosmic energy, organizes a subtle body which forms the template for that will be the physical form. The subtle body is comprised of a vast number of *nadis* (energy channels). The most significant channel is the *sushumna* (the central channel), which corresponds to the spinal cord on the physical plane. Shakti creates and then descends into the sushumna. Shakti descends into the sushumna at the crown of the head and completes her descent at the base of the spine. Then she begins an ascent back up through the sushumna to reach her origin. The descent into manifestation is called *pravritti*, and the ascent back to the source is called *nivritti*.

As Shakti descends, she passes through each of the subtle planes of consciousness. This creates *chakras* (wheels), which are energy vortexes within the sushumna. These seven chakras are:

Chakra	**Location in Sushumna**	**Manifestation in Consciousness**
muladhara	base of spine	I am a being in pursuit of survival.
svadhishthana	behind genitals	I am a being in pursuit of pleasure.
manipura	behind solar plexus	I am a being in pursuit of power.
anahata	behind chest	I am a being of compassion.
vishuddha	behind throat	I am a being of communication.
ajna	behind forehead	I am a being of spiritual wisdom.
sahasrara	crown of head	I am.

When Shakti is ascending within the sushumna of an aspirant, she is known as *kundalini* and is often poetically portrayed as a snake. Kundalini is the pure sense of "I am" within a person. When this pure "I am" interfaces with the energy of any given chakra, a sense of limited personal identity is created and a certain level of consciousness is expressed.

The entire spiritual pilgrimage, therefore, is approximately three feet long—from the top of the skull to the base of the spine, and back again. The work of every aspirant, regardless of particular spiritual path, is the ascent of kundalini. When kundalini returns to the sahasrara chakra, she is enhanced by this journey. She resides there in a union of the ever-still and the ever-active, as the Supreme Divine Self. This is the great cosmic romance, culminating in the reunion of Shakti with her beloved Shiva.

Verses 33–34

arjuna uvāca
yo 'yam yogastvayā proktaḥ sāmyena madhusūdana
etasyāhaṁ na paśyāmi cañcalatvātsthitiṁ sthirām (33)

cañcalaṁ hi manaḥ kṛṣṇa pramāthi balavaddṛḍham
tasyāhaṁ nigrahaṁ manye vāyoriva suduṣkaram (34)

33. Arjuna said: This yoga you teach describes a mind in equilibrium. O Madhusudhana, I do not see how to establish this stable foundation due to restlessness.

34. The mind is so very restless, O Krishna. It is turbulent, wild, and stubborn. It seems to me as difficult to tame as the wind.

Arjuna speaks for every aspirant. The sage describes the joy and peace available to the one who has stabilized the mind, but the aspirant finds himself failing in what seems like an impossible pursuit. Everyone who has ever worked in meditation to quiet the mind knows that Arjuna's statements are not exaggerations. The mind truly is "turbulent, wild, and stubborn" indeed!

Verses 35–36

śribhagavānuvāca
asaṁśayaṁ mahābāho mano durnigrahaṁ calam
abhyāsena tu kaunteya vairāgyeṇa ca gṛhyate (35)

asaṁyatātmanā yogo duṣprāpa iti me matiḥ
vaśyātmanā tu yatatā śakyo 'vāptumupāyataḥ (36)

35. Shri Bhagavan relied: No doubt, O Mahabaho, the mind is difficult to tame and harness. But, O Kaunteya, it can be controlled through repeated practice and non-attachment.

36. Without the control generated by the Self, yoga is hard to attain. But this yoga can be attained when the Self uses the proper means.

In answer to Arjuna's question, Krishna does not argue that the goal is easy. He does, however, try to make the essentials as simple as possible. Krishna encourages Arjuna to arm himself with the two great tools of the yogi: *abhyas* (regular practice) and *vairagya* (non-attachment).

Regular practice means that the aspirant must perform his sadhana, formal practices, on a daily basis. Plus he must engage in karma yoga, selfless activity, during the course of his life. Non-attachment means the aspirant avoids the clinging and codependency that are the hallmarks of egoic relationships. Instead, he finds his fulfillment within; then relationships become ways of joining in joy rather than means of soothing low self-esteem.

Verses 37–39

arjuna uvāca
ayatiḥ śraddhayopeto yogāccalitamānsaḥ
aprāpya yogasaṁsiddhiṁ kāṁ gatiṁ kṛṣṇa gacchati (37)

kaccinnobhayavibhraṣṭaśchinnābhramiva naśyati
apratiṣṭho mahābāho vimūḍho brahmaṇaḥ pathi (38)

etanme saṁśayaṁ kṛṣṇa chettumarhasyaśeṣataḥ
tvadanyaḥ saṁśayasyāsya chettā na hyupapadyate (39)

37. Arjuna said: O Krishna, for one who is unstable, who has faith in these teachings but deviates from yoga and fails to reach accomplishment,

38. Isn't such a one fallen from both the worldly life and the spiritual life? Without stability in either world, doesn't he perish like a spent rain cloud, lost on the path to Infinite Consciousness?

39. My doubt, O Krishna, you should dispel completely. No one else but you can dispel this doubt.

Arjuna accepts Krishna's teaching but ponders the practical matter that most people will simply not achieve the goal of spiritual completion this lifetime. Most aspirants will practice some sadhana and engage in some selfless activity, but they are not yet capable of orienting their consciousness in such a way that their fear and selfishness is completely eradicated. In the spiritual tradition of the Bhagavad Gita, this lack of accomplishment is not considered a sin, but simply a stage on the journey of spiritual evolution. Just as a child has not yet matured into adulthood, an aspirant may have not yet matured into a sage.

Arjuna's concern is based on the fact that most aspirants, regardless of good intentions, will not achieve enlightenment this lifetime. Are their efforts therefore wasted? Plus, he worries, if their labors are not fully successful on the spiritual path, have they ruined their lives further, since the time they spent pursuing spiritual development may have been spent on worldly success? Like all fears that stem from misunderstanding, Arjuna's mind finds misery in every direction.

Verses 40–45

śribhagavānuvāca
pārtha naiveha nāmutra vināśastasya vidyate
na hi kalyāṇakṛtkaściddurgatiṁ tāta gacchati (40)

prāpya puṇyakṛtāṁ lokānuṣitvā śāśvatīḥ samāḥ
śucīnāṁ śrīmatāṁ gehe yogabhraṣṭo 'bhijāyate (41)

athavā yogināmeva kule bhavati dhīmatām
etaddhi durlabhataraṁ loke janma yadīdṛśam (42)

tatra taṁ buddhisaṁyogaṁ labhate paurvadehikam
yatate ca tato bhūyaḥ saṁsiddhau kurunandana (43)

pūrvābhyāsena tenaiva hriyate hyavaśo 'pi saḥ
jijñāsurapi yogasya śabdabrahmātivartate (44)

prayatnādyatamānastu yogī saṁśuddhakilbiṣaḥ
aneka janmasaṁsiddhastato yāti parāṁ gatim (45)

40. Shri Bhagavan said: O Partha, neither in this life nor in the next does such a one meet with destruction. My son, one who earnestly strives to do good never resides permanently in pain.

41. One who loses his way on the yoga path during his life will dwell after death for immeasurable years in the realms of righteous rewards. Then he will be reborn in the home of the pure and respectable.

42. Else he may be born in a family of wise yogis. A birth such as this is

very rare and precious in this world.

43. He regains his intuition born of yoga and strives once more for perfection, O Kurunandana.

44. As a result of previous spiritual efforts, such a one is irresistibly drawn forward. By simply desiring to learn about this authentic yoga, one will rise above traditional religious teachings.

45. The yogi who perseveres with commitment, purified of selfish dross, striving for perfection over many lives, will reach the supreme position.

One can almost hear the gentle chuckle in Krishna's voice as he soothes Arjuna's anxiety. This section of the Bhagavad Gita reveals an intimate dialogue where Arjuna unveils his fears before his guru in order that they be relieved. To have a true teacher or friend to whom one can reveal one's deepest feelings is a great blessing on the path.

Krishna answers Arjuna's fears that spiritual practice would somehow leave one in a nether region, neither in the world of men nor the world of spirit. Krishna points out, matter of factly, that the path to spiritual accomplishment is one that will last many lifetimes. The path is also progressive, with the aspirant regaining each lifetime what was accomplished prior. In addition, the birthplace of the yogi will be perfectly suited to his continued development.

It is worth proposing that this series of verses has special significance for contemporary Western aspirants. Without any seeming familial or societal support, many Westerners have found themselves inspired to pursue the yogic path. These verses state this is the result of spiritual work pursued over previous lifetimes.

Verses 46–47

tapasvibhyo 'dhiko yogī jñānibhyo 'pi mato 'dhikaḥ
karmibhyaścādhiko yogī tasmāyogī bhavārjuna (46)

yogināmapi sarveṣāṁ madgatenāntarātmanā
śraddhāvānbhajate yo māṁ sa me yuktatamo mataḥ (47)

46. This yogi is superior to those of austerity, greater than those of wisdom, greater than those of activity. Therefore, O Arjuna, become such a yogi.

47. Of all the yogis, one who merges his inner Self with me, full of faith and devoted to me, he I deem to enjoy the deepest union.

The yogi of the universal yoga is one who integrates all aspects of his being. He does not segregate yoga from life. He practices a comprehensive yoga which requires a commitment of body, mind, and heart. The yoga of the Bhagavad Gita is not a yoga divided into parcels. It is an expression of the universal whole of the one Self. A yogi described by these verses brings his self into the presence of the Self and, like a piece of wood entering the fire, becomes the fire.

Chapter 7

Jnana-Vijnana Yoga
The Yoga of Wisdom and Knowledge

Verses 1–2

śrībhagavānuvāca
mayyāsaktamanāḥ pārtha yogaṁ yuñjanmadāśrayaḥ
asaṁśayaṁ samagraṁ māṁ yathā jñāsyasi tacchṛṇu (1)

jñānaṁ te 'haṁ savijñānamidaṁ vakṣyāmyaśeṣataḥ
yajñāttvā neha bhūyo 'nyajñātavyamavaśiṣyate (2)

1. Shri Bhagavan said: Hear, O Partha, how by practicing this universal yoga, taking refuge in me, and keeping your mind absorbed in me, you will realize me comprehensively beyond any doubt.

2. I will teach you wisdom together with knowledge, without omission. Understanding this there will be nothing left to understand.

The universal yoga is a comprehensive yoga, which includes insight into the nature of the transcendent Self and the manifest world. Realization of the Self is *jnana* (wisdom) and insight into true nature of the world is *vijnana* (knowledge). The Self is realized by practicing the universal yoga, a realization which spontaneously reveals the workings of nature.

Verse 3

manuṣyāṇāṁ sahasreṣu kaścidyatati siddhaye
yatatāmapi siddhānāṁ kaścinmāṁ vetti tattvataḥ (3)

3. Among thousands, scarcely one strives for spiritual accomplishment. Among those who strive, scarcely one realizes me as the essential truth.

If an individual is preparing to enter the spiritual path, it behooves him to prepare for loneliness. A deep loneliness is often the sole companion of the aspirant. First comes the loneliness of leaving the worldly consensus, when superficial relationships, career, hobbies, and passing fancies stop holding his interest. Friends and family may feel like strangers as one seeks for companions with whom to relate the spiritual quest.

These new companions, however, must not become yet another psychological crutch. The company of other aspirants is crucial at a certain stage of development, but eventually every aspirant must blaze his own path through the night forest. As Krishna advises Arjuna in chapters 1 and 2, even tradition must ultimately be relinquished. The fact that this relinquishment is generally psychological, not requiring physical separation from one's community, does not make it any easier.

Verses 4–6

bhūmirāpo 'nalo vāyuḥ khaṁ mano buddhireva ca
ahaṅkāra itīyaṁ me bhinnā prakṛtiraṣṭadhā (4)

apareyamitastvanyāṁ prakṛtiṁ viddhi me parām
jīvabhūtāṁ mahābāho yayedaṁ dhāryate jagat (5)

etadyonīni bhūtāni sarvāṇītyupadhāraya
ahaṁ kṛtsnasya jagataḥ prabhavaḥ pralayastathā (6)

4. My eightfold primal nature is: earth, water, fire, air, ether, mind, intelligence, and ego.

5. This is my lower nature. Know also my higher nature to be the soul principle, O Mahabaho, by which the world is sustained.

6. Know that all beings share this twofold nature as their common womb. I am the impulse for the creation and dissolution of the world.

The twofold nature of Self is the immanent power of the insentient natural world and the transcendent sentience of the soul. Both arise from, have their being in, and eventually resolve back into the One Self. If the Self is an infinite ocean, the apparently individualized waves are the *jivas* (the souls), and the froth which spits from the top of the waves is the prakriti, the eightfold nature.

Both the souls and nature are part and parcel of the ocean; they are the expression of the ocean and can never be separate from it. Yet, at the same time, the waves do have a temporal existence that is real, so we can say that they exist in an individual manner. Also, as the Self is infinite consciousness, even the froth is conscious and not insentient. For the sake of understanding the dynamics of life as presented in the yogic tradition, however, we can say that the froth has temporarily separated itself from the ocean and is therefore no longer part of sentient consciousness.

Earth, water, fire, air, and ether are the five bhutas, principles of matter. These are not material elements, but forces which produce matter. They are more subtle than even subatomic particles as they have no concrete existence. They are categories of energy which generate physical matter. As discussed before, manas (mind) is the coordinator of sensory impressions; buddhi (intelligence) includes both intellect and intuition; and ahamkara (ego) is the sense of individuality based on identity with the body/mind complex. (See also 2.23–24, 13.5–6.)

That the five principles of matter originate from a divine source is the basis for a spiritual ecology. Matter is sacred energy, born of God. To live in harmony with nature is humanity's religious duty. Ancient peoples have been criticized by modern civilizations for their supposed nature fetishes, for worshipping nature's powers. This critique is biased and prejudiced, failing to understand that prior cultures were more sensitive to the divine energies of our world. Of course a fire will light whether it is prayed over or not, but a person will experience it as a sacred phenomenon only when it is lit with prayer.

Nature and soul are dual partners in the womb of divinity. The soul is "higher" in the sense that matter is the expression of divine power, while the soul is the expression of divine love. In the yogic tradition, love is considered the highest of all values.

Verse 7

ataraṁ nānyatkiñcidasti dhanaṁjaya
mayi sarvamidaṁ protaṁ sūtre maṇigaṇā iva (7)

7. There is nothing higher than I, O Dhananjaya. All creation is strung on me like jewels on a thread.

The Supreme Being finds joy in creative expression through form and finds love through the expression of consciousness. There is no joy higher than divine creativity; there is no love higher than pure consciousness. Finding this joy and love is the path of yoga.

Verses 8–11

raso 'hamapsu kaunteya prabhāsmi śaśisūryayoḥ
praṇavaḥ sarvavedeṣu śabdaḥ khe pauruṣaṁ nṛṣu (8)

puṇyo gandhaḥ pṛthivyāṁ ca tejaścāsmi tapasviṣu
jīvanaṁ sarvabhūteṣu tapaścāsmi tapasviṣu (9)

bījaṁ māṁ sarvabhūtānāṁ viddhi pārtha sanātanam
buddhirbuddhimatāmasmi tejastejasvināmaham (10)

balaṁ balavatāṁ cāhaṁ kāmarāgavivarjitam
dharmāviruddho bhūteṣu kāmo 'smi bharatarṣabha (11)

8. I am the taste of water, O Kaunteya; I am the light of the moon and sun. I am the great sound "aum" described in the wisdom texts; I am vibrating sound in ether and that which is human in humanity.

9. I am the sacred fragrance of the earth and the luminance of fire. I am the soul in all beings, and I am the inner radiance of those who perform austerities.

10. Know me, O Partha, as the eternal seed of all beings. I am the intelligence of those who are intelligent, and I am the luminosity of those who are illuminated.

11. I am the strength of the strong, devoid of selfish desire and passion, and I am the desire in all beings which is not contrary to harmony, O Bharatarshabha.

The same divine essence is found in the natural world and in humanity. The taste of water, the fragrance of the earth, and other expressions of the world arise from the seed of divine power. Intelligence, strength, and righteous desire arise from the seed of divine love. This is not mere poetry; this is a description of the consciousness of the sage and his experience of the love, harmony, and beauty of the universe.

Verses 12–15

ye caiva sāvikā bhāvā rājasātāmasāśca ye
matta eveti tānviddhi na tvahaṁ teṣu ye mayi (12)

tribhirguṇamayairbhāvairebhiḥ sarvamidaṁ jagat
mohitaṁ nābhijānāti māmebhyaḥ paramavyayam (13)

daivī hyeṣā guṇamayī mama māyā duratyayā
māmeva ye prapadyante māyāmetāṁ taranti te (14)

na māṁ duṣkṛtino mūḍhāḥ prapadyante narādhamāḥ
māyayāpahṛtajñānā āsuraṁ bhāvamāśritāḥ (15)

12. Know that all the gunas, the qualities of nature—balance, activation, inertia—arise from me. I am not of them; they are of me.

13. All in the mortal world are deluded by these three qualities of manifest nature and are unable to know me, who is superior to them and unchangeable.

14. This maya of mine, consisting of the three qualities of nature, is hard to surmount. But those who take refuge in me alone cross over this magical display.

15. The foolish and cruel ones, low on humanity's hierarchy, do not attain me, as their wisdom is distracted by my divine magic and they come to align themselves with the energies of conflict.

Two important terms are introduced in this set of verses, and it is worthwhile to understand them before continuing our journey through the Gita. The *gunas* were alluded to in 2.45, but this time they arise as a significant part of the teaching. The gunas, the qualities of nature, are as three strands which make up the rope of nature. The gunas are *rajas* (activation), *sattva* (balance), and *tamas* (inertia).

Rajas is the energy of impulse and creation. It brings forth into physical form the subtle energies of prakriti or nature. Sattva maintains these forms for various periods of time by balancing the forces of growth and decay. Tamas brings the termination of forms by the force of restraint and inertia. Our purpose at this point is to understand the gunas in general terms. The manner in which the gunas are expressed in human life is examined in detail in chapters 14, 17, and 18.

The second significant term is *maya* (she who measures). Measurement refers to the establishment of relative values by which concepts and perceptions are formed. When used philosophically, maya means "illusion," and in some Indian philosophical systems this carries a rather negative connotation. There, the illusion of maya is believed to be the physical world and the various "temptations of the flesh" that accompany life in the world.

The Bhagavad Gita hardly entertains this world-negative philosophy. Here, Krishna calls maya *daivi* (divine) and *mama* (mine). It is obvious from these expressions that maya is sacred, an aspect of divinity, something to be honored.

The maya of the Bhagavad Gita is a divine magic, the power of Brahman to express unity in multiplicity, without which there is no creation.

The maya of the Bhagavad Gita is closely aligned with the maya of tantra and some of the bhakti, or devotional, schools. Shree Maa and Swami Satyananda Saraswati, two contemporary tantra masters, teach that maya has three levels. First, maya is the One Self in relationship to its own unitive consciousness. Second, maya is the relationship of the One to the many and the many to the One. Third, maya is the relationship of the many to the many.

Some of the devotional Vaishnava schools teach that maya is the energy by which the Lord creates the universe for His sport. They believe that maya is utilized by the Lord to manifest a creation, within which he can relate to and entertain his devotees. These relations and entertainments are called *lilas* (divine, playful activities).

God is the only individual soul who is supreme to maya, as it is His energy. All other individual souls, it is taught, are weak and prone to be overwhelmed by maya.

The purport of this set of verses is that maya is a divine energy belonging to the Self which creates a seeming multiplicity from unitary consciousness. It does so through the medium of the three gunas, the qualities of nature. The individual who becomes overwhelmed by the energy of maya literally loses sight of his own Self. In this way he becomes distracted and absorbed in multiplicity. He loses the reality of the foundational unity of all beings and falls into delusion, ending up in conflict with others and his own sense of Self (see 6.6).

Verse 16

caturvidhā bhajante māṁ janāḥ sukṛtino 'rjuna
ārto jijñāsurarthārthī jñānī ca bharatarṣabha (16)

16. There are four types who accrue merit and worship me, O Arjuna: those in distress, those who seek worldly knowledge, those who want wealth, and those who are wise, O Bharatarshabha.

A classification of four types of aspirants is given here. Suffice it to say that the vast majority of people who enter upon the spiritual path do so because they are suffering in some way and are seeking relief. There is certainly no shame in this as even the Buddha entered the path in order to solve the mystery of suffering.

We may flatter ourselves about our motives and intentions, but only the very rare individual embarks on the spiritual journey for the sake of wisdom and service. Virtually everyone at the beginning of their search has some personal desire at the root of their motivation. The guru can perceive this, and it is not cause for undo concern. It only becomes a real problem when an aspirant refuses to acknowledge his own self-centeredness and insists on thinking more highly of himself and his motivations than he actually deserves.

Verses 17–19

teṣāṁ jñānī nityayukta ekabhaktirviśiṣyate
prioy hi jñānino 'tyarthamahaṁ sa ca mama priyaḥ (17)

udārāḥ sarva evaite jñānī tvātmaiva me matam
āsthitaḥ sa hi yuktātmā māmevānuttamāṁ gatim (18)

bahūnāṁ janmanāmante jñānavānmāṁ prapadyate
vāsudevaḥ sarvamiti sa mahātmā sudurlabhaḥ (19)

17. Of these, the most excellent is the wise one, seeking to remain eternally in communion, with his devotion single-pointed. I am exceedingly beloved to him and, likewise, he is exceedingly beloved to me.

18. Certainly all who worship are noble, but the wise one is veritably my own Self. In communion with the Self, he is firmly established in this, of which nothing is higher.

19. After many births the wise one attains me. Such a great being who realizes "Vasudeva is All" is indeed hard to find.

All those who attempt to live the spiritual life are noble, but rare and precious is the soul who lives only for wisdom. He is the epitome of love and devotion. For such a one, selflessness is the norm and virtuous behavior is spontaneous. His accomplishment does not arise with the morning sun, however, but is the result of spiritual development accomplished over many lifetimes. At the peak of his attainment, his separate self becomes the universal Self, and he realizes all existence takes place within his own divine consciousness.

Verses 20–23

kāmaistaistairhṛtajñānāḥ prapadyante 'nyadevatāḥ
taṁ taṁ niyamamāsthāya prakṛtyā niyatāḥ svayā (20)

yo yo yāṁ tanuṁ bhaktaḥ śraddhayārcitumicchati
tasya tasyācalāṁ śraddhāṁ tāmeva vidadhāmyaham (21)

sa tayā śraddhayā yuktastasyārādhanamīhate
labhate ca tataḥ kāmānmayaiva vihitānhi tān (22)

antavattu phalaṁ teṣāṁ tadbhavatyalpamedhasām
devāndevayajo yānti madbhaktā yānti māmapi (23)

20. Those whose wisdom is diverted by selfish desires are distracted by their own limited nature. They seek support from a partial expression of divinity by undertaking specific religious obligations.

21. I support whatever form a devotee worships, making his faith firm.

22. Endowed with this faith, a devotee propitiates his deity and believes this is how to obtain his desires. Actually, however, all is fulfilled by me alone.

23. Transient are the rewards attained by those of lesser understanding. Those who worship partial expressions of divinity enter into the realms of those expressions. My devotees come to me.

Most religious people are not yet prepared to approach the Self. They seek an external form of divinity to worship. Participating in conventional religions and sects, they idealize a form of God or saint, and then seek a communion with this conceptualized deity.

Krishna does not criticize this limited spirituality, as it is appropriate and proper for most people at their stage of development. Most people are simply not spiritually mature enough to pursue their own Self. They need the support of tradition, community, rites, and rituals as well as authorities external to themselves. These paths help develop devotion and virtue, and like-minded followers can congregate together and support one another.

Verses 24–25

avyaktaṁ vyaktimāpannaṁ manyante māmabuddhayaḥ
paraṁ bhāvamajānanto mamāvyayamanuttamam (24)

nāhaṁ prakāśaḥ sarvasya yogamāyāsamāvṛtaḥ
mūḍho 'yaṁ nābhijānāti loko māmajamavyayam (25)

24. Those with an undeveloped intelligence think of me, the unmanifest, as a limited manifest entity. They do not realize my supreme existence—inexhaustible, with nothing higher.

25. I am not revealed to all, as I am veiled by my own yoga of divine magic. The deluded world does not know me as unborn and inexhaustible.

Those who are yet to develop spiritual maturity believe that the limited manifest individual is the highest expression of divinity. This includes the commonly accepted belief that humanity is the crown of creation as well as religions who hold that one form of God is superior to others. All manifest form is limited; it exists within prakriti, or primal nature, and experiences the revolution of nature's cycle of creation, preservation, and dissolution.

Everything that takes place within time belongs to the domain of maya and, hence, has a beginning and an conclusion. The philosophy of the Bhagavad Gita is concerned with the sanatana dharma, the eternal path, which exists independently of man's belief systems and religious institutions.

All holy people, places of pilgrimage, revered scriptures, even visions and prophecies, exist within time and space. Krishna refers to a consciousness which is prior to time, within which time occurs, and which will remain when time is no more. We continue this discussion of time, space, and identity in the next verse.

Verse 26

vedāhaṁ samatītani vartamānāni cārjuna
bhaviṣyāṇi ca bhūtāni māṁ tu veda na kaścana (26)

26. I know the beings of the past, the present, and the future, O Arjuna, but no one knows me.

Modern quantum physics has identified time/space as one integral continuum and has proposed that there exist a variety of time/space continuums. This knowledge is in complete agreement with the teachings of the yogic tradition. The Bhagavad Gita, representing the yogis, encourages the aspirant to seek for the consciousness within which all continuums arise, exist, and dissolve.

This consciousness of the one Self is expressed as individual beings who live at various periods of time, in different parts of the universe. All waves arise from the same ocean regardless of time and place. Krishna does not mean that he knows the infinite number of beings in the same way that a computer can hold vast stores of information. God is not a supercomputer, able to store more binary information than anyone else. The one who knows all beings knows them because they are expressions of his own true identity.

Verses 27–30

icchādveṣasamutthena dvandvamohena bhārata
sarvabhūtāni saṁmohaṁ sarge yānti paraṁtapa (27)

yeṣāṁ tvantagataṁ pāpaṁ jnānaṁ puṇyakarmaṇām
te dvandvamohanirmūktā bhajante māṁ dṛḍhavratāḥ (28)

jarāmaraṇamokṣāya māmāśritya yatanti ye
te brahma tadviduḥ kṛtsnamadhyātmaṁ karma cākhilam (29)

sādhibhūtādhidaivaṁ māṁ sādhiyajñaṁ ca ye viduḥ
prayāṇakāle 'pi ca māṁ te viduryuktacetasaḥ (30)

27. The pairs of opposites arise as selfish will and repulsion, O Bharata. All beings naturally drift into this delusory influence, O Parantapa.

28. Those whose perform positive deeds and whose self-centeredness has come to an end are free of the delusions arising from the pairs of opposites. They worship me with firm resolve.

29. Those who seek my shelter and strive for liberation from decay and death come to know the Divine Essence—Infinite Consciousness, Self-Consciousness, and the nature of activity.

30. Those who know me as the essence of Existence, the essence of Divinity, and the essence of Offering are in conscious communion with me, even at the time of death.

The spiritual realization of the Bhagavad Gita is a comprehensive, inclusive, holistic consciousness. This is the Infinite Consciousness which is the essence of all things—of every sentient being and material object. Those who have attained to this state pass through all of life's changes, even through the portal of death, in communion with the Self.

In these two verses, Krishna uses several Sanskrit terms which are worth understanding more fully. Arjuna lends the student of the Bhagavad Gita a hand, in a manner of speaking, by opening the next chapter asking Krishna for greater clarification of these terms.

Chapter 8

Akshara Brahman Yoga
The Yoga of the Imperishable Infinite Consciousness

Verses 1–2

arjuna uvāca
kiṁ tadbrahma kimadhyātmaṁ kiṁ karma puruṣottama
adhibhūtaṁ ca kiṁ proktamadhidaivaṁ kimucyate (1)

adhiyajñaḥ kathaṁ ko 'tra dehe 'sminmadhusūdana
prayāṇakāle ca kathaṁ jñeyo 'si niyatātmabhiḥ (2)

1. Arjuna asked: What is the Infinite Consciousness? What is the essence of Self-consciousness? What is the nature of activity? O Purushottam (Krishna as Supreme Spiritual Being), what is the essence of existence? What is that which is taught to be the essence of divinity?

2. While one is embodied, how is one to understand the essence of spiritual offering, O Madhusudhana? Also, how are you to be known by those Self-directed persons at the time of their departure into death?

At the conclusion of the previous chapter, Krishna briefly described to Arjuna the holistic nature of spirituality, encompassing transcendent divinity, immanent divinity, and the divinity of the individual soul. Arjuna, lacking enlightenment, could not possibly understand Krishna's teachings on first hearing, so here he asks for clarification.

These questions demonstrate that Arjuna has reached a stage of spiritual readiness. His mind has entered into subtle spheres, and he seeks to know the purpose and meaning of life. He is engaged in the great quest for authentic spiritual realization.

Verses 3–4

śribhagavānuvāca
akṣaraṁ brahma paramaṁ svabhāvo 'dhyātmamucyate
bhūtabhāvodbhavakaro visargaḥ karmasaṁjñitaḥ (3)

adhibhūtaṁ kṣaro bhāvaḥ puruṣaścādhidaivatam
adhiyajño 'hamevātra dehe dehabhṛtāṁ vara (4)

3. Shri Bhagavan said: The imperishable Infinite Consciousness is the ultimate, whose essential nature is known as Self-consciousness. Activity is the spontaneous creative urge which is the cause and origin of all being.

4. The essence of manifest existence is the transient principle. Spiritual Being is the essence of divinity. I alone am making the essential offering here in the body, O Dehabhritam Vara (Arjuna as Supreme among the Embodied).

Brahman, the imperishable Infinite Consciousness, is the divine transcendent, unchanging principle. It is described as ultimate because it is absolutely inclusive; a consciousness which includes within itself all and everything and embraces all and everything, yet remains beyond the time/space continuum and all phenomena.

Adhyatman, also known as jiva, is the individual soul and is described as the essence of Brahman. Brahman manifests the individual souls in the same way a bonfire expresses itself as sparks.

Karma, or action, is described as *visargah*: the spontaneous impulse which inspires the fire of divinity to burn, to seek fuel, to consume, and to illuminate. It is the intrinsic spirit of Brahman to creatively manifest. This creation is non-purposeful, playful folly since Brahman is already whole and complete with no purpose to achieve. *Adhibhutam* is the subtle energy which manifests as creation. This is nature in her never-ceasing dance of creating, preserving, and destroying, in order to create anew.

Purusha, or Spiritual Being, is described as the very essence of divinity. Divinity is not only the transcendent Brahman as an abstract impersonal consciousness. Divinity is also purusha, Being with personality. This personality is presented in the various yogic myths as loving, sublime, powerful, protective, and full of joy. This personality permeates all aspects of divinity. (See also verses 20–22 and chapter 15 for a discussion of purusha.)

God is both transcendent and immanent, impersonal and personal. He is She. The God of the Bhagavad Gita is the all-inclusive consciousness which is the abode of paradox, inconsistency, ambiguity, subtlety, and mischief—all of the ingredients necessary to create the stew of cosmic love. If this rings true in your heart, dear reader, it is because this God is being expressed through the core of your being, as you. It is none other than God who is making the supreme spiritual offering, the *adhiyajnah*, embodying himself in a limited world, undergoing a pilgrimage through creation for the sheer joy of reawakening to unlimited consciousness.

Verses 5–7

antakāle ca māmeva smaranmuktvā kalevaram
yaḥ prayāti sa madbhāvaṁ yāti nāstyatra saṁśayaḥ (5)

yaṁ yaṁ vāpi smaranbhāvaṁ tyajatyante kalevaram
taṁ tamevaiti kaunteya sadā tadbhāvabhāvitaḥ (6)

tamātsarveṣu kāleṣu māmanusmara yudhya ca
mayyarpitamanobuddhirmāmevaiṣyasyasaṁśayam (7)

5. One who leaves the body at the time of death thinking of me alone comes into my state of being. Of this there can be no doubt.

6. Whatever one thinks of at the time of death, to that he goes, O Kaunteya, as this reflects the nature of his disposition.

7. Therefore, at all times remember me and fight. With your mind and intelligence surrendered to me, you shall come to me alone, have no doubt.

In verse 2, Arjuna asked Krishna how one is to direct his consciousness in order to make death a successful passage. Krishna answers by explaining that the transition of death is pivotal and the orientation of one's mind will determine the direction taken into the next realm of existence. To maintain an inner equilibrium during the death process is a task that must be rehearsed during life. This rehearsal is meditation. The process of meditation is explained below in verses 11–14.

As verse 6 explains, the attitude of mind at death is of critical importance at the time of death (pun intended). Those unfamiliar with the operation of the mind may conclude that they can live any way they desire during life, then just make sure to turn their mind to spirituality at the time of death and, magically, they will attain their goal. Those who have practiced meditation know that the mind is difficult to make tranquil even under the best of conditions. Under the stress of death, with the dissolving of all relationships, identities, and possessions, it is impossible for the untrained person to focus the mind.

Verse 8

abhyāsayogayuktena cetasā nānyagāminā
paramaṁ puruṣaṁ divyaṁ yāti pārthānucintayan (8)

8. O Partha, one goes to the Supreme Spiritual Being through a contemplation which involves repeatedly bringing his full awareness to this yoga, without being distracted by anything else.

The attainment of the Supreme Spiritual Being does not arise by belief or mere acceptance of the teachings of the Bhagavad Gita. It takes sadhana, spiritual practice. The aspirant must learn to direct his mind and heart toward his goal. This focus must become one-pointed, without being diluted by petty distractions. If the arrow is to hit the bull's eye, the archer must have a steady gaze.

Verses 9–10

kaviṁ purāṇamanuśāsitāramaṇoraṇīyāṁsamanusmaredyaḥ
sarvasya dhātāramacintyarūpamādityavarṇaṁ tamasaḥ parastāt (9)

prayāṇkāle manasācalena bhaktyā yukto yogabalena caiva
bhruvormadhye prāṇamāveśya samyak sa taṁ paraṁ puruṣamupaiti divyam (10)

9. One who contemplates the Seer, the Ancient One, the Ruler, more subtle than an atom, the Supporter of All, Whose Form is Beyond Conception, Bright Like the Sun, Beyond Darkness;

10. At the time of departure from the body, steadying the mind, harmonized in devotion and the strength of yoga, firmly setting his life-force in the center between the eyebrows, he reaches the Supreme Spiritual Being.

Here is the instruction on meeting death with a controlled consciousness. By fixing the mind on any of the various qualities of the Supreme Being, bringing the awareness to the root of the externalization of mind (between the eyebrows), and utilizing the devotion and strength garnered by yoga practice during the lifetime, one can consciously pass through the portal of death.

The Supreme Being, the one Self, has infinite qualities, a few of which are described poetically in verse 9. For instance, the Supreme Being is poetically described as Bright Like the Sun, as he is Self-luminous, and as being Beyond Darkness, as he is beyond the darkness of delusion.

Verses 11–14

yadakṣaraṁ vedavido vadanti viśanti yadyatayo vītarāgaḥ
yadicchanto brahmacaryam caranti tatte padaṁ saṁgraheṇa pravakṣye (11)

sarvadvārāṇi saṁyamya mano hṛdi nirudhya ca
mūrdhnyādhāyātmanaḥ prāṇamāsthito yogadhāraṇam (12)

omityekākṣaraṁ brahma vyāharanmāmanusmaran
yaḥ prayāti tyajandehaṁ sa yāti paramāṁ gatim (13)

ananyacetāḥ satataṁ yo māṁ smarati nityaśaḥ
tasyāhaṁ sulabhaḥ pārtha nityayuktasya yoginaḥ (14)

11. I shall concisely describe to you the way to that imperishable of which the vedic sages spoke. This is what those who are self-controlled and obsession-free desire and thus lead a life focused on the Infinite Consciousness.

12. Constraining the sensory gates and constraining the mind in the spiritual heart, with the life force focused in the head, established in yogic concentration,

13. Uttering the single-syllabled *aum* and remembering me, brings one to the supreme path when abandoning the body.

14. One whose mind is not drawn elsewhere but is constantly remembering me is a yogi ever in communion. To such a one, I am easily attained, O Partha.

The path of meditation is one of a progressive internalization of consciousness. The aspirant first withdraws his attention from external influences and centers his mind in his spiritual heart, the sense of "I am." He then raises his energy into the higher energy centers in the head and vibrates aum, the vibration of Infinite Consciousness. He rises above identity with his personal life, realizing his body/mind as nothing more than a temporary vehicle he occupies during his incarnation in this world.

The realization of the soul as separate from the bodily vehicle makes the passage into death a continuation of the spiritual path engaged in during the lifetime. Those who have continually practiced spiritual consciousness by remembering God and engaging in yogic disciplines attain communion with the Infinite Consciousness. The work performed by a yogi during his life will definitely bear fruit at his death.

Verses 15–16

māmupetya punarjanma duḥkhālayamaśāśvatam
nāpnuvati mahātmānaḥ saṁsiddhiṁ paramāṁ gatāḥ (15)

ābrahmabhuvanāllokāḥ punarāvartino 'rjuna
māmupetya tu kaunteya punarjanma na vidyate (16)

15. Having attained me, these great souls are not born again in a transitory realm of suffering, having gone beyond to the supreme station.

16. All realms, from that of Brahma, the Creator, to the material world are involved in the cycle of rebirth, O Arjuna. But on reaching me, O Kaunteya, there is not another compulsive rebirth.

Tradition holds that pain is intrinsic to the transitory realms of matter. As everything is constantly changing, there exists nothing that can bring lasting comfort or peace to the weary soul. This has lead several schools of thought to conclude that the realms of matter are the cause of suffering. The true cause, however, is mental attachment.

The great souls who do not cling to anything in transitive form, even their own body and mind, experience the world as a creative venture. The world of form can be an abode of misery or a "carnival of joy," said Paramahamsa Ramakrishna. It all depends on the level of consciousness.

Those who identify with a personal history will experience suffering. Be they the highest god or ordinary individual, attachment to form results in pain. To be an individual is to be apart from the one Self. To be a sage is to be a part of the one Self. The path from being a common person to becoming a sage is to identify with the consciousness of Krishna, the Supreme Being, who is imperishable, eternal, and not subject to compulsive birth and death.

Verses 17–19

sahasrayugaparyantamaharyadbrahmaṇo viduḥ
rātriṁ yugasahasrāntāṁ te 'horātravido janāḥ (17)

avyaktādvyaktayaḥ sarvāḥ prabhavantyaharāgame
rātryāgame pralīyante tatraivāvyaktasaṁjñake (18)

bhūtagrāmaḥ sa evāyaṁ bhūtvā bhūtvā pralīyate
rātryāgame 'vaśaḥ pārtha prabhavantyaharāgame (19)

17. Those who understand the day of Brahma, which is a thousand ages, and his night, which is also a thousand ages, truly know day and night.

18. From the unmanifest all that is manifest arises at the arrival of day; at the arrival of night it all merges back into the unmanifest.

19. This very same constellation of beings comes into existence repeatedly and merges compulsively at the arrival of cosmic night. O Partha, they yet again arise at the arrival of the next day.

Yogic cosmology is vast in its scale. A cosmic cycle is traditionally said to last 4,320,000 years. Each of these cycles is one day in the life of the creator god, Brahma. Another full cycle comprises his night. Brahma lives for one hundred years of these immense periods of time.

The essential teaching here is that time is cyclical: all beings arise into manifestation and eventually return to an unmanifest state, only to manifest again. The value of this teaching is not historic but yogic. An aspirant who appreciates that his brief life is as fleeting as a drop of dew is able to maintain the appropriate degree of perspective. His accomplishments and failures are not imagined to hold vast significance. The aspirant finds it easy to be humble before the grandeur of eternity.

Verses 20–22

parastasmāttu bhāvo 'nyo 'vyakto 'vyaktātsanātanaḥ
yaḥ sa sarveṣu bhūteṣu naśyatsu na ninaśyati (20)

avyakto 'kṣara ityuktastamāhuḥ paramāṁ gatim
yaṁ prāpya na nivartante taddhāma paramaṁ mama (21)

puruṣaḥ sa paraḥ pārtha bhaktyā labhyastvananyayā
yasyāntaḥ sthāni bhūtāni yena sarvamidaṁ tatam (22)

20. Beyond this cyclic unmanifest, there is another eternal unmanifest state of being which does not transform when other states transform.

21. This unmanifest is termed the Imperishable and is spoken of as the supreme condition, gaining when there is no more compulsive return. Such is my supreme abode.

22. This is the state of the Supreme Being, O Partha, within whom abide all beings and by whom all creation is pervaded. Attainable he is by unswerving devotion.

The cyclic manifestation of individual identities and their eventual reabsorption back into the unmanifest is the subject of the previous set of verses. Here, Krishna teaches that there exists a consciousness beyond anything occurring within the realms of form. While personalities and entire worlds are engaged in the cycle of manifestation, the Supreme Being is not subject to change. The waves on the ocean arise, exist, and return to the ocean, but the great force which causes the swelling of the waters exists forever.

This force, the essence of primal activity and power, arises from a conscious being—the Supreme Being, Purushottama. In this sense we can refer to a personal God, but only because this God is no different from the one Self. There exists a personality within the Infinite Consciousness of the impersonal Brahman, but a personality so vastly incomprehensible to the human mind that sages are often reluctant to discuss the issue for fear of being misunderstood. Those trapped in egoic identification cannot understand the nature of their own soul, let alone the supreme soul. Only the great yogis whose devotion is unswerving and universal can realize the Supreme Being.

Verses 23–27

yatra kāle tvanāvṛttimāvṛttiṁ caiva yohinaḥ
prayātā yānti taṁ kālaṁ vakṣyāmi bharatarṣabha (23)

agnirjyotirahaḥ śuklaḥ ṣaṇmāsā uttarāyaṇam
tatra prayātā gacchanti brahma brahmavido janāḥ (24)

dhūmo rātristathā kṛṣṇaḥ ṣaṇmāsā dakṣiṇāyanam
tatra cāndramasaṁ jyotiryogī prāpya nivartate (25)

śuklakṛṣṇe gatī hyete jagataḥ śaśvate mate
ekayā yātyanāvṛttimanyayāvartate punaḥ (26)

naite sṛtī pārtha jānanyogī muhyati kaścana
tasmātsarveṣu kāleṣu yogayukto bhavārjuna (27)

23. I will now tell you, O Bharatarshabha, the times which yogis depart from this world and which result in their return or non-return.

24. Those who go forth when there is divine fire, divine light, during daytime, during the waxing moon, and during the six months of the sun's northern course are knowers of Infinite Consciousness and reach Infinite Consciousness.

25. Those yogis who go forth when there is smoke, night, the dark and waning moon and during the six months of the southern course of the sun attain the lunar light and return again.

26. These two—the bright and dark—are known to be the world's perennial paths. By one there is the attainment of non-return, while by the other there is coming back again.

27. Understanding these two paths, O Partha, a yogi is not at all confused. Therefore, O Arjuna, at all times be in communion through yoga.

In this set of verses, Krishna describes symbolically the two alternative paths available at the time of death. One path, the way of the ascending light, leads to Infinite Consciousness. This is the way of the universal yoga as taught in the Bhagavad Gita. The other path, within the realms of shadows, leads to a rebirth in the world. This is the way of selfishness. For the sincere yogi, the path of the ascending light is the appropriate path. It is the goal and result of a life of spiritual aspiration.

Verse 28

vedeṣu yajñeṣu tapaḥsu caiva dāneṣu yatpuṇyaphalaṁ pradiṣṭam
atyeti tatsarvamidaṁ viditvā yogī paraṁ sthānamupaiti cādyam (28)

28. A yogi who realizes this teaching transcends whatever meritorious reward can be gained by traditional religious practices such as ceremonies, austerities, and giving charitable gifts. He attains to the Supreme Primal State.

Traditional religious practices, no matter how meritorious or benign, support the sense of individuality which the yogi must transcend if he seeks the path of Infinite Consciousness. Anything that keeps one's identity in a conceptual box during life leads to an actual box—a casket—at the end of life. A yogi practices this authentic yoga, beyond the confines of man's religious creations, and passes over the chasm of death without confusion or dismay. The path of social conventions is proper for the citizen whose home is the world. The path of immortality is for the yogi who belongs to the whole universe.

Chapter 9

Rajavidya Rajaguhya Yoga
The Yoga of the Majestic Science and the Majestic Mystery

Verses 1–2

śrībhagavānuvāca
idaṁ tu te guhyatamaṁ pravakṣyāmyanasūyave
jñānaṁ vijñānasahitaṁ yajjñātvā mokṣyase śubhāt (1)

rājavidyā rājaguhyaṁ pavitramidamuttamam
pratyakṣāvagamaṁ dharmyaṁ suskhaṁ kartumavyayam (2)

1. Shri Bhagavan said: To you who are without duplicity, I shall reveal this profound mystery—a wisdom along with practical application, realizing that you will be liberated from all misgivings.

2. This majestic science and majestic mystery is the highest sanctity, accessible by direct experience, completely harmonious, is simple to live, and does not degrade over time.

The teacher acknowledges the sincerity of the student. Arjuna has asked serious questions and has paid attention to Krishna's answers. Now is the time for Krishna to begin to drop the curtain, revealing to Arjuna the reality of Infinite Consciousness and its actual attainment.

The experience of the teacher will not suffice, however, nor will scriptures or traditions. The student must know for himself, by firsthand experience, the nature of Infinite Consciousness. Direct experience alone is the manner by which the yogic tradition stays alive and continues to remain vital generation after generation.

Verse 3

aśraddadhānāḥ puruṣā dharmasyāsya paraṁtapa
aprāpya māṁ nivartante mṛtusaṁsāravartmani (3)

3. Those souls who have no faith in the way of harmony, O Parantapa, do not reach me and are forced to return to the cycle of mortality, death, and ignorance.

The world is a school in which souls are educated in spiritual reality. The result of a lack of interest in spirituality during one lifetime is a return to the mortal world. Just as most people will not attain a Ph.D. during the course of their lifetime, so likewise most will not attain Infinite Consciousness. The development of a soul takes time. Since this is the eternal game, there is no hurry at all.

This perspective on spiritual development is vastly different from that presented by the Abrahamic religions of Judaism, Christianity, and Islam. Although there are certain sects within these traditions that acknowledge reincarnation, the general teaching is that an individual experiences just one human life. Then, depending on the appropriateness of a person's beliefs and behavior, he or she will enjoy eternal reward or punishment. The teaching is not consistent with the experiences of the great yogis who have completed their spiritual evolution.

Verses 4–6

mayā tatamidaṁ sarvaṁ jagadavyaktamūrtinā
matsthāni sarvabhūtāni na cāhaṁ teṣvavasthitaḥ (4)

na ca matsthāni bhūtāni paśya me yogamaiśvaram
bhūtabhṛnna ca bhūtastho mamātmā bhūtabhāvanaḥ (5)

yathākāśasthito nityaṁ vāyuḥ sarvatrago mahān
tathā sarvāṇi bhūtāni matsthānītyupadhāraya (6)

4. I pervade all this world by my unmanifest form. All beings abide in me, and yet I do not abide in them.

5. Behold my divine yoga by which it appears that these beings do not abide in me nor am I dwelling in them. But look closer—I am the cause and sustainer of them all.

6. As the great expanse of air travels everywhere and permeates space, similarly you might understand how all beings have their basis in me.

There truly exists nothing but the Supreme Being in infinite forms. Unmanifest, He/She manifests as all forms. As verse five indicates, though all abide within the supreme, the supreme cannot be said to abide in any of the forms, as nothing in form can fully and completely manifest that which is ever unmanifest.

The Indian religious tradition permits people to generate their own personal conception of the transcendent, called an *ishtadevata* (chosen form of God). The ishtadevata serves as a conceptual link by which a person can relate to the supreme. As we shall see, it is very difficult for most aspirants to relate to the unmanifest (see 12.2). Some form is usually helpful in directing one's mind and heart on the spiritual path.

The "divine yoga" of verse 6 is maya, the extraordinary magical power wielded by the supreme. By maya the infinite, unitary, and unmanifest appears to be finite, diverse, and manifest—existing everywhere as the wind blows throughout the sky, yet seeming to be nowhere. Such an amazing game—the Supreme Being playing hide and seek with Himself! God plays the fool when he becomes man; then man becomes the sage when he finds God.

Verses 7–10

sarvabhūtāni kaunteya prakṛtiṁ yānti māmikām
kalpakṣaye punastāni kalpādau visṛjāmyaham (7)

prakṛtiṁ svāmavaṣṭabhya visṛjāmi punaḥ punaḥ
bhūtagrāmamimaṁ kṛtsnamavaśaṁ prakṛtervaśāt (8)

na ca māṁ tāni karmāṇi nibadhnanti dhanaṁjaya
udāsīnavadāsīnamasaktaṁ teṣu karmasu (9)

mayādhyakṣeṇa prakṛtiḥ sūyate sacarācaram
hetunānena kaunteya jagadviparivartate (10)

7. All beings pass into my primal nature at the end of a cosmic cycle, O Kaunteya, and at the beginning of the next cycle I again emanate them.

8. By virtue of my primal nature, I emanate again and again this entire multitude of beings, all subject to the laws of my nature.

9. This activity does not bind me, O Dhananjaya, for I am seated as if indifferent and unattached.

10. Under my guidance, primal nature gives birth to all that is animate and inanimate. This is the means, O Kaunteya, by which the world creation revolves.

The cyclic nature of prakriti, primal nature, in creation and destruction has previously been discussed. Here Krishna informs Arjuna how the Supreme Being utilizes prakriti to bring to life all that is animate (breathing) and all that is inanimate (without breath). Remaining transcendent, the Self is like a magnet which causes metal filings to move. The magnet does not actually do anything; by its inherent power activity occurs.

The Supreme Being as both transcendent and immanent is superbly depicted in the figure of Shiva Mahayogi, "The Great Yogi." Shiva is eternally enjoying both dancing wildly and sitting in meditation, at the very same time. Simultaneously, he is both "seated as if indifferent" as well as expressing himself as prakriti.

Shiva is meditated upon with the great five-syllabled *mantra* (sacred phrase) *na-ma-shi-va-ya*. Na is creation, ma is preservation, shi is destruction, va is cloaking his reality, ya is revealing his reality. This mantra is constantly being repeated by prakriti as she dances with her Lord, the transcendent Shiva. The cycles of nature, therefore, are nothing more than na-ma-shi-va-ya. The yogi who realizes the truth of this mantra realizes Shiva and the unity of the transcendent and the immanent.

Verses 11–12

avajānanti māṁ mūḍhā mānuṣīṁ tanumāśritam
paraṁ bhāvamajānanto mama bhūtamaheśvaram (11)

moghāśā moghakarmāṇo moghajñānā vicetasaḥ
rākṣasīmāsurīṁ caiva prakṭiṁ mohinīṁ śritāḥ (12)

11. The foolish do not understand me when I adopt a human form. They are ignorant of my supreme existence as the Great Lord of all beings.

12. Their petty and superficial hopes, acts, and wisdom are based on false assumptions. Like thugs and enemies they submit themselves to an illusory nature.

Those who do not have the eyes to see that it is none other than God who has become all beings are spiritually ignorant. To mortal eyes it seems impossible that the Great Lord could have become the petty human being. Yet, exclaim the realized yogis, it is indeed the one Self who has become all. In a gesture of love and abandon, God has descended into human form, in order to later ascend and realize Himself.

Verses 13–15

mahātmānastu māṁ pārtha daivīṁ prakṛtimāśritāḥ
bhajantyananyamanaso jñātvā bhūtādimavyayam (13)

satataṁ kīrtayanto māṁ yatantaśca dṛḍhavratāḥ
namasyantaśca māṁ bhaktyā nityayuktā upāsate (14)

jñānayajñena cāpyanye yajanto māmupāsate
ekatvena pṛthaktvena bahudhā viśvatomukham (15)

13. But the great souls, O Partha, submit themselves to my divine primal nature and worship me with an undistracted mind, realizing me as the inexhaustible source of all beings.

14. They are always singing of me, ever striving, firm in their vows, respecting me, forever devoted in communion, drawing ever near.

15. Others also perform the wisdom-offering and draw near to me by seeking my face in union, in duality, and in multiplicity.

Verse 14 describes bhakti yoga, the yoga of spiritual devotion, which is more fully discussed in chapter 12. The devotee cherishes the sense of separation from God in order that he may feel the joy of worship. To quote a common expression in this area: "He wants to taste sugar; he does not want to become sugar." The devotee enjoys the relationship of lover and beloved, drawing ever-nearer toward an embrace which is never quite reached—infinitely halved—forever yearned for—enjoyed by its non-satisfaction. The devotee does not want to become a wave returning to the sea; he wants to be like a grain of sand, retaining a trace of individuality in order to experience the grandeur of the beach.

Verse 15 describes a more comprehensive experience of Infinite Consciousness through the wisdom offering, jnana yoga, the yoga of wisdom discussed in chapter 4. Seeking God's face in union references the experience of the yogi in samadhi, meditative absorption. One is reminded of the Zen teaching that when a meditator attains enlightenment, his eyebrows mingle with those of the Buddha. In other words, those of realization "see through the same eyes" when they experience the same vision.

Realization of only the unity of Infinite Consciousness in jnana, like realization of only the duality of Infinite Consciousness in bhakti, are both less than integral. Realization must be unitary, dual, and multiple if it is to include all aspects of the Supreme. One is reminded of Hanuman's pronouncement to his guru and God, Shri Rama. When Ram asked, "Hanuman, who are you?" Hanuman answered, "When I feel myself a body, I serve you. When I feel myself an individual soul, I worship you. When I know who I am, I am you."

Verses 16–19

ahaṁ kraturahaṁ yajñaḥ svadhāhamahamauṣadham
mantro 'hamahamevājyamahamagnirahaṁ hutam (16)

pitāhamasya jagato mātā dhātā pitāmahaḥ
vedyaṁ pavitramoṅkāra ṛksāma yajureva ca (17)

gatirbhartā prabhuḥ sākṣī nivāsaḥ śaraṇaṁ suhṛt
prabhavaḥ pralayaḥ sthānaṁ nidhānaṁ bījamavyayam (18)

tapāmyahamahaṁ varṣaṁ nigṛhṇāmyutsṛjāmi ca
amṛtaṁ caiva mṛtyuśca sadasaccāhamarjuna (19)

16. I am the ritual act, I the offering, I the ancestral respect, I the healing herb, I the sacred phrase, I the butter, I the sacrament.

17. I am the father of the world, the mother, the supporter, the ancestor, the one who is to be known, the purifier. I am aum, and I am the sacred writings.

18. I am the goal, the upholder, the master, the witness, the abode, the refuge, the friend. I am the cycle of creation and dissolution, the foundation, the basis, and the imperishable seed.

19. I radiate heat; rain I withhold and send forth. I am the nectar of immortality and I am death. O Arjuna, I am eternal reality and temporal illusion.

In this section of verses, the aspirant may find it helpful to read the text while identifying with Krishna. As a meditation, dear reader, try to recite Krishna's words as your own. Rising above the confusion and concern of Arjuna, bring consciousness to the level of the one Self who is all beings and energies. For the Self shared by all is the father, mother, friend, all that is sought. This Self is not outside but resides within as your true identity.

When an individual realizes himself as the Self, the fears and confusion of superficial life fall away. The primal fear of death, a seeming external power before which one is powerless, is recognized as yet another expression of the Self. All phenomena of nature, including death, belong to the Self. Infinite Consciousness is the bliss of this eternal reality as well as the confusion which takes place within the temporal illusion. All is well; all is the play of God.

Verses 20–22

traividyā māṁ somapāḥ pūtapāpā yajñarṣṭvā svargatiṁ prārthayante
te puṇyāmāsādyā surendrālokamaśnanti divyāndivi devabhogān (20)

te taṁ bhuktvā svargalokaṁ viśālaṁ kṣīṇe puṇye martyalokaṁ viśanti
evaṁ trayīdharmamanuprapannā gatāgataṁ kāmakāmā labhante (21)

ananyāścintayanto māṁ ye janāḥ paryupāsate
teṣāṁ nityābhiyuktānāṁ yogakṣemaṁ vahāmyaham (22)

20. Practitioners of traditional religious systems drink the soma nectar and are purified of error. They worship by traditional ceremonies and pray to enter heaven after death. They accrue merit, which qualifies them for their next birth in the realm of Indra, Lord of Heavens, where they enjoy the divine pleasures of the gods.

21. Having enjoyed that vast and expansive heavenly realm, their merit is depleted, and they re-enter the realm of mortality. This is consistent with the

teachings of the scriptures that one can certainly attain great pleasures which are, ultimately, fleeting.

22. But those who meditate exclusively on me and always seek communion solely with me, I bring them the supreme good of yoga.

Those who practice a traditional religious system live a moral lifestyle and enjoy a heavenly reward after death. The various heavens are created by the power of the minds of adherents who share similar beliefs. Their stay in heaven, however extensive by human years, is still transient, concluding with rebirth. Good karma, produced by an ethical lifestyle, will produce its positive rewards. The goal of the teachings of the Bhagavad Gita is not good karma or reward, no matter how heavenly, but the freedom that comes from transcendence of all personally driven motivations. Religion can bring one to a visit in the heaven of his desires, but yoga can bring one to freedom.

The nature of the soma nectar mentioned in verse 20 is debatable. Some believe it is a symbol of the nectar of devotion, the joy that arises within from devotion to God. It is equally plausible, however, based on traditional testimony and ancient writings, that soma was some sort of intoxicating herbal preparation. The inebriation from drinking this libation brought an enhancement of perception and devotional feelings.

Regardless of whether soma is a symbol of divine emotions and/or an external aid to producing devotional feelings, the essential teaching remains the same. All realms are transitory, all perceptions pass, all moods arise and fall; only the imperishable Infinite Consciousness is eternal. Those alone who meditate on the Self, renouncing the desire for personal enjoyment on earth and in heaven, enjoy the supreme good of yoga.

Verses 23–25

ye 'pyanyadevatā bhaktā yajante śraddhayānvitāḥ
te 'pi māmeva kaunteya yajantyavidhipūrvakam (23)

ahaṁ hi sarvayajñānāṁ bhoktā ca prabhureva ca
na tu māmabhijānanti tattvenātaścyavanti te (24)

yānti devaratā devānpitṛnyānti pitṛvratāḥ
bhūtāni yānti bhūtejyā yānti madyājino 'pi mām (25)

23. Those who are devoted to partial expressions of divinity are displaying a faith which is ultimately directed to me, O Kaunteya, though they are not in abidance with the true standard.

24. For I am the true enjoyer and the master of all offerings. They fall who do not understand me as the essence.

25. Followers of partial expressions of divinity go to the realms of these partial expressions, followers of their ancestors go to the realms of their ancestors, and followers of the nature spirits go to the nature spirits. My worshippers attain me.

There are a variety of ways by which people express their devotion which are not consistent with the highest principles of the yogic tradition. Krishna teaches Arjuna to seek his own Self and in this seeking discover the universal Self. This is a path of going inward into the source of one's being, becoming ever more autonomous and independent.

Religious followers who worship particular forms of God, those who worship their ancestors, those who revere local nature spirits or any other man-made cults, keep their members dependent on community, tradition, and external forces. Followers of these paths, if they be people of good will and ethical behavior, accrue positive karma during their life, enabling them to enjoy a period of respite in their heavenly ideal. As discussed before, none of these heavens is eternal, any more than a paradisiacal vacation on the earth. At the end of the vacation, the soul returns to the classroom of life and resumes the assignment of seeking his true nature in the one Self.

Verses 26–28

patraṁ puṣpaṁ phalaṁ toyaṁ yo me bhaktyā prayacchati
tadahaṁ bhaktyupahṛtamaśnāmi prayatātmanaḥ (26)

yatkaroṣi yadaśnāsi yajjuhoṣi dadāsi yat
yattapasyasi kaunteya tatkuruṣva madarpaṇam (27)

śubhāśubhaphalairevaṁ mokṣyase karmabandhanaiḥ
saṁnyāsayogayuktātmā vimukto māmupaiṣyasi (28)

26. One who offers to me with loving devotion a leaf, flower, fruit, or water from a pure heart makes an offering I accept.

27. Whatever you do, whatever you eat, whatever you offer, whatever you give, whatever austerity you undertake, O Kaunteya, do this as an offering to me.

28. In this way you will be liberated from the bonds of action and reaction and from positive and negative consequences. This yoga of renunciation through Self-communion will free you, and you will come to me.

The quantity of service offered to God, guru, and humanity is insignificant in comparison to the quality of the service. The important factor is the love with which an act is imbued. Something as simple as offering a tender leaf or budding flower with reverence and respect conveys more than a complex ritual. A loving heart brings forth simplicity; the clever and methodical mind produces elaborate plans and complications.

When action is an offering of communion, one becomes free of karmic results because there is no personal motivation driving the behavior. When there is no seed of personal drive, no plant of reward or consequence can possibly grow.

Selfless service is such a simple idea, though not always easy to act upon.

Verse 29

samo 'ham sarvabhūteṣu na me dveṣyo 'sti na priyaḥ
ye bhajanti tu māṁ bhaktyā mayi te teṣu cāpyaham (29)

29. I regard all beings equally. For me there is none to hate or hold special. However, those who worship me with loving devotion are of me, and I am expressed through them.

There are no special ones to God. There are no chosen people, no deluxe privileges, no love bestowed upon one and not another. The sun of Infinite Consciousness shines upon all equally. It is simply up to the individual to choose to step into the fresh air and enjoy the warming rays.

Verses 30–33

api cetsudurācāro bhajate māmananyabhāk
sādhureva sa mantavyaḥ samyagvyavasito hi saḥ (30)

kṣipraṁ bhavati dharmātmā śaśvacchāntiṁ nigacchati
kaunteya prati jānīhi na me bhaktaḥ praṇaśyati (31)

māṁ hi pārtha vyapāśritya ye 'pi syuḥ pāpayonayaḥ
striyo vaiśyāstathā śūdrāste 'pi yānti parāṁ gatim (32)

kiṁ punarbrāhmaṇāḥ puṇyā bhaktā rājarṣayastathā
anityamasukhaṁ lokamimaṁ prāpya bhajasva mām (33)

30. If one of extensive depravity comes to worship me with intense loving devotion, he should be considered to be a legitimate practitioner, for he has properly resolved.

31. In a moment of resolution, he turns toward Self-harmony and enters the way of abiding peace. Trust me, O Kaunteya; my loving devotees need not fear destruction.

32. Whosoever resorts to me for refuge, O Arjuna—including those of low caste, women, businessmen, and the uneducated—they attain the supreme goal.

33. How much more, then, the pious seekers of Infinite Consciousness and the devoted royal sages. Having appeared into this transient realm of sorrow, offer your worship to me.

The buddhi, the intelligence, is like a two-way mirror. When tilted toward the manas, the cognizing mind, perceptions and conceptualizations create confusion about the nature of the Self. When buddhi turns towards the Self, it reflects the Self, and the reality of love is apparent.

The instant the buddhi offers itself to the influence of the Self, in that same moment it enters into the reality of Infinite Consciousness. Though buddhi may not stay in deliberate relationship with the Self for long, still the moment is valid. In fact, spiritual progress is essentially a matter of keeping buddhi turned towards the Self for increasingly more extensive periods of time. When the light enters a room, it matters not how dark it was nor how long it was dark. The light has come.

Verse 32 describes the universal nature of the authentic yoga of the Bhagavad Gita. Race, gender, occupation, and other biological and social identities are irrelevant. To be an aspirant, one must simply desire to progress on the spiritual path. No artificial, manmade barriers stand as obstructions on this path.

Verse 34

manmanā bhava madbhakto madyājīmāṁ namaskuru
māmevaiṣyasi yuktvaivamātmānaṁ matparāyaṇaḥ (34)

34. Fix your mind on me, direct your love and devotion to me, adore me, welcome me with respect. Being in communion with your own Self, you will come to me, the climactic achievement.

To come into communion with the Self requires full attention. Meditation must be focused, enthusiastic, and endowed with devotion and reverence. In this way the aspirant will rise above his egoic identifications and realize the Self within. The pinnacle of achievement reveals the non-dual, one Self within all. The wave discovers it has always been the ocean.

Chapter 10

Vibhuti Yoga
The Yoga of Divine Manifestations

Verses 1–3

śrībhagavānuvāca
bhūya eva mahābāho śṛṇu me paramaṁ vacaḥ
yatte 'haṁ prīyamāṇāya vakṣyāmi hitakāmyayā (1)

na me viduḥ suragaṇāḥ prabhavaṁ na maharṣayaḥ
ahamādirhi devānāṁ maharṣīṇāṁ ca sarvaśaḥ (2)

yo māmajamanādiṁ ca vetti lokamaheśvaram
asaṁmūḍhaḥ sa martyeṣu sarvapāpaiḥ pramucyate (3)

1. Shri Bhagavan said: Listen to my supreme word again, O Mahabaho, for you are my dear one and are receptive. I desire only your well-being.

2. Neither the pantheon of gods nor the great sages know my origin, for I am truly the source of the gods and the sages.

3. Who understands me as unborn, beginningless, and the great lord of the world is undeluded among mortals and is emancipated from selfish errors.

The sage, having attained the spiritual goal, has no personal needs that can be met by his students. He holds the treasure of peace and joy, willingly sharing with whoever is interested. His only need is that the aspirant be receptive, for only with open hands can a gift be received. The closed minds of the egotistical do not allow them to consider that the sages hold the key to the palace of happiness.

Everyone will die. Every kingdom passes with time. The sun, moon, and stars will, someday, cease to exist. But the Self was, is, and will forever be. The goal of the yogic tradition is the realization of the Self as the Infinite Consciousness. This realization raises a mortal man to the status of immortal being.

Verses 4–5

buddhijñānamasaṁmohaḥ kṣamā satyaṁ damaḥ śamaḥ
sukhaṁ duḥkhaṁ bhavo 'bhāvo bhayaṁ cābhayameva ca (4)

ahiṁsā samatā tuṣṭistapo dānaṁ yaśo 'yaśaḥ
bhavanti bhāvā bhūtānāṁ matta eva pṛthagvidhāḥ (5)

4. Intuitive intelligence, wisdom, non-delusion, forgiveness, truthfulness, self-restraint, composure, happiness and suffering, eternal reality and temporal illusion, fear and fearlessness,

5. Non-violence, equanimity, contentment, austerity, generosity, fame, and shame are various states of being that proceed from me alone.

All states of being arise from within. Emotions, aspirations, perceptions of reality and illusion—these are all modes of experience which have no ontological existence. Rather, they arise from consciousness, exist within consciousness, and then recede back into their source. As such, it is essential that the individual aspirant take full responsibility for his emotions and perceptions if he wishes to cultivate spiritual consciousness and rise to a higher plane of reality.

Verses 6–8

maharṣayaḥ sapta pūrve catvāro manavastathā
madbhāvā mānasā jātā yeṣāṁ loka imāḥ prajāḥ (6)

etāṁ vibhūtiṁ yogaṁ ca mama yo vetti tattvataḥ
so 'vikampena yogena yujyate nātra saṁśayaḥ (7)

ahaṁ sarvasya prabhavo mattaḥ sarvaṁ pravartate
iti matvā bhajante māṁ budhā bhāvasamanvitāḥ (8)

6. The seven great sages of old and the four law-givers are parcel of my existence and born of my mind. From these come all the creatures of creation.

7. One who understands the essentials of my divine manifestations is a yogi. Through his own unfaltering practice of yoga he comes into communion. Of this there is no doubt.

8. I am the source of all; from me all creation extends. Understanding this, the wise worship me with an attitude of confidence.

Not only emotions and perceptions, but the entire world arises and exists only within consciousness. Just as someone asleep can dream an entire world, very similarly does an individual dream his own reality. Modern physics confirms that the external world is actually nothing but quantum energy which is literally given its form by the mind. This form is then colored by attachments, desires, and subjective values. This results in a perceptual world that exists solely in the mind.

When a yogi realizes that all existence manifests within his consciousness, he perceives the world as an expression of the energy of the Self. In communion with the Self, he feels all beings are a part of him. His compassion becomes universal in a natural expression of identity and love for the All in all.

Verses 9–11

maccittā madgataprāṇā bodhayantaḥ parasparam
kathayantaśca māṁ nityaṁ tuṣyanti ca ramanti ca (9)

teṣāṁ satatayuktānāṁ bhajatāṁ prītipūrvakam
dadāmi buddhiyogaṁ taṁ yena māmupayānti te (10)

teṣāmevānukampārthamahamajñānajaṁ tamaḥ
nāśayāmyātmabhāvastho jñānadīpena bhāsvatā (11)

9. Their individual consciousness fixed on me, their life force endowed to me, enlightening one another, and ever sharing with each other their feelings about me, they are content and they rejoice.

10. To those established in undisturbed communion and sweet worship, I grant the yoga of intuitive insight by which they come to me.

11. Because of my compassion for them, I abide as the feeling of their own Self and destroy the darkness of ignorance by the shining lamp of wisdom.

That all creation arises within the consciousness of the one Self does not mean that every person has actually realized this truth. There is a vast difference between the typical ego-centered individual, who believes his personal self is the center of the universe, and the realized sage, who realizes the one Self is the center of the universe. In fact, the sage who realizes the one Self will still behave as a normal human being while in the world. He adopts a sattvic ego, a pure individuality, by which he lives as a devotee of God and guru. Recognizing that his individuality is a but a wave on the ocean of Infinite Consciousness, he no longer lives a personal life. He lives, rather, a life of selfless service.

The sole joy of a sage is to share his realization with others. The joining together in communion is called *satsang* (gathering in truth). Most gatherings of worldly people are to support each other's superficial interests, bad habits, and anger against others. Satsang is for the purpose of joining together with other aspirants for the purpose of healing the illusions of ego-centered life. Satsang is a precious treasure in a world of ego-relationships, a means for establishing healthy relationships whereby one can communicate with vulnerability and integrity.

Verse 12

arjuna uvāca
paraṁ brahma paraṁ dhāma pavitraṁ paramaṁ bhavān
puruṣaṁ śāśvataṁ divyamādidevamajaṁ vibhum (12)

12. Arjuna said: You are the supreme absolute, supreme abode, supreme purifier, the eternal divine spiritual being, the primal divinity, the unborn, and all-pervading.

To Arjuna's credit, he recognizes the Infinite Consciousness in Krishna. His problem, however, as we will see in the next chapter, is that he fails to recognize that same consciousness within himself. Because of this artificial duality, Arjuna will become frightened when he perceives the totality of Krishna's being. For now, though, let us congratulate Arjuna that he has reached the level of spiritual advancement where he can appreciate how the Infinite Consciousness can manifest in a human being.

Verses 13–18

āhustvāmṛṣayaḥ sarve devarṣināradastathā
asito devalo vyāsaḥ svayaṁ caiva bravīṣi me (13)

sarvametadṛtaṁ manye yanmāṁ vadasi keśava
na hi te bhagavanvyaktiṁ vidurdevā na dānavāḥ (14)

svayamevātmanātmānaṁ vettha tvaṁ puruṣottama
bhūtabhāvana bhūteśa devadeva jagatpate (15)

vaktumarhasyaśeṣeṇa divyā hyātmavibhūtayaḥ
yābhirvibhūtibhirlokānimāṁstvaṁ vyāpya tiṣṭhasi (16)

kathaṁ vidyāmahaṁ yogiṁstvāṁ sadā paricintayan
keṣu keṣu ca bhāveṣu contyo 'si bhagavanmayā (17)

vistareṇātmano yogaṁ vibhūtiṁ ca janārdana
bhūyaḥ kathaya tṛptirhi śṛṇvato nāsti me 'mṛtam (18)

13. All the seers say this of you—the divine sage Narada as well as Asita, Devala, and Vyasa—just as you have declared to me.

14. I believe all this which you say to me is the truth, O Keshava. Neither the gods nor the demons, O Bhagavan, fully know your true nature.

15. Only you yourself know your Self by the Self, O Purushottama. You are the origin of all beings and existences, the God of gods, the Lord of the world.

16. Please tell me without omission of the divine manifestations of your Self whereby you pervade these worlds while still abiding beyond.

17. In what ways shall I constantly contemplate you? How shall I know you, O Yogi? Are you expressed in specific forms by which I can cognize you, O Bhagavan?

18. Relate to me in detail, O Janardana, the yoga of your Self and divine manifestations. I never cease to enjoy listening to your nectarine teachings.

Arjuna understands the revelation of the Self is not a new teaching; it has been acknowledged by ancient sages for time immemorial (see 4.1–3). He also knows that no individualized being—not man, god, or demon—can know the Self. The part cannot fully apprehend the whole. Only the Self can know the Self, after egoic individuality is sacrificed on the altar of love.

Arjuna asks Krishna for some sort of handle by which he can direct his mind towards Infinite Consciousness. Because Arjuna has not yet understood how to direct his own consciousness inward toward the Self, he asks Krishna to provide him with an external form on which he can channel his outward-directed mind.

Krishna agrees to Arjuna's request, as the compassionate guru must meet the disciple at the level of his development. As we will see in chapter 11, it is very difficult for most aspirants to meditate on the formless Infinite Consciousness. Most aspiring yogis need some form to which they can direct their mind and yearning heart.

Verses 19–39

śrībhagavānuvāca
hanta te kathayi.syāmi divyā hyātmavibhūtayaḥ
prādhānyataḥ kuruśreṣṭha nāstyanto vistarasya me (19)

ahamātma guḍākeśa sarvabhūtāśayasthitaḥ
ahamādiśca madhyaṁ ca bhūtānāmanta eva ca (20)

ādityānāmahaṁ viṣnṇurjyotiṣāṁ raviraṁśumān
marīcirmarutāmasmi nakṣatrāṇāmahaṁ śāśī (21)

vedānāṁ sāmvedo 'smi devānāmasmi vāsavaḥ
indriyāṇāṁ manaścāmi bhūtānāmasmi cetanā (22)

rudrāṇāṁ śaṅkaraścāsmi vitteśo yakṣarakṣasām
vasūnāṁ pāvakaścāsmi meruḥ śikhariṇāmaham (23)

purudhasāṁ ca mukhyaṁ māṁ viddhi pārtha bṛhaspatim
senānīnāmahaṁ skandaḥ sarasāmsami sāgaraḥ (24)

maharṣīṇāṁ bhṛgurahaṁ girāmasmyekamakṣaram
yajñānāṁ japayajño 'smi sthāvarāṇāṁ himālayaḥ (25)

aśvattaḥ sarvavṛkṣāṇāṁ devarṣīṇāṁ ca nāradaḥ
gandharvāṇāṁ citrarathaḥ siddhānāṁ kapilo muniḥ (26)

uccaiḥśravasamaśvānāṁ viddhi māmamṛtodbhavam
airāvataṁ gajendrāṇāṁ narāṇāṁ ca narādhipam (27)

āyudhānāmahaṁ vajraṁ dhenūnāmasmi kāmadhuk
prajanaścāsmi kandarpaḥ sarpāṇāmasmi vāsukiḥ (28)

anaśtaścāsmi nāgānāṁ varuṇo yādasāmaham
pitṝṇāmaryamā cāsmi yamaḥ saṁyamatāmaham (29)

prahlādaścāsmi daityānāṁ kālaḥ kalayatāmaham
mṛgānāṁ ca mṛgendro 'haṁ vainateyaśca pakṣiṇam (30)

pavanaḥ pavatāmasmi rāmaḥ śastrabhṛtāmaham
jhaṣāṇāṁ makaraścāsmi srotasāmasmi jāhnavī (31)

sargāṇāmādirantaśca madhyaṁ caivāhamarjuna
adhyātmavidyā vidyānāṁ vādaḥ pravadatāmaham (32)

akṣarāṇāmakāro 'smi dvaṁdvaḥ sāmāsikasya ca
ahamevākṣayaḥ kālo dhātāhaṁ viśvatomukhaḥ (33)

mṛtyuḥ sarvaharaścāhamudbhavaśca bhaviṣyatām
kīrtiḥ śrīrvākca nārīṇāṁ smṛtirmedhā dhṛtiḥ kṣamā (34)

bṛhatsāma tathā sāmnāṁ gāyatrī chandasāmaham
māsāṇāṁ mārgaśīrṣo 'hamṛtūnāṁ kusumākaraḥ (35)

dyūtaṁ chalayatāmasmi tejastejasvināmaham
jayo 'smi vyavasāyo 'smi sattvaṁ sattvavatāmaham (36)

vṛṣṇīnāṁ vāsudevo 'smi pāṇḍavānāṁ dhanaṁjayaḥ
munīnāmapyahaṁ vyāsaḥ kavīnāmuśanā kaviḥ (37)

daṇḍo damayatāmasmi nītirasmi jigīṣatām
maunaṁ caivāsmi guhyānāṁ jñānaṁ jñānavatāmaham (38)

yaccāpi sarvabhūtānāṁ bījaṁ tadahamarjuna
na tadasti vinā yatsyānmayā bhūtaṁ carācaram (39)

19. Shri Bhagavan said: Ah! Indeed! I shall relate for you the brilliant manifestations of my Self, but only the most significant, O Kurushreshtha (Arjuna as Grandest of Kauravas), for there is no end to me.

20. I am the Self, O Gudakesha, seated in the heart of all beings; and I am their origin, middle, and conclusion.

21. Of the *adityas* (twelve effulgent beings), I am Vishnu (God as Preserver); of luminaries I am the radiant sun; I am Marichi (most beneficial wind) of the *maruts* (forty-nine wind gods); among heavenly bodies, I am the moon.

22. Of the vedas (wisdom texts) I am *Sama Veda* (volume of harmonious songs); of the gods, I am Indra (chief of heavens); in the senses, I am mind; and in living beings, I am consciousness.

23. Of the *Rudras* (storm gods), I am Sankara (Shiva as Giver of Peace); of the *Yakshas* and *Rakshasas* (spirits of material longings), I am Vittesha (god of wealth); of the *Vasus* (eight shining gods), I am Pavaka (god of fire); and among the heights, I am Mt. Meru (mountain at center of the world).

24. Of household priests, O Arjuna, know me as the chief priest Brihaspati; of military leaders, I am Skanda (general of the gods); of bodies of water, I am the ocean.

25. Of the great seers, I am Bhrighu (a great sage); of what can be spoken, I am aum (the primal sound); of divine offerings I am japa (repetition of sacred phrases); of the immoveable, I am the Himalayas.

26. Of all trees, I am Ashvattha (ever-exisiting cosmic tree, see 15.1–3); of divine seers, I am Narada (a messenger between gods and men); of the *gandharvas* (celestial singers), I an Chitraratha (chief gandharva); of the perfected ones, I am the silent Kapila (author of Samkhya text, see chapter 2).

27. Of horses, know me to be Uccaihshravas (Indra's horse), born of the nectar of immortality; of noble elephants, I am Airavata (Indra's elephant); and of men, I am the emperor.

28. Of weapons, I am the thunderbolt; of cows, I am the heavenly cow which fulfills all desires; of the progenitors, I am Cupid; of serpents, I am Vasuki (chief serpent).

29. Of *naga* snakes, I am Ananta (naga king); of those of the water, I am Varuna (ocean god); of the ancestors, I am Aryama (chief ancestor); of those who regulate, I am Yama (god of death).

30. Of the *daityas* (giants and demons), I am Prahlada (a daitya devotee of God); among systems of measurment, I am time; among beasts, I am the lion; and of birds, I am Garuda (Vishnu's eagle).

31. Of that which purifies, I am the wind; of warriors, I am Rama (an incarnation of Vishnu); of fish, I am Makara (the shark vehicle of Varuna); and of rivers, I am the Ganga (India's most sacred river).

32. Of creations, I am the origin, middle, and conclusion; of knowledge, I am the knowledge of the Self; and of debate, I am the dialectic.

33. Of letters, I am A (the first letter); of compounds, I am the connective; I am unexpended time; I am creation's maintainer whose face is turned everywhere.

34. I am all-engulfing death and the source of all that is born; of the feminine, I am fame, prosperity, eloquence, memory, intelligence, stability, and forgiveness.

35. Of hymns, I am Brihat-saman; of poetic meters, I am the gayatri (the two chief sacred recitations); of months, I am post-harvest; and of seasons, I am the flower-bearing spring.

36. I am the nerve of the gambler; I am the inner luster of the lustrous; I am victory, I am decisiveness, I am the essence of purity.

37. Of the Vrishnis (a powerful dynasty), I am Vasudeva (Krishna); of the Pandavas, I am Dhananjaya (Arjuna); of the silent sages, I am Vyasa (author of the Bhagavad Gita); of poets, I am Ushana (a guru poet).

38. I am the scepter of the ruler; of those who seek success, I am the diplomat; of esoteric teaching, I am silence; and I am the wisdom of all who are wise.

39. I am the seed of all created beings, O Arjuna. There is nothing moving or unmoving which exists without my support.

This is a listing of various symbolic forms in which the Infinite Consciousness manifests. The mythology here is oriented toward the time and place of ancient India, the land in which the Bhagavad Gita was composed. The universal teaching, however, is that Infinite Consciousness is the alpha and omega of all mythological constructs. The Self is the "hero with a thousand masks," said Joseph Campbell. The one Being is the highest archetype, which serves as the template from which all varieties of creation spring and toward which humanity directs its religious imagination.

The sensitive student will find corollaries for the spiritual path with the mythological symbols here presented. In yoga, the macrocosm and microcosm are reflections of each other, so there are certainly correspondences between many of the external symbols and internal yogic processes. To explore this subject and all of its symbolism and ramifications, however, would require a complete treatise of its own. For our purposes, we will allow the student to contemplate the imagery in private and reach inspiration relevant to his unique personality and quest.

Verses 40–42

nānto 'sti mama divyānāṁ vibhūtīnāṁ paraṁtapa
eṣa tūddeśataḥ prokto vibhūtervistaro mayā (40)

yadyadvibhūtimatsattvaṁ śrīmadūrjitameva vā
tattadevāvagaccha tvaṁ mama tejoṁ 'śasaṁbhavam (41)

athavā bahunaitena kiṁ jñātena tavārjuna
viṣṭabhyāhamidaṁ kṛtsnamekāṁśena sthito jagat (42)

40. There is no end to my divine manifestations, O Parantapa. What I have spoken of is only illustrative of my infinite nature.

41. Any being that manifests divinity, grace, and prowess is expressing a fragment of my luminosity.

42. But what use is this detailed knowledge for you, O Arjuna? The essence is: I support the entire world with a fraction of my power, while ever remaining myself.

In this set of three verses, Krishna gives Arjuna two teachings. First, the divine manifestations of the infinite are also infinite. Wherever there is a spark of genius, creativity, brilliance, or greatness in any form, we are seeing the germinal expression of the Infinite Consciousness. This Infinite Consciousness permeates all life, while effortlessly abiding in awareness of being one Self. Creation is the full and complete expression of the one Self, yet the Self remains forever full and complete. This is the great teaching of vedanta, the conclusion of all the wisdom texts, summarized so beautifully in this Bhagavad Gita.

The second teaching is for the aspirant to not get lost in the ancillary discussions but to remain focused on the essence. Regardless of specific details of philosophy, the aspiring yogi is still left with the task at hand—to gain realization. It matters not how many angels can dance on the head of a pin. When the Buddha was asked philosophical questions not actually related to the questioners' needs, he answered by offering a "noble silence."

The questioning mind is supported by the infinite, and thus questions can be infinite in number. The aspirant is encouraged to develop discrimination to perceive which questions will lead to his freedom from illusions and which are just mental chatter, defense mechanisms distracting him from spiritual work. The key to peace is not found in answers to intellectual questions; it is found in the profound silence discovered in deep meditation.

Chapter 11

Vishvarupa Darshan Yoga
The Yoga of the Vision of the Universal Form

Verses 1–4

arjuna uvāca
madanugrahāya paramaṁ guhyamadhyātmasaṁjñitam
yattvayoktaṁ vacastena moho 'yaṁ vigato mama (1)

bhavāpyayau hi bhūtānāṁ śrutau vistaraśo mayā
tvattaḥ kamalapatrākṣa māhātmyapi cāvyayam (2)

evametadyathāttha tvamātmanaṁ parameśvara
draṣṭumicch'ami te rūpamaiśvaraṁ puruṣottama (3)

manyase yadi tacchakyaṁ mayā draṣṭumiti prabho
yogeśvara tato me tvaṁ darśayātmānamavyayam (4)

1. Arjuna said: The teachings you have spoken out of kindness for me have revealed the supreme secret of the Self. By this my confusion has vanished.

2. Your depiction of the origin and dissolution of beings has been heard by me, O Kamalapattraksha (Krishna as Lotus-Eyed), as also of your ever-existing magnificence.

3. You have declared yourself as Supreme Lord. I desire to see your divine form, O Purushottama.

4. If you think it possible for me to perceive, O Prabho (Krishna as Master), O Yogeshvara (Krishna as Lord of Yogis), show to me your ever-existing Self.

Arjuna has intellectually understood Krishna's teachings, and his confusion has apparently been cleared. He has successfully conceptualized the teachings, and this will certainly help to inspire him. He will be able to move ahead in the right direction on his spiritual journey. Significant indeed is Arjuna's understanding, but his premature self-congratulation will cause him problems.

Arjuna, like virtually all aspirants, is still seeking some sort of experience. He wishes to obtain a vision, a phenomenon, a thrill. Though Arjuna's desire may appear to be sublime, it is a desire nonetheless. All desires, however base or noble they may seem, have their roots in the personal self, the individual personality. They are motivated, in some way, to protect the reality of the separate self. In this way the wave of individuality attempts to keep from acknowledging its identity with, and dependance upon, the ocean.

Arjuna correctly identifies Krishna as a Lord of Yoga, but he fails to grasp the full extent of his Lord's teaching. Krishna has not been encouraging Arjuna to worship him or seek external experiences. The guru wants the disciple to journey inward, through the personal self, to realize the One Self, the disciple's true identity. The guru wants the aspirant to enjoy the same Infinite Consciousness in which the guru lives.

Verses 5–8

śrībhagavānuvāca
paśya me pārtha rūpāṇi śataśo 'tha sahasraśaḥ
nānāvidhāni divyāni nānāvarṇākṛtīni ca (5)

paśyādityānvasūnrudrānaśvinau marutastathā
bahūnyadṛṣṭapūrvāṇi paśyāścaryāṇi bhārata (6)

ihaikasthaṁ jagatkṛtsnaṁ paśyādya sacarācaram
mama dehe guḍākeśa yaccānyaddraṣṭumicchasi (7)

na tu māṁ śakyase draṣṭumanenaiva svacakṣuṣā
divyaṁ dadāmi te cakṣuḥ paśya me yogamaiśvaraṁ (8)

5. Shri Bhagavan said: Behold, O Partha, my forms by the hundreds and thousands, full of variety, all divine, in various colors and forms.

6. Behold the *adityas* (twelve shining gods), the *vasus* (eight ancient gods), the *rudras* (storm gods), the two *ashvins* (healing gods), and the *maruts* (wind gods); behold so many marvels never before seen, O Bharata.

7. Now behold here unified in my body, O Gudakesha, the entire world—the moving and unmoving, and whatsoever else you wish to see.

8. But you are unable to perceive this with your mortal eyes. I bestow unto you a divine eye that you may behold my awesome yoga.

Note again how Arjuna asks Krishna to show him Krishna's true Self and not his own. This is a key to understanding what will take place in the verses that follow when Krishna does show Arjuna the manifestations of the Self. Arjuna's request is noble, but it is not of the highest caliber. Krishna still provides Arjuna with the experience, because the guru meets the disciple at the disciple's current level of development. This is reminiscent of Sridi Sai Baba, a great yogi of the nineteenth century, who performed many miracles before his devotees. When asked about his miracles, he said, "I give them what they want so they will want what I have to give."

In order for Arjuna to have the vision he requested, Krishna must help him transcend his mortal sight and attain spiritual vision. The path of the disciple requires two traits: intense personal effort and receptivity to grace. The effort of the aspirant consists in applying unremitting energy to his own development. Beyond a certain point, however, grace is necessary to lift the earnest disciple.

Grace is a particular energy, called *kripa*, which is wielded by those who have realized Infinite Consciousness. The disciple must gather the wood and construct the fire-pit, but it is the guru who offers the spark. This neither denigrates the position of the disciple nor falsely elevates that of the guru. It is simply a fact, part of the divine plan to ensure that all who enter into Infinite Consciousness will have first bathed in the waters of humility.

Verse 9

saṁjaya uvāca
evamuktvā tato rājanmahāyogeśvaro hariḥ
darśayāmāsa pārthāya paramaṁ rūpamaiśvaram (9)

9. Sanjaya said: Having thus spoken, O King Dhritarashtra, Hari (Krishna as Remover of Ignorance), the great Yogeshvara displayed to Partha the supreme awesome form.

As a literary device, we return to the initial scene from chapter 1 where blind King Dhritarashtra asks Sanjaya to describe the events on the battlefield. We are reminded that the dialogue between Arjuna and Krishna is being presented by Sanjaya to his King. This reintroduction of characters at this junction is to highlight the drama of what is now to occur. The aspiring Arjuna has been prepared by Krishna for a stunning experience of the Universal Form. He will perceive the totality of the Supreme Being in an awe-inspiring vision.

Verses 10–14

anekavaktranayanamanekādbhutadarśanam
anekadivyābharaṇaṁ divyānekodyatāyudham (10)

divyamālyāmbaradharaṁ divyagandhānulepanam
sarvāścaryamayaṁ devamanantaṁ viśvatomukham (11)

divi sūryasahasrasya bhavedyugapadutthitā
yadi bhāḥ sadṛśī sā syādbhāsastasya mahātmanaḥ (12)

tatraikasthaṁ jagatkṛtsnaṁ pravibhaktmanekadhā
apaśyaddevadevasya śarīre pāṇḍavastadā (13)

tataḥ sa vismayāviṣṭo hṛṣṭaromā dhanaṁjayaḥ
praṇamya śirasā devaṁ kṛtāñjalirabhāṣata (14)

10. With a multitude of faces and eyes, marvelous displays, divine ornaments, and many uplifted weapons,

11. Adorned with divine garlands and cloth, and anointed with divine perfumes and balms, appears the awesome, boundless, divine face of the universe.

12. If the light of a thousand suns were to blaze forth in the sky, such might resemble the splendor of that Great Self.

13. There the Pandava beheld the entire world with its manifold divisions, established as one in the body of the God of Gods.

14. Then he, Dhananjaya, dazed in amazement with his hairs standing on end, reverently bowed his head to God before him and with palms together spoke.

Arjuna's divine vision is of the unity of the one Being whose face is all faces and who sees through all eyes. Arjuna is dazed and, as we shall see, overwhelmed. With good reason, as the vision before him is experienced at first like a vast, impersonal ocean crushing down upon the shore of his personality. Arjuna is described as having his hairs standing on end, the same state he experienced at the beginning of the text (1.29). The line between spiritual ecstasy and agony is thin.

It is worth noting the reference in verse 12 to the light of a thousand suns blazing forth. This line was cited by Robert Oppenheimer upon witnessing the first explosion of an atomic bomb in 1945, at St. Alamos, New Mexico. The scientist became aware that the primal power before him was unleashed by man but not created by him.

Humanity is forever in relationship with the awesome forces of creation. The lesson of humanity is to learn how to live in peaceful harmony with this energy and not abuse it in a mad march of collective destruction.

Verses 15–31

arjuna uvāca
paśyāmi devāṁstava deva dehe sarvāṁistathā bhūtaviśeṣasaṁghān
brahmāṇamīśaṁ kamalāsanasthamṛṣīṁśca sarvānuragāṁśca divyan (15)

anekabāhūdaravaktranetraṁ paśyāmi tvāṁ sarvato 'nantarūpam
nāntaṁ na madhyaṁ na punastavādiṁ paśyāmi viśveśvara viśvarūpa (16)

kirīṭinaṁ gadinaṁ cakriṇaṁ ca tejorāśiṁ sarvato dīptimantam
paśyāmi tvāṁ durnirīkṣyaṁ samantāddīptānalārkadyutima prameyam (17)

tvamakṣaraṁ paramaṁ veditavyaṁ tvamaśya viśvasya paraṁ nidhānam
tvamavyayaḥ śāśvatadharmagoptā sanātanastvaṁ puraṣo mato me (18)

an[adimadhyāntamanantavīryamanantabāhuṁ śaśisūryanetram
paśyāmi tvāṁ dīptahutāṣavaktraṁ śvatejasā viśvamidaṁ tapantam (19)

yāvāpṛthivyoridamantaraṁ hi vyāptaṁ tvayaikena diśaśca sarvāḥ
dṛṣṭvādbhutaṁ rūpamugraṁ tavedaṁ lokatrayaṁ pravyathitaṁ mahātman (20)

amī hi tvāṁ surasaṁghā viśanti kecidbhītāḥ prāñjalayo gṛṇanti
svastītyuktvā maharṣisiddhasaṁghāḥ stuvanti tvāṁ stutibhiḥ puṣkalābhiḥ (21)

rudrādityā vasavo ye ca sādhyā viśve 'śvinau marutaścoṣmapāśca
gandharvayakṣāsurasiddhasaṁghā vīkṣante tvāṁ vismitāścaiva sarve (22)

rūpaṁ mahatte bahuvaktranetraṁ mahābāho bahubāhūrupādam
bahūdaraṁ bahudaṁṣṭrākarālaṁ dṛṣṭvā lokāḥ pravyathitāstathāham (23)

nabhaḥspṛśaṁ dīptamanekavarṇaṁ vyāttānanaṁ dīptaviśālanetram
dṛṣṭvā hi tvāṁ pravyathitāntarātmā dhṛtiṁ na vindāmi śamaṁ ca viṣṇo (24)

daṁṣṭrākarālāni ca te mukhāni dṛṣṭvaiva kālānalasaṁnibhāni
diśo na jāne na labhe ca śarma prasīda deveśa jagannivāsa (25)

amī ca tvāṁ dhṛtarāṣṭrasya putrāḥ sarve sahaivāvanipālasaṁghaiḥ
bhīṣmo droṇaḥ sūtaputrastathāsau sahāsmadīyairapi yodhamukhyaiḥ (26)

vaktrāṇi te tvaramāṇā viśanti daṁṣṭrākarālāni bhayānakāni
kecidvilagnā daśanāntareṣu saṁdṛśyante cūrṇitairuttamāṅgaiḥ (27)

yathā nadīnāṁ vahavo 'mbuvegāḥn samudramevābhimukhā dravanti
tathā tavāmī naralokavīrā viśanti vaktrāṇyabhivijvalanti (28)

yathā pradīptaṁ jvalanaṁ pataṁgā viśanti nāśāya samṛddhavegāḥ
tathaiva nāśāya viśanti lokāstavāpi vaktrāṇi samṛddhavegāḥ (29)

lelihyase grasamānaḥ samantāllokānsamagrānvadanairjvaladbhiḥ
tejobhirāpūrya jagatsamagraṁ bhāsastavogrāḥ pratapanti viṣṇo (30)

ākhyāhi me ko bhavānugrarūpo namo 'stu te devavara prasīda
vijñātumicchāmi bhavantamādyaṁ na hi prajānāmi tava pravṛttim (31)

15. Arjuna said: O God, in your body I see Brahma, the Lord of Creation, established on his lotus seat. I see the gods along with the various other types of beings. I see all the seers, all the divine serpents.

16. I behold you of infinite form, boundless, with numberless arms, stomachs, faces, and eyes. But I do not see your conclusion, nor middle, nor origin.

17. I behold you with crown, mace, and discus (as Vishnu, God of Preservation)—a massive radiance shining everywhere, blinding everywhere, blazing with the light of fire and sun, immeasurable.

18. You are the imperishable, the supreme, that which is to be known. You are the ultimate, the foundation of the universe, the inexhaustible protector of harmony. I recognize you as the eternal spiritual being.

19. I behold you as having no beginning, middle, or end. You have infinite power, infinite arms for activity, with the sun and moon as eyes, your face glowing as a roaring fire energizing this universe with your essential radiance.

20. Heaven, earth, and all the directions are pervaded by you alone. Having seen this wondrous, terrible form of yours, the three worlds tremble, O Mahatma (Krishna as Great Soul).

21. The multitude of gods enter into you. Supplicating, awestruck, praying, the great seers are crying out, "All is well," singing your praises in beautiful hymns.

22. The rudras (storm gods), adityas (twelve effulgent beings), vasus (eight shining gods) and *sadhyas* (patron gods), the *vishvadevas* (ancestral gods) and two ashvins (healing gods), the maruts (wind gods) and *ushmapas* (guardian spirits) as well as the multitude of gandharvas (celestial musicians), yakshas (destructive entities), asuras (opponents of light), and siddhas (perfected ones) all gaze at you, wonderstruck.

23. Seeing your great form with many mouths and eyes, O Mahabaho (Krishna as Mighty Armed), of many arms, legs, and feet; with many stomachs, many fearful teeth, the worlds are terrified and tremble in fear, and so do I.

24. On seeing you stretching into the void, a radiant spectrum of colors, with mouths wide open and immense radiant eyes, my inner self becomes terrified. I find no courage nor contentment, O Vishnu (Krishna as Preserver of Life).

25. Having seen your mouths filled with fearful teeth, ready to devour as the flames of time, I lose my bearings in space and find no happiness. Be gracious, O Devesha (Krishna as Lord of Gods), O Jagannivasa (Krishna as Abode of the Worlds).

26. All the sons of Dhritarashtra, together with the multitude of worldly leaders such as Bhishma, Drona, and Karna, along with other chief warriors,

27. Are rushing into your dreadful jaws with terrible teeth. Some are caught between your teeth with their heads crushed to dust.

28. As so many torrents of rivers rush towards the ocean, so do these worldly heroes rush into your flaming mouth.

29. As moths speed into a blazing fire to perish, so do these temporal worlds speed into your jaws to perish.

30. You lick up all the temporal worlds throughout space, devouring them in your flaming mouth. The entire world is filled with your glorious illumination and is gleaming with your intense radiation, O Vishnu.

31. Reveal to me who you are in this fierce form. I offer my respects, O Devara (Krishna as Great God). I want to understand your graciousness, O Adyam (Krishna as Primal One), for I know not the nature of your evolutionary activities.

Arjuna receives from Krishna a vision of the Universal Form, and he gets more than he bargained for. In a series of provocative verses, the vast and awesome nature of reality is presented before Arjuna. He experiences his own naked vulnerability when confronted with the reality of time, the all-devouring energy of existence. Arjuna experiences all too directly the fact that everything that has form will meet its demise. Whatever power man may feel is impotent before the ravages of time.

All living beings—gods, mankind, astral beings—arise, exist, and return to the *Adyam* (the Primal One). All clinging to individual existence is vain folly. The waves all subside back into the ocean. Arjuna, like all of us, trembles before the vision of death as conqueror. He came to the battlefield a brave and renowned warrior; now he quivers on the cliff of his own insignificance.

One who has had this experience knows that it is not a joking matter and can appreciate Arjuna's fear. When all that is felt to be oneself is being torn asunder, when all that one holds dear as "me and mine" is felt to be wrenched away, the aspirant is left alone with his soul.

Disoriented at first, he will eventually realize this vision is the transforming event which turns him from chrysalis into butterfly. But first, as we shall see, there is a period of instability, confusion, and continued questioning. The vision is significant, but it is a starting point and not the finish line. There is still much for the aspirant to accomplish.

Verse 32

śrībhagavānuvāca
kālo 'smi lokakṣayakṛtpravṛddho lokānsamāhartumiha pravṛttaḥ
ṛte 'pi tvāṁ na bhaviṣyanti sarve ye 'vasthitāḥ pratyanīkeṣu yodhāḥ (32)

32. Shri Bhagavan said: I am time, destroyer of all temporal worlds, ripened into maturity, acting as the annihilator of these worlds. Even without you, none of these arrayed warriors in either army will continue to live.

Krishna is generally considered to be one of the ten incarnations of Vishnu, the God of Preservation, who protects creation and maintains balance. He is depicted in other sources, such as the Bhagavat Purana, as being a darling boy, a romantic youth, and a kind adult. There is an esoteric tradition, however, which views Krishna as an incarnation of the Goddess Kali, the Goddess of Destruction. From this perspective, Krishna is regarded as more of a warrior, wrecking havoc upon the foes of harmony. Regardless of mythological status, Krishna certainly describes himself in a Kali-like manner in this verse. As such, let us explore the nature of Goddess Kali, for without understanding divine destruction it is impossible to understand divine creation. The aspirant must fathom the lion if he wishes to lie with the lamb.

Kali, literally "She who is beyond time," is depicted as being pitch black. She is shown dancing ecstatically, bare breasted, wearing a garland of human skulls and a skirt of human arms, with her tongue hanging out of her mouth in order to drink blood. In her four arms she carries a sword, a trident, and a freshly severed human head, and one arm is upraised with the palm forward. This depiction is symbolic in a manner which often disturbs the Western mind, unfamiliar as it is with divine destruction and mythological symbolism.

Kali is black because she lives in the deepest, darkest recesses of consciousness. She dances naked in Her own bliss as Mother Nature, in an orgasmic ecstasy of the creation, preservation, and destruction of the universe. Her skirt of arms symbolize the supposed "mighty deeds" accomplished by men, and her garland of decapitated heads depicts the various personalities which a person may wear in order to garner praise and reward. All activities and personalities exist within time, and, since Kali is beyond time, She is not impressed with petty temporal phenomena. Her tongue hangs out as She is drinking the blood of the great demon, Raktabija, the essence of imprisoning selfishness.

Her trident represents creation, preservation, and destruction; or the three periods of time: past, present, and future. Her sword is used to cut away the fears and attachments which keep aspirants bound. The severed head represents the human ego, the false sense of individuality which will one day be destroyed. For the common person, this destruction takes place at death. The yogi offers his head to Kali prior to his physical death, in order that he be reborn and rise up to join her in her cosmic dance.

Verses 33–34

tasmāttvamuttiṣṭha yaśo labhasva jitvā śatrūn bhuṅkṣva rājyaṁ samṛddham
mayaivaite nihatāḥ pūrvameva nimittamātraṁ bhava savyasācin (33)

droṇaṁ ca bhīṣmaṁ ca jayadrathaṁ ca karṇaṁ tathānyānapi yodhavīrāṇ
mayā hatāṁstvaṁ jahi mā vyathiṣṭhā yudhyasva jetāsi raṇe sapatnān (34)

33. Therefore, arise, gain glory, conquer your foes, enjoy an opulent kingdom. By me alone have these warriors already been slain; O Savyasacin (Arjuna as Ambidextrous), be my instrument.

34. Drona and Bhishma, old Jayadata and Karna, too, as well as the other heroic warriors will be slain as a result of my will. Do not be distressed. Fight and conquer in this battle with your enemies.

When the aspirant awakens from the sleep of his fear and confusion, he gains glory by defeating the egoic inner enemies. With their defeat, he enjoys the kingdom of heaven. God's kingdom does not wait for death; it waits, as said in Zen, "For eyes unclouded by yearning."

In the literature associated with the figure of Krishna, there exist two other Gitas. One is the *Uddhava Gita*, in which Krishna shares with his friend, Uddhava, a very similar message as that which he presents to Arjuna. In the *Venu Gita*, "The Song of the Flute," various devotees of Krishna extol the flute as Krishna's ideal instrument. The flute is essentially a hollow tube through which the master can express himself. Similarly, the goal of the aspirant is not to become someone great and renowned: it is to become a simple vessel into which the guru can pour his teachings. With time, the vessel may take the form of a suitable instrument through which the divine love can be played and divine deeds accomplished.

Verse 35

saṁjaya uvāca
etacchrutvā vacanaṁ keśavasya kṛtāñjalirvepamānaḥ kirīṭī
namaskṛtvā bhūya evāha kṛṣṇaṁ sagadgadaṁ bhītabhītaḥ praṇamya (35)

35. Sanjaya said: Having heard that speech of Keshava, Kiriti (Arjuna as Crowned One), in worship and trembling, bowed repeatedly to Krishna, and with his voice choking, prostrating in awe, he spoke:

The narrator, Sanjaya, is re-introduced in order to describe Arjuna's emotional state. Notice how Arjuna again experiences many of the same symptoms he demonstrated in the beginning of the text. There he was in despair; here he is in awe. To his credit, Arjuna is an aspirant capable of deeply experiencing his own emotions. In this regard, he is not a timid man, but a true warrior capable of advancing onto the battlefield of his own feelings.

Verses 36–44

arjuna uvāca
sthāne hṛṣīkeśa tava prakīrtyā jagatprahṛṣyatyanurajyate ca
rakṣāṁsi bhītāni diśo dravanti sarve namasyanti ca siddhasaṁghāḥ (36)

kasmaca te na nameranmahātman garīyase brahmaṇo 'pyādikartre
ananta deveśa jagannivāsa tvamakṣaraṁ sadasattatparaṁ yat (37)

tvamādidevaḥ puruṣaḥ purāṇastvamasya viśvasya paraṁ nidhānam
vettāsi vedyaṁ ca paraṁ ca dhāma tvayā tataṁ viśvamanantarūpa (38)

vāyuryamo 'gnirvaruṇaḥ śaśāṇkaḥ prajāpatstvaṁ prapitāmahaśca
namo namaste 'stu sahasrakṛtvaḥ punaśca bhūyo 'pi namo namaste (39)

namaḥ purastādatha pṛṣṭhataste namo 'stu te sarvata eva sarva
anantavīryāmitivakramastvaṁ sarvaṁ samāpnoṣi tato 'si sarvaḥ (40)

sakheti matvā prasabhaṁ yaduktaṁ he kṛṣṇa he yādava he sakheti
ajānatā mahimānaṁ tavedaṁ mayā pramādātpraṇayena vāpi (41)

yacāvahāsārthamasatkṛto 'si vihāraśayyāsanabhojaneṣu
eko 'thavāpyacyuta tatsamakṣaṁ tatkṣāmaye tvāmahamaprameyam (42)

pitāsi lokasya carācarasya tvamasya pūjyaśca gururgarīyān na
tvatsamo 'styabhyadhikaḥ kṛto 'nyo lokatraye 'pyapratimaprabhāva (43)

tasmātpraṇamya praṇidhāya kāyaṁ prasādaye tvāmahamīśamīḍyam
piteva putrasya sakheva sakhyuḥ priyaḥ priyāyārhasi deva soḍhum (44)

36. Arjuna said: O Hrishikesh, rightly so does the world rejoice and delight in glorifying you. Negativity flees in fear in all directions, while the community of accomplished yogis offer their love and respect.

37. Why would they not offer you homage, O Mahatman, more venerable than even Brahma, the Creator. You are the primal creator, the eternal God of gods, the foundation of the universe; you are the imperishable one. You are that which is eternal reality and that which is temporal illusion, and you are supreme beyond that.

38. You are the primal god and the ancient spiritual being. You are the supreme foundation of the universe; you are both knower and that which is to be known as well as the supreme transcendent. The manifest universe is the expression of your infinite form.

39. You are Vayu (wind god), Yama (god of death), Agni (fire god), Varuna (god of oceans), Shashanka (moon god), Prajapati (first progenitor), and the Great Grandfather. Honor to you, honor to you offered a thousand times. Again and again, honor to you, honor to you.

40. Prostrations to you in the front and behind, prostrations to you on all sides. You are all, of infinite potency, immeasurable strength; you are all-pervading and everything is your manifestation.

41. Whatever I may have said in casualness, or even in affection, saying, "Hey, Krishna, Hey, Yadava, member of our tribe, Hey, my friend," thinking of you as a peer and ignorant of your grandeur,

42. For whatever disrespect I may have jokingly expressed toward you while playing, relaxing, sitting around, or eating, while I was alone with you, or while we were with others, I ask for your forgiveness, O Achutya (Krishna as Without Lapse), O Aprameyam (Krishna as Immeasurable).

43. You are the father of the worlds, of all that is animate and inanimate. You are the one to be worshipped; you are the venerable guru; none is your equal. How could there possibly be another in the three worlds greater, O Apratimaprahbava (Krishna as One of Incomparable Greatness)?

44. I prostrate my body and bow, seeking your grace, O Idyam Isham (Krishna as Adorable Lord). Please consider, O God, to bear with me as a father toward a son, a friend toward a friend, a lover to his beloved.

Arjuna has been blessed with the universal vision in the form of Krishna. He understands now the sage is not an ordinary mortal but the manifestation in human form of the Infinite Consciousness, the all-inclusive reality. Arjuna asks Krishna to forgive any unintentional errors in etiquette he may have exhibited in failing to perceive his guru's magnitude.

This apology is unnecessary, however, for two reasons. First, the sage is pure compassion and stunning wisdom. Krishna already understands Arjuna's state of mind and knows Arjuna is an honest and innocent man. Second, the true guru goes out of his way to help the disciple feel comfortable. For there to be intimacy between people, hierarchies based on prestige and status must fall away. Certainly the guru deserves the greatest possible respect from the aspirant. Like a caring parent who gets down on the floor to play with his child, meeting the child on his own level, the guru is more concerned with love than with respect.

Verses 45–46

adṛṣṭapūrvaṁ hṛṣito 'smi dṛṣṭvā bhayena ca pravyathitaṁ mano me
tadeva me darśaya deva rūpaṁ prasīda deveśa jagannivāsa (45)

kirīṭinaṁ gadinaṁ cakrahastamicchāmi tvāṁ drṣṭumahaṁ tathaiva
tenaiva rūpeṇa cathurbhujena sahasrabāho bhava viśvamūrte (46)

45. I am gladdened to have seen what has never been seen before, but my mind is disturbed by fear. O God, be pleased to show me only that other form, O Devesha, O Jagannivasa.

46. I wish to see you again with a crown on your head, with mace and discus in your hands. Assume your four-limbed form, O Sahasrabaho (Krishna as Thousand-Armed One).

Arjuna acknowledges his joy with the universal vision, but his feelings of awe drive him to seek something more comforting. He asks Krishna to resume his familiar human form. The mind reels before the awesome majesty of the impersonal cosmos; it longs to dive back to the familiar, to the personal, to that which it knows and understands. This is a natural human dynamic experienced by Arjuna, and one which every aspirant will face in his own development.

These verses also deserve some attention in that they are frequently translated as Arjuna asking Krishna to reveal his "four-armed" rather than "four-limbed" form. This reading would mean Arjuna is asking Krishna to present himself in a form consistent with mythological depictions of the four-armed Vishnu, of whom Krishna is often considered to be an incarnation.

While it is true that *caturbhujena* could mean "four-armed," the problems with this translation are significant within the greater context of Arjuna's experience. First, Arjuna asks Krishna to return to a form he has previously seen. He is seeking comfort and consolation, not the excitement of another visionary experience. Second, as we shall see in the following verses, Krishna resumes his human form, not a four-armed mythological form. In verses 49–51, Krishna acknowledges Arjuna's request, displays what is described as his gentle *manusam rupam*, which can only be translated as "human form," and is then thanked by Arjuna. Arjuna's gratitude only makes sense if his initial desire has been fulfilled.

Verses 47–51

śrībhagavānuvāca
mayā prasannena tavārjunedaṁ rūpaṁ paraṁ darśitamātmayogāt
tejomayaṁ viśvamanantamādyaṁ yanme tvadanyena na dṛṣṭapūrvam (47)

na vedayajñādhyayanairna dānairna ca kriyābhirna tapobhirugraiḥ
evaṁrūpaḥ śakya ahaṁ nṛloke draṣṭuṁ tvadanyena kurupravīra (48)

mā te vyathā mā ca vimūḍhabhāvo dṛṣṭvā rūpaṁ ghoramīdṛṅmamedam
vyapetabhīḥ prītamanāḥ punastvaṁ tadeva me rūpamidaṁ prapaśya (49)

saṁjaya uvāca
ityarjunaṁ vāsudevastathoktvā svakaṁ rūpaṁ darśayāmāsa bhūyaḥ
āśvāsayāmāsa punaḥ saumyavapurmahātmā (50)

arjuna uvāca
dṛṣṭvedaṁ mānuṣaṁ rūpaṁ tava saumyaṁ janārdana
idānīmasmi saṁvṛttaḥ sacetaḥ prakṛtiṁ gataḥ (51)

47. Shri Bhagavan said: I have expressed my favor with you, O Arjuna. By the yoga of my own Self, you have been shown my supreme form: luminous, universal, endless, primal, never seen by another before you.

48. Neither by observances of the scriptures, by sacrifice, by study, by charity, by ritual, nor by severe austerities can I possibly be seen in this form in the human realm by anyone other than you, O Arjuna.

49. Be free from turmoil; be not confused having seen this apparently horrific form of mine. Have no fear, and put your mind at ease as you behold my form of your desire.

50. Sanjaya said: Having thus spoken to Arjuna, Vasudeva (Krishna as God Within) again displayed his own form. The Mahatman showed his gentle form and consoled the frightened one.

51. Arjuna said: Beholding your gentle human form, O Janardana, my mind calms down and is restored to a calm state.

In this section, Krishna returns to human form, and Arjuna's awe is resolved back into calm. Krishna also teaches that solely by grace is this universal vision granted. The aspirant must climb the mountain of spiritual development by himself, but at the pinnacle there is a cliff over which he will be lifted by those already on the peak above. The aspirant must prepare himself, but the grand vision is ultimately the result of grace. The aspirant who has prepared himself through self-effort has become Arjuna, the one with eyes to see.

Verses 52–55

sudurdarśamidaṁ rūpaṁ dṛṣṭavānasi yanmama
devā apyasya rūpasya nityaṁ darśanakāṅkṣiṇaḥ (52)

nāhaṁ vedairna tapasā na dānena ca cejyayā
śakya evaṁvidho draṣṭuṁ dṛaṣṭavānasi māṁ yathā (53)

bhaktyā tvananyayā śakya ahamevaṁvidho 'rjuna
jñātuṁ draṣṭuṁ ca tattvena praveṣṭuṁ ca paraṁtapa (54)

matkarmakṛnmatparamo madbhaktaḥ saṅgavarjitaḥ
nirvairaḥ sarvabhūteṣu yaḥ sa māmeti pāṇḍava (55)

52. Shri Bhagavan said: This form of mine which you have seen is very rarely perceived. Even the gods desire to behold this form.

53. Not by scriptural study, nor by austerity, nor by charity, nor by offerings can I be seen in the form that you have seen me.

54. By single-pointed devotion, O Arjuna, I can be known and seen, and my essence entered into, O Parantapa.

55. He who is active for me, for whom I am the supreme, whose devotion is to me, devoid of attachment, free of enmity towards anyone, such a one reaches me, O Pandava.

Krishna reiterates the preciousness of the vision experienced by Arjuna. He concludes with a theme which will be developed in the next chapter: devotion holds the key to spiritual accomplishment. Krishna has taught Arjuna about activity, philosophy, wisdom, and meditation; now he prepares Arjuna to enter the inner chambers where lovers dwell.

Chapter 12

Bhakti Yoga
The Yoga of Devotion

Verse 1

arjuna uvāca
evaṁ satatayuktā ye bhaktāstvāṁ paryupāsate
ye cāpyakṣaramavyaktaṁ teṣāṁ ke yogavittamāḥ (1)

1. Arjuna said: Of devotees who worship you and those who worship the imperishable and unmanifest, who has the supreme knowledge of yoga?

After his stunning vision in the previous chapter, Arjuna is confused as to how to proceed. His vision was based on the expansion of Krishna into the universal form. Now Arjuna wonders as to whether he should worship and contemplate upon the vision of the universal One or the one who led him to the vision.

Verses 2–5

śrībhagavānuvāca
mayyāveśya mano ye māṁ nityayuktā upāsate
śraddhayā parayopetāste me yuktatmā matāḥ (2)

ye tvakṣaramanirdeśyamavyaktaṁ paryupāsate
sarvatragamacintyaṁ ca kūṭasthamacalaṁ dhruvam (3)

saṁniyamyendriyagrāmaṁ sarvatra samabuddhayaḥ
te prāpnuvabti māmeva sarvabhūtahite ratāḥ (4)

kleśo 'dhikatarasteṣāmavyaktāsaktacetasām
avyaktā hi gatirduḥkhaṁ dehavadbhiravāpyate (5)

2. Shri Bhagavan said: Those whose minds are devoted to me in an eternal union, who worship me with utmost faith, I regard to be in the greater union.

3. And those who contemplate the imperishable, the indefinable, the unmanifest and all-pervasive, beyond conception, the spiritually stable, the unmovable and permanent,

4. Having restrained the senses, equal in attitude towards all, intent on the welfare of all beings, they also reach me.

5. Those whose consciousness is directed toward the unmanifest have a more difficult path, as the unmanifest is difficult for the embodied to reach.

Krishna answers Arjuna by suggesting that those who are devoted to a form of God or guru have properly channelled their emotions. He definitely acknowledges those who venerate the unmanifest Infinite Consciousness will also reach the goal, but he points out that this path is very difficult. It is extremely difficult for most yogis to progress on the spiritual path without some form they can visualize and toward which they can direct their aspirations and yearnings.

Verses 6–8

ye tu sarvāṇi karmāṇi mayi saṁnyasya matparāḥ
ananyenaiva yogena māṁ dhyāyanta upāsate (6)

teṣāmahaṁ samuddhartā mṛtyusārasāgarāt
bhavāmi nacirātpārtha mayyāveśitacetasām (7)

mayyeva mana āhatsva mayi buddhiṁ niveśaya
nivasiṣyasi mayyeva ata ūrdhvaṁ na saṁśayaḥ (8)

6. Those who worship me and renounce all activities to me, who make me supreme and meditate on me with an unswerving yogic commitment,

7. Directing their consciousness unto me, I become before long, O Partha, their deliverance from the ocean of delusion and death.

8. Place your mind solely in me, place your intelligence and intuition in me, and without doubt you will come to dwell in me.

Krishna describes the ideal form of devotion to God or guru. The guru or worshipped form of God is the external manifestation of the one Self, which the aspirant has not yet been able to access within his own being. The inner guru of the disciple manifests as the outer guru, who instructs the disciple in such a way that he comes into contact with his own inner guru. A true guru wants the disciple to become free, not to remain dependent on any external person as a crutch. The relationship of the inner and outer dimensions of this experience were described well by Ramana Maharshi, who said, "God, guru, and Self are one."

Verses 9–12

atha cittaṁ samādhātuṁ na śaknoṣi mayi sthiram
abhyāsayogena tato māmicchāptuṁ dhanaṁjaya (9)

abhyāse 'pyasamartho 'si matkarmaparamo bhava
madarthamapi karmāṇi kurvansiddhimavāpsyasi (10)

athaitadapyaśakto 'si kartuṁ madyogamāśritaḥ
sarvakarmaphalatyāgaṁ tataḥ kuru yatātmavān (11)

śreyo hi jñānamabhyāsājjñānāddyānaṁ viśiṣyate
dhyānātkarmaphalatyāgastyāgācchāntiranantaram (12)

9. If you are unable to absorb your consciousness entirely in me, then by means of persistent practice seek to reach me, O Dhananjaya.

10. If you are incapable of persistent practice, make it your passion to perform activities for my sake. Doing all activities on my behalf shall lead you to perfection.

11. If you are unable to do this, then seek solace in my yoga, act from Self-directedness and relinquish the rewards of your activities.

12. Better indeed is direct wisdom than practice, better than wisdom is meditation, better even than meditation is relinquishing the rewards of activities, for relinquishment brings peace.

For those aspirants who are not capable of the complete relinquishment of self necessary to realize the Self, Krishna offers alternatives. Even the greatest of yogis generally undergo years and years of extensive training before realization. So a lack of immediate awakening does not indicate any failure but rather the universal condition of the human aspirant.

Krishna describes a practical hierarchy for those struggling to ascend the ladder of spirituality. Most aspirants will require significant amounts of practice before being able to absorb their individual consciousness in the Self. This practice will require karma yoga, as described in chapter 3, to help purify the mind. To be truly selfless in karma yoga, one will need to understand the tenets of this universal yoga and develop an intuitive sense of how to behave.

The pinnacle of practice is the relinquishment of desire for personal reward. Without this relinquishment, even the deepest meditation will remain unsuccessful at untying the knot of ego. Meditation done solely for one's own benefit still reinforces the selfish individuality which the aspirant is to untangle. Through a relinquishment of concern for personal reward or benefit, one undertakes all activities, both in the world and in his personal sadhana, as an offering of service to the one Self which abides in all beings.

Verses 13–20

adveṣṭā sarvabhūtānāṁ maitraḥ karuṇa eva ca
nirmamo nirahaṅkāraḥ samaduḥkhasukhaḥ kṣamī (13)

saṁtuṣṭaḥ satataṁ yogī yatātmā dṛḍhaniścayaḥ
mayyarpitamanobuddhiryo madbhaktaḥ sa me priyaḥ (14)

yasmānnodvijate loko lokānnodvijate ca yaḥ
harṣāmarṣabhayodvegairmukto yaḥ sa ca me priyaḥ (15)

anapekṣaḥ śucirdakṣa udāsīno gatavyathaḥ
sarvārambhaprityāgī yo madbhaktaḥ sa me priyaḥ (16)

yo na hṛṣyati na dveṣṭi na śocati na kāṅkṣati
śubhāśubhaparityāgī bhaktimānyaḥ sa me priyaḥ (17)

samaḥ śatrau ca mitre ca tathā mānāpamānayoḥ
śītoṣṇasukhaduḥkheṣu samaḥ saṅgavivarjitaḥ (18)

tulyanindāstutirmaunī saṁtuṣṭo yena kenacit
aniketaḥ shiramatirbhaktimānme priyo naraḥ (19)

ye tu dharmyāmṛtamidaṁ yathoktaṁ paryupāsate
śraddadhānā matparamā bhaktāste 'tiva me priyāḥ (20)

13. One who has no hatred toward other beings, who is friendly and compassionate, free from possessiveness and selfish self-centeredness, equal in pain and pleasure, forgiving;

14. The yogi who is ever-content, Self-directed, firmly committed, whose mind and intellect are given unto me, such a one is my devotee and is dear to me.

15. One who does not disturb the world and who is undisturbed by the world, who is free of superficial happiness, resentment, and fear, such a one is dear to me.

16. One who is without expectation, pure, competent, untroubled, having relinquished selfish initiatives, such a one is my devotee and is dear to me.

17. One who does not rejoice in worldly gain, who neither hates nor grieves, who has relinquished care for worldly advantages and disadvantages, such a one is my devotee and is dear to me.

18. Equal to those acting as friend or foe, equal in honor or dishonor, the same in cold and heat, pleasure and pain, free from attachment,

19. To whom blame and praise are alike, practicing inner silence, content with everything, without a sense of a permanent abode, inwardly firm, such a one is my devotee and is dear to me.

20. One who cherishes this nectar-like teaching of the path of harmony, endowed with faith, holding me as supreme, these devotees are exceedingly dear to me.

This set of verses describes the character of the accomplished one. An individual who demonstrates these qualities is, in the best sense of the term, a saint. The typical aspirant wavers between selfish and selfless impulses, between fear and love. The sage described in these verses, however, has transcended the selfish impulse of clinging to individuated ego needs. He or she is the most rare and precious spiritual flower. Such a one is the fruit of the entire enterprise of the universe.

It is worth noting that Krishna nowhere identifies his devotee as one who has joined a particular sect or adopted a certain set of beliefs and codes.

The yoga of the Bhagavad Gita is for all. It is a universal path. Krishna does not care about the particular form of worship or practice. His concern is with the content of the individual's mind.

All religious forms and formulas are prone to abuse by fallible and selfish human beings. When an aspirant is filled with love, whatever practices or traditions he might engage in become useful means for expressing his bhakti, his devotion.

Chapter 13

Kshetra-Kshetrajnana Vibhaga Yoga
The Yoga of the Field of Activity and the Knower of the Field

arjuna ūvāca
prakṛtiṁ puruṣaścaiva kṣetraṁ kṣetrajñameva ca
etadveditumicchāmi jñānaṁ jñeyañca keśava

Arjuna said: Primal nature and consciousness, the field and the knower of the field, wisdom and what is to be known—these I very much want to understand, O Keshava.

This verse is not included in all versions of the Bhagavad Gita. Its exclusion would allow for the total number of verses to a be tidy 700. I have included it here as I think it serves as a positive literary device, contributing to the sense of dialogue between Arjuna and Krishna.

Verses 1–2

śrībhagavānuvāca
idaṁ śarīraṁ kaunteya kṣetramituamidhīyate
etadyo vetti taṁ prāhuḥ kṣetrajña iti tadvidaḥ (1)

kṣetrajñaṁ cāpi māṁ viddhi sarvakṣetreṣu bhārata
kṣetrakṣetrajñayorjñānaṁ yatrajjñānaṁ mataṁ mama (2)

1. Shri Bhagavan said: This body, O Kaunteya, is called the field. The one who knows the activities which take place on the field is called by the wise as the "knower of the field."

2. Know that I am the knower of the field in all fields, O Bharata. I hold that the wisdom which illuminates the relationship of the field and the knower of the field to be real wisdom.

The field of all experiences, called the *kshetra*, is the body/mind complex. All that occurs during a lifetime arises, exists, and then passes away within the parameters of this field. The entire world of perceptions and activities is simply phenomena based on the interplay of external matter with the body's senses and mind.

This viewpoint is not materialistic or nihilistic, however, for the field does not exist without the knower of its activities, the *kshetrajnana*. Consciousness is not an epi-phenomenon within the field of nature. Rather, like a magnet whose energy causes the metal filings of a motor to spin, the knower is the force behind activity. This knower in all beings is none other than the one Self. It is the Infinite Consciousness shining upon the body/mind complex which causes the field to activate.

Verses 3–4

tatkṣetraṁ yacca yādṛkca yadvikāri yataśca yat
sa ca yo yatprabhāvaśca tatsamāsena meśṛṇu (3)

ṛṣibhirbahudhā gītaṁ chandobhirvividhaiḥ pṛthak
brahmasūtrapadaiścaiva hetumadbhirviniścitaiḥ (4)

3. Hear from me a concise explanation of the field—its characteristics, experiences, and transformations—and also of the knower of the field and his expressions.

4. This teaching has been presented by seers in many ways, with a variety of melodies, and in the rational and conclusive wisdom scriptures.

Krishna will now present that which he has declared in verse 2 to be wisdom: the relationship of the field and the knower of the field. Notice how he reiterates the point made earlier that the teachings here are not new (see 4.1–3). They are consistent with the great wisdom tradition of the sages, presented in original manners to meet the needs of particular cultures and times.

Verses 5–6

mahābhūtānyahaṅkāro buddhiravyaktameva ca
inmdriyāṇi daśaikaṁ ca pañca cendriyagocarāḥ (5)

icchā dveṣaḥ sukhaṁ duḥkhaṁ saṁghātaścetanā dhṛtiḥ
etatkṣetraṁ samāsena savikāramudāhṛtam (6)

5. The five great elements, the ego, intelligence, and also the unmanifest, the ten and the one senses, and the five sensations of sense perception,

6. Selfish will and repulsion, pleasure and pain, the aggregate of individual consciousness, and a sense of personal continuity—these concisely describe the field and its modifications.

Verse 5 provides a list of the traditional twenty-four *tattvas* (essential principles) which constitute nature, the field of all experience. This is the philosophical vision of samkhya, first presented in a cursory manner in chapter 2, for differentiating between prakriti or nature, here called kshetra (the field); and purusha or consciousness, here called kshetrajnana (the knower of the field). These twenty-four essentials are the forces which build the perceptual universe, essentials which cannot be reduced any further. The tattvas are:

1–5. *Bhutas* —The five elements:
Earth—the principle of solidity
Water—the principle of liquidity
Fire—the principle of heat
Air—the principle of gas
Ether—the principle of space

6. *Ahamkara*—Ego—the principle of separate identity based on the body/ mind complex.

7. *Buddhi*—Intelligence—the principle of intellect and intuition.

8. *Avyakta*—Unmanifest—the principle of nature as a great holistic phenomenon, without separate parts. Also known as Mahat or Cosmic Mind.

9–19. *Indriyanis*—Senses—the principles of the five jnanendriyas, the organs of reception; the five karmendriyas, the organs of action; and the manas, the cognitive mind.

Eyes
Ears
Nose → *Jnandriyas*
Mouth
Skin

Arms
Legs
Tongue → *Karmendriyas*
Genitals
Anus

Manas—Cognitive mind.

20–24. *Tanmatras*—the principles of perceivable sensations:

Seen
Heard
Tasted → *Tanmatras*
Touched
Felt

Perceptions and experiences of the world are based entirely on the interaction of the tattvas with each other. The elements interface with the organs of reception, resulting in the sensations. The mind takes these sensations and produces a composite picture of an external world. The intelligence applies labels to the various forms perceived, thereby giving the world names and meanings. The ego comes into being as the grand finale of the intercourse of the gross phenomenal world with the subtle phenomenon of mind and intelligence.

Individuality, therefore, is nothing but another exhibition of nature, like a leaf on a tree. Individuality is not permanent; it arises, exists, and passes away. Problems with ego arise when someone takes his individuality as being great and acts selfishly. Every leaf on the tree has equal meaning and value. The selfish, unhealthy ego feels itself to be alone. The selfless, healthy ego experiences itself as part of a greater whole.

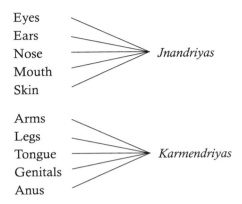

Transcending the limited ego does not leave one as some sort of amorphous pool of non-personality. Just the opposite. One who recognizes his identity as consciousness independent of limited identity becomes free of the obsessions and compulsions of the anxious ego. He is able to live in the world without being imprisoned by the world. Individuality ceases to be something to protect and, instead, becomes something to celebrate. The quirks, traits, and unique characteristics of incarnation are seen as evidence of the infinite creativity of the divine energy. Just as every snowflake is unique, so is every individual manifestation precious and joyous, having its own part in the cosmic play.

Verses 7–11

tamānitvamadambhatvamahiṁsā kṣāntirārjavam
ācāryopāsanaṁ śaucaṁ sthairyamātmavinigrahaḥ (7)

indriyārtheṣu vairāgyamanahaṅkāra eva ca
janmamṛtyujarāvyādhiduḥkhadoṣānudarśanam (8)

asaktiranabhiṣvaṅgaḥ putradāragṛhādiṣu
nityaṁ ca samacittatvamiṣṭāniṣṭopapattiṣu (9)

mayi cānyanyayogena bhaktiravyabhicāriṇī
viviktadeśasevitvamaratirjanasaṁsadi (10)

adhyātmajñānanityatvaṁ tattvajñānārthadarśanam
etajjñānamiti proktamajñānaṁ yadato 'nyarthā (11)

7. Absence of pride and self-importance, nonviolence, forbearance, straightforwardness, loyal support of one's teacher, purity, stability, and Self-directedness;

8. Detachment from sensual allurements, absence of egoism, insight into the suffering and limitations in birth, death, old age, and illness;

9. Without clinging and excessive attachment to children, spouse, or home; a continual equilibrium of consciousness when confronted with apparently desirable or undesirable events;

10. Unswerving, constant devotion to me, resorting to solitude, a distaste for superficial society;

11. Continually seeking the wisdom of the Self, seeking the wisdom vision of the divine essence—this I declare to be wisdom, and all that is otherwise is ignorance.

These verses provide a concise list of positive traits arising from the wisdom which differentiates between the knower and the known. These are the characteristics of a cultured, refined individual. Those who pursue these traits and those of great attainment in whom they spontaneously appear are considered to be wise. The yogic tradition holds that all other types of knowledge, particularly those which draw the knower away from realization of the Self, are actually forms of ignorance. Ignorance immerses an individual deeper into the confusion of identifying himself with the field; wisdom frees the knower to abide in the Self.

Verse 12

jñeyaṁ yattatpravakṣyāmi yajjñātvāmṛtamaśnute
anādimatparaṁ brahma na sattannāsaducyate (12)

12. I shall declare that divine essence which is to be known, knowing which one attains the nectar of immortality. The beginningless, supreme, absolute consciousness which cannot be described completely as being eternal reality nor temporal illusion.

Thus far in this chapter we have descriptions of the field of experience (verses 5–6) and the symptoms of wisdom (verses 7–11). Now Shri Krishna will review the essential characteristics of the knower of the field. His description cannot be complete, as the absolute cannot be described in relative language. The whole set of consciousness cannot be contained within the subset of mind, intellect, and speech.

Verses 13–17

sarvataḥpāṇipādaṁ tatsarvato 'kṣiśiromukham
sarvataḥśrutimalloke sarvamāvṛtya tiṣṭhati (13)

sarvendriyaguṇābhāsaṁ sarvendriyavivarjitam
asaktaṁ sarvabhṛccaiva nirguṇaṁ guṇabhoktṛ ca (14)

bahirantaśca bhūtānāmacaraṁ carameva ca
sūkṣmatvāttadavijñeyaṁ dūrasthaṁ cāntike ca tat (15)

avibhaktaṁ ca bhūteṣu vibhaktamiva ca sthitam
bhūtabhartṛ ca tajjñeyaṁ grasiṣṇu prabhaviṣṇu ca (16)

jyotiṣāmapi tajjyotistamasaḥ paramucyate
jñānaṁ jñeyaṁ jñānagamyaṁ hṛdi sarvasya viṣṭhitam (17)

13. With hands and feet everywhere, with eyes and heads and mouths everywhere, hearing everything, the divine essence pervades all.

14. Without any senses, yet reflected in the senses and their natural qualities; unattached, yet the sustainer of all; not influenced by the qualities of nature, while enjoying these qualities of nature.

15. Within and without all beings, moving and immobile, too subtle to be known, the divine essence is both near and far.

16. Undivided, yet seemingly divided as separate beings; the support of existence and the divine essence which is to be known; repeatedly drawing all into the Self and then expressing all again into being.

17. The light of lights beyond darkness, knowledge, the object of knowledge, and what is to be reached by knowledge, situated in the hearts of all.

This description of the conscious knower of the field of nature is mind-boggling in its vastness. Everything and everyone is an expression of this knower, yet he still remains complete, unexpended. He is all beings, and still he remains transcendent and independent. These verses are dark to the manas, the cognitive mind, but the aspirant recognizes this truth by the intuitive function of the buddhi, the intelligence.

Verse 18

satkāramānapūjārthaṁ tapo dambhena caiva yat
kriyate tadiha proktaṁ rājasaṁ calamadhruvam (18)

18. Thus the field, wisdom, and that divine essence which is to be known have briefly been described. Realizing this, my devotee attains my state.

All knowledge can be classified as being worldly, psychological, or spiritual. Worldly knowledge is information about the functions of nature and the manipulation of matter and forms. This is the domain of the kshetra, the field. This includes the physical sciences, engineering, computers, architecture, mechanics, and so forth. Accomplishment in this realm produces increased physical comfort and prosperity.

Psychological knowledge is anything related to the mind of humans. Examples include psychology, politics, sociology, anthropology, and so forth. Accomplishment in this realm brings about an increased appreciation of the mind and its powers.

Spiritual knowledge is related to the realization of the divine essence. This is not found in religious institutions, which are more concerned with worldly and psychological issues. It is the realm of the sages, yogis, and mystics, those who tread the path of the inner pilgrimage. Accomplishment in this realm brings one into the state of the one Self.

Verses 19–23

prakṛtiṁ puruṣaṁ caiva viddyanādī ubhāvapi
vikārāṁśca guṇāṁścaiva viddhi prakṛtisambhavān (19)

kāryakaraṇakartṛtve hetuḥ prakṛtirucyate
puruṣaḥ sukhaduḥkhānāṁ bhoktṛtve heturucyate (20)

puruṣaḥ prakṛtistho hi bhuṁkte prakṛtijānguṇān
kāraṇaṁ guṇasaṅgo 'sya sadasadyonijanmasu (21)

upadraṣṭānumantā ca bhartā bhoktā maheśvaraḥ
paramātmeti cāpyukto dehe 'sminpuruṣaḥ paraḥ (22)

ya evaṁ vetti puruṣaṁ prakṛtiṁ ca guṇaiḥ saha
sarvathā vartamāno 'pi na sa bhuyo 'bhijāyate (23)

19. Know that both primal nature and consciousness are beginningless. Know also that the transformations and qualities of nature arise from primal nature.

20. Primal nature is the origin of the trinity of cause, effect, and agent. Consciousness is the origin of the experiences of happiness and unhappiness.

21. Consciousness is situated in primal nature and experiences nature's qualities. Attachment to these qualities is the cause of birth in wombs conducive to eternal reality or temporal illusion.

22. Consciousness, when related to the body, is called the witness, sanctioner, supporter, enjoyer, the great Lord, and the supreme Self.

23. One who thus understands consciousness and nature, along with the manner in which nature's qualities function, whatever the manner of his life-style, he will not be forced into birth again.

This is an extremely important set of verses. It outlines the character, functions, and relationship of the field of experience and the knower of the field. Kshetra, the field, is nature, matter, ever-changing form. Kshetrajnana, the knower of the field, is consciousness, being, ever-stable existence. The field and the knower are both eternal manifestations of One Divine Being. They interpenetrate one another, yet at the same time retain their autonomy. They are not like black and white, which blended together make a dull gray. They are more like a rich blue and bright red, which blended together generate a royal purple.

Within the field arises all phenomena, including the appearance of the individual identity. The knower is the root of happiness and sadness in that these experiences can only occur to a sentient being. Matter can be stimulated to react, but only a conscious being can respond with happiness or sadness.

Nature operates due to a natural stimulation by consciousness. The sun of Infinite Consciousness shines on cups of water, and the reflected light in the cups are called jivas, individual souls. The jiva is not an eternal entity but the manifestation of the union of consciousness and nature. At some point the cup will break and the reflection will cease, though the sun remains luminous and unaffected.

If consciousness identifies in any way with the fluctuations of nature, an individual ego is formed. Why this happens is the domain of paradox, ambiguity, and intuition. The cognitive mind will ask, "How can the supreme, unlimited consciousness become confused and lose its sense of supremacy and unlimitedness? If there is only One Divine Blissful Being, why does there appear to be a world with billions of souls who experience suffering?"

The myth of Krishna's life, told in the Bhagavad Purana and other texts, provides a sublime answer to these questions. The entire drama of the universe, with all its attendant phenomenon, is simply lila, God's play. The supreme, unlimited consciousness deliberately undertakes the great sacrifice of offering itself into the fire of its own love in order that it become cloaked in limitation. The purpose of this limitation is for the sake of the great adventure of creation, culminating in the reawakening of the one Self to Infinite Consciousness.

What would prompt the Divine Being to engage in such sport? The answer is love. Love alone. The very nature of love is to constantly expand its limits and reach out to contain that which is currently beyond its reach. The apparent demarcation of where love has not yet reached is the universe of limited beings and their attendant sufferings.

On the field of creation, the knower seeks to know himself. Like a drop of rain which falls from a cloud, courses through a river to the sea, and then evaporates back into the cloud, so does Infinite Consciousness become limited into separate raindrops for the sake of a grand exploration. The knower eternally explores the field, and the field eternally expresses the consciousness of the knower.

Do not be concerned if this is difficult to comprehend. It is a truth which is dark to the mind but light to the heart. Questions in the mind about the field and the knower cannot be answered within the mind. They will, however, be resolved through the direct experience of love and Self-realization.

Verses 24–25

dhyānenātmani paśyanti kecidātmānamātmanā
anye sāṁkhyena yogena karmayogena cāpare (24)

anye tvevamajānantaḥ śrutvānyebhya upāsate
te 'pi cātitarantyeva mṛtyuṁ śrutiparāyaṇāḥ (25)

24. By meditation some behold the Self in the Self, others attain through the yoga of essential principles, and others by the yoga of selfless action.

25. Still others, not themselves yet realized, worship based on the testimonies of spiritual authorities. By commitment to what they have heard they also cross beyond death.

The means to realization will vary based on the temperament of the aspirant. Some will realize the Self through dhyana, the yoga of meditation; others through samhkya yoga, the yoga of essential principles; and others via karma yoga, the yoga of selfless service. For those who have not achieved success, the path of commitment to the tradition of realized teachers is also possible. The sincere aspirant who can apply himself obediently to his guru, conforming to the guru's teachings of behavior and sadhana (spiritual practices), will also eventually achieve the goal.

Verse 26

yāvatsaṁjāyate kiṁcitsattvaṁ sthāvarajaṅgamam
kṣetrakṣetrajñasaṁyogāttadviddhi bharatarṣabha (26)

26. Whatever arises in manifestation, O Bharatarshabha, realize that as a production of the union of the field of activity with the knower of the field.

Nothing exists in all of creation but the interplay of consciousness and nature. All is the expression of these two characteristics of One Divine Being. Infinite Consciousness, the Self of all, is the director and producer of the play of life. Even more, the Self becomes all the actors, the props, even the stage of the world itself. The wheel of life is the grand display of the magnificence of the essence of everyone and everything. Everywhere is the center of consciousness, infinite the circumference of nature's display.

Verses 27–30

samaṁ sarveṣu bhūteṣu tiṣṭhantaṁ parameśvaram
vinaśyatsvavinaśyantaṁ yaḥ paśyati sa paśyati (27)

samaṁ paśyanhi sarvatra samavasthitamīśvaram
na hinastyātmanātmānaṁ tato yāti parāṁ gatim (28)

prakṛtyaiva ca karmāṇi kriyamāṇāni sarvaśaḥ
yaḥ paśyati tathātmānamakartāraṁ sa paśyati (29)

yadā bhūtapṛthagbhāvamekasthamanupaśyati
tata eva ca vistāraṁ brahma saṁpadyate tadā (30)

27. The aspirant who perceives the supreme Lord abiding equally in all beings as that which does not perish within the perishable, such a one, verily, perceives.

28. The aspirant who perceives the Lord abiding equally everywhere does no harm to the Self by the Self (during incarnation) and so attains the supreme goal.

29. The aspirant who perceives that all activities are actually performed by nature alone and, correspondingly, the Self as consciousness is not the doer, he truly perceives.

30. The aspirant who perceives that apparently separate beings are actually established in the one Self and are expansions of the one Self, he merges into Infinite Consciousness.

The supreme Lord is described in these verses as abiding equally in all beings, imperishable, not the performer of activities, and the root of all other beings. This supreme Lord is the Self of all. The atman or jiva, the apparently individual soul, is discovered to be none other than Brahman, Infinite Consciousness.

Nature, the power of the Lord, performs the dance of creation, preservation, and destruction. The Lord, however, remains eternally settled in the eternal consciousness of joy. The realization of this eternal consciousness is the goal of the yogic path. The attainment of this goal makes one capable of correct perception; he is endowed with eyes that truly see.

Verses 31–34

anāditvānnirguṇatvātparamātmāyamavyayaḥ
śarīrastho 'pi kaunteya na karoti na lipyate (31)

yathā sarvagataṁ saukṣmyādākāśaṁ nopalipyate
sarvatrāvasthito dehe tathātmā nopalipyate (32)

yathāprakaśayatyekaḥ kṛtsnaṁ lokamimam raviḥ
kṣetraṁ kṣetrī tathā kṛtsnaṁ prakaṣayati bhārata (33)

kṣetrakṣetrajñayorevamantaraṁ jñānacakṣuṣā
bhūtaprakṛtimokṣaṁ ca ye viduryānti te param (34)

31. With no beginning, with no qualities of nature, this supreme Self never diminishes even while abiding in the body, O Arjuna. It neither acts nor is affected by activity.

32. As the all-pervading space remains ever undiluted due to its subtlety, likewise so the Self, pervading the entire body, remains ever undiluted.

33. As the one sun illumines the entire world, so does the lord of the field, O Bharata, illumine the entire field.

34. Those who thus behold by the eye of wisdom the difference between the field and knower of the field and how this wisdom brings about liberation from primal nature's matter attain the supreme.

The supreme Self, the one Divine Being, is all-pervasive and contains all within. The typical human being feels himself an isolated individual confronting a vast external universe. The realized soul experiences the universe as occurring within his heart, his own consciousness.

The average person feels himself to be inhabiting a body, forced to submit to the dictates of nature and the iron law of death. The sage knows that the body is simply a phenomenon of nature which arises, exists, and passes away within his own consciousness. With this realization, he is liberated from the fear of death and abides in supreme peace.

Chapter 14

Gunatraya Vibhaga Yoga
The Yoga of Transcending the Qualities of Nature

Verses 1–2

śrībhagavānuvāca
paraṁ bhūyaḥ pravakṣyāmi jñānānāṁ jñānamuttamam
yajjñātvā munayaḥ sarve parāṁ siddhimito gatāḥ (1)

idaṁ jñānamupāśritya mama sādharmyamāgatāḥ
sarge 'pi nopajāyante pralaye na vyathanti ca (2)

1. Shri Bhagavan said: I shall once more clarify for you that supreme wisdom, the highest wisdom, realizing which sages have risen above worldly confusion to the supreme perfection.

2. Having resorted to this wisdom and having come into harmony with me, they are not involuntarily born again in creation, nor troubled by its dissolution.

The ripe student is like dry kindling, ready to blaze into fire with the merest spark. Most aspirants, like Arjuna, need repeated instruction and clarification.

The job of the guru is to present the teachings in such a way that the student will be inspired to undertake the sadhana necessary to obtain his own realization. Questions and doubts are not necessarily negative. They may well be indicators that the aspirant is sincerely struggling to bring his consciousness in line with the teachings of the guru.

Verses 3–4

mama yonirmahadbrahma tasmingarbhaṁ dadhāmyaham
saṁbhavaḥ sarvabhūtānāṁ tato bhavati bhārata (3)

sarvayoniṣu kaunteya mūrtayaḥ saṁbhavanti yāḥ
tāsāṁ brahma mahadyonirahaṁ bījapradaḥ pitā (4)

3. My womb is the great creative source in which I place the seed that brings about the birth of all beings, O Bharata.

4. Whatever representative forms are generated in all the worlds, O Kaunteya, the creative source is their common womb, and I am the seed-bestowing father.

There is a great axiom: "As above, so below; as below, so above." What we see manifest in the microcosm of the visible universe is a reflection of subtle phenomena taking place in the higher spheres. Cause takes place in the spiritual realms, effect results on the material plane. Since cause and effect are one sequence, we can understand one by studying the other.

We see in our world that all living beings—animals, birds, amphibians, humans—arise from the union of male and female energies. The seed is somehow planted in a womb, and a new life is grown. This takes place on the level of species regeneration because it is reflective of the dynamics of the spiritual realm.

Purusha, the consciousness knower, impregnates prakriti, the field of nature. As the sun penetrates the soil of the earth to arouse the seed, the light of purusha invigorates the dormant lives resting in the womb of prakriti.

Those familiar with Hindu art may have seen the hermaphroditic figure of Ardhanari, literally "half-female." Half Shiva, the male god, and half Parvati, the female goddess, Ardhanari depicts the unity of the seed-bestowing father and the creative source mother—eternally in union, yet eternally possessing unique energies.

Male and female are the positive and negative poles of the one divine energy which courses throughout creation. This divine couple is symbolically depicted in many ways: as Ram and Sita, Radha and Krishna, Jesus and Mary, the Sun and the Moon.

Verse 5

sattvaṁ rajastama iti guṇāḥ prakṛtisaṁbhavāḥ
nibadhnanti mahābāho dehe dehinamavyayam (5)

5. The three qualities generated from primal nature are balance, activation, and inertia. These bind the ever-existing One, O Mahabaho, to bodily identification.

The subject of the gunas, the modes of nature, was first introduced in 2.45 and 7.12. It may be helpful for the reader to refer to these verses and their commentary before contemplating the following discussion. The point being made in this verse is that the gunas serve as three strands of an imprisoning rope to one who identifies with their operation. The gunas are the modes of nature, expressed by the incessant revolution of creation, preservation, and destruction.

One who is caught in the bonds of nature has lost his transcendent consciousness into bodily identity. The result is a fear of bodily harm and, ultimately, a fear of death. Since death is inevitable, life for such a one is permeated on a deep level by a sense of dread. No amount of worldly security or pleasure can overcome this persistent unease. The path to freedom is to relinquish identification with the operation of the gunas and realize the Self as transcendent consciousness.

The subject of the three gunas is a significant topic of the Bhagavad Gita, with additional material presented in chapters 17 and 18. The entire subject has been summarized and presented in a chart in Appendix 2.

Verses 6–9

tatra sattvaṁ nirmalavāt prakaśakamanāmayam
sukhasaṅgena badhnāti jñānasaṅgena cānagha (6)

rajo rāgātmakaṁ viddhi tṛṣṇāsaṅgasamudbhavam
tannibadhnāti kaunteya karmasaṅgena dehinam (7)

tamastvajñānajaṁ viddhi mohanaṁ sarvadehināṁ
pramādālasyanidrābhistannibadhnāti bhārata (8)

sattvaṁ sukhe saṁjayati rajaḥ karmaṅi bhārata
jñānamāvṛtya tu tamaḥ pramāde sañjayatyuta (9)

6. Balance, by its essential purity, brings illumination and well-being. It binds by creating attachment to happiness and knowledge.

7. Know that activation is the very nature of attachment, generated by a primal thirst for experience and attachment. It binds the embodied one, O Kaunteya, by creating attachment to activity.

8. Know that inertia is born of ignorance and is the deluder of all embodied beings. It binds, O Bharata, through negligence, indolence, and sleep.

9. Balance binds one through happiness, activation through activity, O Bharata, and inertia cloaks wisdom through negligence.

Here is a description of how the three gunas generate bondage in their own particular ways. Sattva, balance, binds through attachment to goodness. The individual bound by sattva is imprisoned by chains of his own identification with purity. He may be a religious or charitable person, but attachment to producing good in the world falls short of the profundity of authentic karma yoga. The person attached to sattva frequently fails to discern the subtle selfishness lurking in his apparently positive worldly work.

The person bound by rajas, activation, is imprisoned by a need for activity. The spectrum of rajas-inspired activity can go from the worldly "workaholic" to the religious fanatic who cannot rest until he feels everyone has been blessed by the Lord. It matters not the form of behavior; rajas binds through selfish motivation for action.

Tamas, inertia, makes a person lethargic. He will not have the energy or gumption to probe spiritual teachings to find how he might improve his life. His hungers are basically food, sex, and money, and his vision of happiness centers around fulfilling these desires.

Verses 10–13

rajastamaścābhibhūya sattvaṁ bhavati bhārata
rajaḥ sattvaṁ tamaścaiva tamaḥ sattvaṁ rajastathā (10)

sarvadvāreṣu dehe 'sminprakāśa upajāyate
jñānaṁ yadā tadā vidyādvivṛddhaṁ sattvamityuta (11)

lobhaḥ pravṛttirārambhaḥ karmaṇāmaśamaḥ spṛhā
rajasyetāni jāyante vivṛddhe bharatarṣabha (12)

aprakāśo 'pravṛttiśca pramādo moha eva ca
tamasyetāni jāyante vivṛddhe kurunandana (13)

10. At various times balance prevails, overpowering activation and inertia, O Bharata. Other times activation prevails over balance and inertia, and then inertia prevails over balance and activation.

11. When the light of wisdom streams forth from the doors of the senses, it may be understood that balance is dominant.

12. When activation dominates, there arises greed, frantic activity, selfishness motivated by desire for rewards, impatience, and cravings, O Bharatarshabha.

13. When inertia dominates, there arises dullness, laziness, delusion, and infatuation, O Kurunandana.

The gunas rise and fall like a seesaw. One side is activation (rajas) and on the other is inertia (tamas). At a certain midpoint these two come into a balanced state (sattva). This is not a perfect analogy as sattva is not just a passive state between two imbalances; it possess its own intrinsic energy. This illustration should suffice, however, to give an idea of how the gunas relate.

These verses describe the different experiences a person will have based on which of the gunas is predominant at any given time. As we learned in chapter 13, the pure consciousness of the knower is reflected in the pool of the field of nature. When inertia is predominate, the pool is torpid and muddy. When activation is predominate, the pool is filled with turbulent waves. When balance is predominate, the pool is still and clear. Only when balance is dominate can the knower see his reflection accurately in the field of nature. Thus, the aspirant will be encouraged to develop the sattvic qualities in body, mind, and character as described below and in chapter 18.

Verses 14–15

yadā sattve pravṛddhe tu pralayam yāti dehabhṛt
tadottamavidāṁ lokānamalānpratipadyate (14)

rajasi pralayaṁ gatvā karmasaṅgiṣu jāyate
tathā pralīnastamasi mūḍhayoniṣu jāyate (15)

14. If the embodied one meets with the dissolution of death when balance is dominant, he attains the pure worlds of those who know the highest.

15. Experiencing the dissolution of death while activation is dominant, one is reborn among those attached to selfish activities. Likewise, if the dissolution of death occurs in a state of inertia, he will be reborn in the wombs of the deluded.

Through a lifetime of habitual patterns, an individual will cultivate a predominance of one or the other gunas. At the time of death, when the karmic fruit ripens and falls from the vine, the energy of the dominate guna will direct the individual towards his next birth. Balance brings one to a station in which spirituality is sought, activation brings one to the arena of karmic activity, and inertia toward delusion and indulgence.

Verses 16–18

karmaṇaḥ sukṛtasyāhuḥ sāttvikaṁ nirmalaṁ phalam
rajasastu phalaṁ duḥkhamajñānaṁ tamasaḥ phalam (16)

sattvātsaṁjāyate jñānaṁ rajaso lobha eva ca
pramādamohau tamaso bhavato 'jñānameva ca (17)

ūrdhvaṁ gacchanti sattvasthā madhye tiṣṭhanti rājasāḥ
jaghanyaguṇavṛttisthā adho gacchanti tāmasāḥ (18)

16. The result of positive actions arising from balance is purity, the result of activity arising from activation is pain, and the result of activity arising from inertia is ignorance.

17. From balance arises wisdom, from activation arises greed, and from inertia arises infatuation and delusion.

18. Those who abide in balance progress, those in activation remain stationary, those in inertia—being steeped in the lowest quality of nature—regress.

This set of verses describes the result of actions springing from the different gunas. Balance, the tranquil state, brings purity, wisdom, and an increase in spiritual maturity. Activation, being inherently selfish, invariably produces pain, greed, and an inability to develop spiritually. Inertia, being dull, brings forth ignorance, delusion, and a decrease in spiritual development.

Verses 19–20

nānyaṁ guṇebhyaḥ kartāraṁ yadā draṣṭānupaśyati
guṇebhyaśca paraṁ vetti madbhāvaṁ so 'dhigacchati (19)

guṇānetānatītya trīndehī dehasamudbhavān
janmamṛtyujarāduḥkhairvimukto 'mṛtamaśnute (20)

19. When the seer beholds no agent other than the qualities of nature and knows what is superior to the qualities, such a one attains to my being.

20. Transcending the three qualities of nature which cause identification with the body, one is liberated from the suffering of birth, death, and old age and attains the nectar of immortality.

The relationship between the seer and the seen, the knower and the field of knowledge, is the relationship of consciousness and nature. The three gunas, the qualities of nature, revolve due to the presence of consciousness. The exhibition of nature's dance takes place only under the light of awareness.

On a practical level, an individual has only two directions he can turn his mind to. One way is toward nature, the world of form, and the source of his body. The other direction is toward consciousness, the world of spirit, and the source of his sentience. Identifying with the external world inevitably leads to attachment with the body/mind complex, resulting in fear and the suffering arising from the vicissitudes of life. One who turns his attention inward, particularly in meditation, will transcend body/mind identification and eventually find the genesis of nature and the root of his true identity—Brahman, Infinite Consciousness.

Verse 21

arjuna uvāca
kairliṅgaistrīnguṇānetānatīto bhavati prabho
kimācāraḥ kathaṁ caitāṁstrīnguṇānativarte (21)

21. Arjuna said: What are the indicators, O Prabho, of one who has risen above the three qualities? How does he behave? How does he transcend the three qualities?

Arjuna, in a demonstration of honesty and humility, asks Krishna to help him understand the identifying feature of the sage. Even after the myriad of answers he has received as well as experiencing the universal vision, Arjuna is still confused. In spite of the teachings and grace from Krishna, Arjuna still can't quite quiet his mind and accept the truth. Perhaps Arjuna's continuing difficulty can bring some consolation to the aspirant who struggles with the teachings of the sages and the instructions of his guru.

Verses 22–25

śrībhagavānuvāca
prakāśaṁ ca pravṛttiṁ ca mohameva ca pāṇḍava
na dveṣṭi saṁpravṛttāni na nivṛttāni kāṅkṣati (22)

udāsīnavadāsīno guṇairyo na vicālyate
guṇa vartanta ityeva yo 'vatiṣṭhati neṅgate (23)

samaduḥkhasukhaḥ svasthaḥ samaloṣṭāśmakāñcanaḥ
tulyapriyāpriyo dhīrastulyanindātmasaṁstutiḥ (24)

mānāpamānayostulyastulyo mitrāripakṣayoḥ
sarvārambhaparityāgī guṇātītaḥ sa ucyate (25)

22. Shri Bhagavan said: When one is not repulsed when any of the three qualities arise—balance, which brings illumination; activation, which brings activity; and inertia, which brings delusion—and when he does not crave for them in their absence,

23. When he is seated objectively and is not disturbed by the qualities, when he recognizes the qualities progressively rotate and that he is distinct and unmoving,

24. When he is the same in pleasure and pain, content within; to whom a lump of dirt, a stone, or a piece of gold are equal in value; steady in mood, accepting praise and blame equally,

25. When he is equal in honor or dishonor, favoring neither friend nor foe, not initiating selfish ventures—he is said to have transcended the three qualities of nature.

Krishna answers Arjuna's question about how to recognize a sage in relationship to the three qualities of nature. Essentially, the sage has realized his identity as the calm center of the tornado of nature's energy and movement. Regardless of how the wind blows and swirls, the eye of the tornado remains still. When the calm center is realized and maintained, one lives in harmony with nature's patterns. Nature is then experienced as a divine enjoyment.

Verses 26–27

māṁ ca yo 'vyabhicāreṇa bhaktiyogena sevate
sa guṇānsamatītyaitānbrahmabhūyāya kalpate (26)

brahmaṇo hi pratiṣṭhāhamamṛtasyāvyayasya ca
śāśvatasya ca dharmasya sukhasyaikāntikasya ca (27)

26. One who serves me with an unswerving yoga of devotion passes beyond the three qualities and is spiritually mature enough to become Infinite Consciousness.

27. I am the basis of Infinite Consciousness, of the unexpended nectar of immortality, of the eternal path of spirituality, and of ultimate happiness.

The highest realization is the identity of purushottama, the Supreme Being. Purushottama was originally discussed in 8.20–22 and will be the primary subject of the next chapter. The way to the attainment of purushottama is through bhakti yoga, the path of spiritual devotion. Only he who is devoted to service can dwell in the foundation of immortality and joy. Love is the genesis of all existence, and the expression of love is service. Loving service is the path, for it reaches the One, the Supreme Being, purushottama, who is love.

Chapter 15

Purushottama Yoga
The Yoga of the Supreme Being

Verses 1–4

śrībhagavānuvāca
ūrdvamūlamadhaḥśākhamaśvatthaṁ prāhuravyayam
chandāṁsi yasya parṇāni yastaṁ veda sa vedavit (1)

adhaścordhvaṁ prasṛtāstasya śākhā guṇapravṛddhā viṣayapravālāḥ
adhaśca mūlānyanusaṁtatāni karmānubandhīni mauṣyaloke (2)

na rūpamasyeha tathopalabhyate nānto na cādirna ca saṁpratiṣṭhā
aśvatthamenaṁ suvirūḍhamūlamasaṅgaśastreṇa dṛḍhena chittvā (3)

tataḥ padaṁ tatprimārgitavyaṁ yasmingatā na nivartanti bhūyaḥ
tameva cādyaṁ puruṣaṁ prapadye yataḥ pravṛttiḥ prasṛtā purāṇī (4)

1. Shri Bhagavan said: There is taught to be an ever-existing cosmic tree, with roots above and branches below, the leaves of which are the world's religious hymns. Who knows this tree is one of traditional religious wisdom.

2. Below and above, its branches are perceived to be spread, nourished by the three qualities of nature. Sensory attractions are the buds when the roots stretch downward into the human realm, binding men to karma.

3. The form of this tree is not perceived in this human realm as it has no end and no beginning, no material basis. Cut down this strongly rooted cosmic tree with the weapon of detachment.

4. Then take the path toward that from which you will not return again. Ponder: "I take refuge in that primal spiritual being from whom originally streamed the activities of evolution."

This description of the cosmic tree is a mythological presentation of prakriti, primal nature. Prakriti is rightly described as ever-existing, with origins in the subtle realms beyond the sight of mortal eyes. Nature and her manifestations are the basis of the concerns and desires of worldly people and also most culturally sanctioned religious systems. Consider how many of the world's religions are occupied with making adherents more comfortable on earth and promising a paradise of enjoyment in the afterlife.

The yogi lives in harmony with nature and respects her power, but he also realizes his self as transcendent to all of nature's energy and manifestations. Shiva, sitting alone and naked, atop Mt. Kailash, is a common yogic symbol for the ability of the yogi to abide above all of the world's allures and impulses. Shiva, the accomplished yogi, is detached from any rewards offered in the world of form. He seeks only the peace and love existing within his own Self, the primal spiritual being.

Verses 5–6

nirmānamohā jitasaṅgadoṣā adhyātmanityā vinivṛttakāmāḥ
dvandvairvimuktāḥ sukhaduḥkhasaṁjñairgacchantyamūḍhāḥ
padamavyayaṁ tat (5)

na tadbhāsayate sūryo na śaśāṅko na pāvakaḥ
yadgatvā na nivartante taddhāma paramaṁ mama (6)

5. Those who are without pride or delusion, who have overcome the flaws of attachment, who constantly adhere to the Self, whose selfish desires are stilled, who are free from the duality known as pleasure and pain, they proceed toward the perennial state.

6. The sun does not illumine that state, nor the moon, nor fire. That is my supreme abode from which, having reached, there is no regression.

The yogi desires not effects; he seeks cause. The buds on the cosmic tree do not satisfy his quest, he yearns for the roots of experience. To use another analogy, the yogi travels upstream from the dwelling places of humanity, seeking the bubbling spring, the source of the sacred rivers of love and wisdom. In this abode all transitory powers—such as sun, moon, and fire—are seen in their proper perspective. They are phenomena of nature, part of the play of creation, but their existence or nonexistence does not impinge upon his perennial consciousness.

Verses 7–9

mamaivāṁśo jīvaloke jīvabhūtaḥ sanātanaḥ
manaḥṣaṣṭhānīndriyāṇi prakṛtisthāni karaṣati (7)

śarīraṁ yadavāpnoti yaccāpyutkrāmatīśvaraḥ
gṛhītvaitāni saṁyāti vāyurgandhānivāśayāt (8)

śrotraṁ cakṣuḥ sparśanaṁ ca rasanaṁ ghrāṇameva ca
adhiṣṭhāya manaścāyaṁ viṣayānupasevate (9)

7. An eternal fraction of mine arises as the individual being in the realm of beings and draws to itself the senses, including the mind, which are part of nature.

8. When the Lord takes on a body and also upon leaving it, he takes the mind and senses and goes forth, as does the wind carry fragrances from flowers.

9. Presiding over the ear, eye, touch, taste, smell, and mind, he participates in the sensory experience.

This is a key set of verses for understanding the yogic vision. The individual soul is a parcel of the eternal divine consciousness. In fact, what is often believed to be an individual soul is actually a composite of characteristics of prakriti, nature, for there truly exists but one sentient being, one consciousness, which is distributed throughout creation.

The fire of consciousness sends forth flames which spark into space. These sparks, having leapt into apparent separate existence, are the jivas, individual souls. Keeping in mind that the sparks have their origin in the fire and will eventually descend back into their source, we can avoid confusing a semantic and conceptual distinction with reality. For fire and sparks are non-different; sparks are simply a form of fire, and the nature of fire is to flame and spark.

The One Divine Being, purushottama, extends himself into the forms created by nature. Expressions of the Divine Being in individual bodies are the sparks which enliven the activity of nature. The jiva is the spark which experiences the universe through the mechanisms of the senses and mind. In an unenlightened being, in whom consciousness maintains an egoic identification with the body/mind, reincarnation will take place. The unenlightened being carries his attachments into the death experience, and these attachments draw to him another body/mind.

It is difficult for the ordinary person, and even the typical religious person, to believe that his seemingly miniscule consciousness is actually part of eternal and infinite being. All thoughts of littleness and limitation, however, occur within the closed system of egoic beliefs. The yogic enlightenment cracks the apparent solidity of this belief system and shines the light of realization into the darkness of the ego's fear and sense of isolation.

Verse 10

utkrāmantaṁ sthitaṁ vāpi bhuṅjānaṁ vā guṇānvitam
vimūḍhā nānupaśyanti paśyanti jñānacakṣuṣaḥ (10)

10. The deluded have no divine vision, as they are conditioned by the three qualities of nature. They do not perceive the One engaged in departing, remaining, or experiencing. Those with the eyes of wisdom have vision.

Those in the thrall of avidya, primal ignorance, have no true vision. They see with their eyes and minds, but their inner eye is closed to spiritual sight. From the perspective of the yogis, they are blind. Worse than blind, actually, as they do not even acknowledge their blindness. The three qualities of nature present the dance of creation, preservation, and destruction, but this is only the activity on the stage of life. The One who witnesses the play is the Self.

Verse 11

yatanto yoginaścainaṁ paśyantyātmanyavasthitam
yatanto 'pyakṛtātmāno nainaṁ paśyantyacetasaḥ (11)

11. Aspiring yogis will perceive the One established in the Self. Those not in accord with the Self are still undeveloped; they may strive but will not perceive Him.

One need not be a fully accomplished sage to achieve some degree of realization of the Self of all beings. The sincere aspirant is certain to achieve levels of insight during the course of his development. His visions of spiritual reality will be fleeting at first, but through continued meditation and spiritual living he will enhance and stabilize his consciousness.

Those who are not on a path of inner journey—who are involved with conventional social religions and preoccupied with external rites and rituals—will not realize the Self. Their perceptions will be limited to the conditioning of their personal sect. They may be decent citizens, practicing a religion based on good will, but they are not yet prepared for the radical experience of the yogis—the realization of one Self, abiding equally in saint and sinner.

Verses 12–13

yadādityagataṁ tejo jagadbhāsayate 'khilam
yaccandramasi yaccāgnau tattejo viddhi māmakam (12)

gāmāviśya ca bhūtāni dhārayāmyahamojasā
puṣṇāmi cauṣadhīḥ sarvāḥ somo bhūtvā rasātmakaḥ (13)

12. That radiance is mine which comes from the sun and brightens the entire world as well as that radiance which is in the moon and fire.

13. I permeate the earth and sustain the life of all beings by my vital potency. I become the nectar which nurtures all plants as flowing sap.

Yogic consciousness is the highest environmental consciousness. The yogi recognizes that all energy originates in divine consciousness. Energy is an expression of the Self and when in harmony with the Self produces beauty, love, and healing and dissolves fear. When energy is manipulated through selfishness, disaster arises both ecologically and socially.

Humanity is intended to be a co-creator of the world, alongside the higher beings (3.10–13). When people accomplish this task, they enjoy the four boons of life: *kama* (pleasure), *artha* (prosperity), *dharma* (harmonious relationships), and *moksha* (spiritual freedom). When people fail to complete this creative mission, they suffer the lack of these four boons, and life becomes a miserable burden of mundane existence.

The rational mind can respect the power of nature and inspire one to seek to live in harmony with her. The yogi, however, with his enhanced intuition, takes respect further: into the realms of love. The yogi is a lover of nature and a beloved of nature. He knows his world is alive and responds to him. He has a relationship with the sun, moon, and fire as well as with plants and the very earth. His relationship with his environment is intimate and tender, a spiritual sensuality based on love and care.

Verses 14–15

ahaṁ vaiśvānaro bhūtvā prāṇināṁ dehamāśritaḥ
prāṇāpānasamāyuktaḥ pacāmyannaṁ caturvidham (14)

sarvasya cāhaṁ hṛdi saṁniviṣṭo mattaḥ smṛtirjñānamapohanaṁ ca
vedaiśca sarvarahameva vedyo vedāntakṛdvedavideva cāham (15)

14. Acting as the flame of life and entering the body of living things, united with the inflowing and outflowing energies, I integrate the four types of experience.

15. I am situated in the heart of all. From me comes spiritual memory and wisdom and their withdrawal. I am what is to be known by the wisdom texts. Indeed, I am the knower of the texts and their author, too.

It is one divine fire that exists as the Self of all beings. The Self stimulates the operation of the breath, the primary form of inflowing and outflowing energies, and brings about the experience of manifest existence. The "four types of experience" is a translation of what literally means "four types of food." These "foods" are the four experiences of nature: earth, water, fire, and air (13.5). The Self "digests" or integrates these primary manifestations via life experiences, interacting with solids, liquids, heat, and gas, respectively.

The Self is the actor of all roles on the stage of creation. Abiding in the heart of all beings, the Self is the goal of all spiritual aspirations and what is pointed to in the wisdom texts. In the lila, the divine play of creation, the Self cloaks his own identity in a withdrawal of spiritual wisdom. For the sake of entering the world as an ordinary jiva, the Supreme Being wears the cloak of ignorance. The Lord is disguised first as a fool, then as an aspirant, and finally as a sage. Such an amazing play!

Verses 16–18

dvāvimau puruṣau loke kṣaraścākṣara eva ca
kṣaraḥ sarvāṇi bhūtāni kūṭastho 'kṣara ucyate (16)

uttamaḥ puruṣastvavyaḥ paramātmetyudāhṛtaḥ
yo lokatrayamāviśya bubhartyavyaya īśvaraḥ (17)

yaśmātkṣaramatīto 'hamakṣarādapi cottamaḥ
ato 'smi loke vede ca prathitaḥ puruṣottamaḥ (18)

16. There are two aspects to consciousness in the world: the perishable and the imperishable. The perishable are the individuated beings of nature, and the imperishable is that which is unmanifest and unchangeable.

17. The highest degree of consciousness, however, is another, called the Supreme Self—the eternal Lord, who pervades and sustains the three worlds.

18. Because I am beyond the perishable and superior even to the imperishable, I am declared by the world and by the wisdom texts to be the Supreme Being.

We have examined in chapter 13 the distinction between the field of experience and the knower of the field, between primal nature and pure consciousness. Here these are identified as the perishable and imperishable. Primal nature is labeled perishable, as her material manifestations are ever-changing. Pure consciousness is imperishable; it is ever-stable as nonmaterial consciousness.

Higher than these dual aspects is purushottama, the Supreme Being. This Being is the true Self of all beings. Purushottama is the experience of Brahman, Infinite Consciousness with personality (see 8.20–22). Purushottama is the alpha and omega of experience, the pinnacle of reality, from which all life descends. It is also the outermost expression of form and the creative impulse. Purushottama is the cosmic dancer whose movement is nature. It is the consciousness which imbibes forms and brings them to life.

Purushottama, dear reader, is your true identity. You are the source of primal nature, delighting in ever seeking new forms with which to express your creative impulse. You are the consciousness within bodies, which appear as individual souls traversing the breadth of the cosmos over vast eons of time in the spiritual pilgrimage. You are the omniscient, omnipresent, omnipotent Supreme Being.

This teaching may be blasphemous to the orthodox, just as it was when Christ proclaimed: "I and my Father are one." But condemnation by conventional traditions does not change the teachings of the sages. This eternal truth of the yogis is for those prepared to awaken and arise. Awake, aspirant; realize you are not the little self of one small lifetime—you are the Life that lives forever as all lives! Arise, Arjuna; realize you are not the frightened man on the battlefield—you are eternal lover and beloved, Shri Krishna!

Verse 19

yo māmevamasaṁmūḍho jānāti puruṣottamam
sa sarvavidbhajati māṁ sarvabhāvena bhārata (19)

19. The one who is undeluded and realizes me as the all-knowing Supreme Being is able to lovingly worship me from all perspectives, O Bharata.

The key to appreciating the nature of the purushottama is to remember that all individual souls are sparks from the one fire of divinity. As such, the sparks and fire are of identical disposition. The jivas, souls, are microcosmic reflections of the macrocosmic Being, purushottama. What exists within the souls exists in the Supreme Being, and vice versa. The only difference, however, is the consciousness of purushottama is infinite while that of the jiva is limited.

The jiva experiences itself as living in a limited form on finite levels of consciousness. Purushottama exists in unlimited forms on all levels of consciousness, in all dimensions of reality. Existing as all beings, all experience, and all activity, purushottama is truly omnipresent, omniscient, and omnipotent.

Purushottama might also be thought of as an infinite snowman, made of an infinite number of snow flakes, the jivas. In order to love the snowman, it is necessary to love each and every snowflake. By loving the snowman completely, one will automatically love all the snowflakes. When people complain they have not seen God, it is simply that they have not qualified themselves to do so. They cannot see the snowman because they have not yet learned to love all of its flakes.

Verse 20

iti guhyatamaṁ śāstramidamuktaṁ mayānagha
etadbuddhvā buddhimānsyātkṛtakṛtyaśca bhārata (20)

20. Thus have I taught to you this most secret spiritual teaching, O Anagha. One who knows this becomes realized and has completed the purpose of all activities, O Bharata.

The Bhagavad Gita began with Arjuna confused about his proper course of action. The realization of the identity of the purushottama as the true Being within all jivas is the culmination of Arjuna's quest. When one realizes his own identity in the Supreme Being and realizes that all others are different forms of the same Supreme Being, proper conduct becomes clear. He only wishes to love and serve his beloved, whether this be in his home, in his community, or even on the battlefield. Arjuna sought for directions on how to behave; Krishna taught him to know himself. Harmonious behavior naturally follows.

Chapter 16

Daivasura Sampad Vibhaga Yoga

The Yoga of the Endowments of Illumination and Darkness

Verses 1–3

śrībhagavānuvāca
abhayaṁ sattvasaṁśuddhirjñānayogavyavasthitiḥ
dānaṁ damaśca yajñaśca svādhyāyastapa ārjavam (1)

ahiṁsā satyamakrodhastyāgaḥ śantirapaiśunam
dayā bhūteṣvaloluptvaṁ mārdavaṁ krīracāpalam (2)

tejaḥ kṣamā dhṛtiḥ śaucamadroho nātimānitā
bhavanti saṁpadaṁ daivīmabhijātasya bhārata (3)

1. Shri Bhagavan said: Fearlessness, purity and truthfulness, steadfastness on the path of yogic wisdom, generosity, self-control, self-giving, Self-contemplation, self-discipline, integrity,

2. Nonviolence, truthfulness, without anger, relinquishing selfishness, peacefulness, not fault-finding, compassion for all beings, free of covetousness, gentleness, modesty, stability,

3. Vigor, forgiveness, endurance, cleanliness, and absence of enmity and pride are the constitutional endowments of illumination, O Bharata.

In this chapter, Krishna makes it easy for Arjuna to differentiate between the two poles of influence within the human psyche. One he calls "illumination," and the other "darkness." Illumination is the force of selflessness, by which an individual understands the path of love, service, and the essential unity of all beings. Darkness is the force of selfishness, which prompts a person toward greed, egocentric behavior, and a desire to create unnecessary divisions and conflicts among people.

These three verses are a brief summary of qualities to be found in a person under the influence of the force of illumination. Worth mentioning is *yajna*, which is translated here as "self-giving." Yajna also refers to a type of traditional ceremony in which various items such as flowers, fruit, and incense are offered to God. Here, in the context of the universal yoga, yajna refers to the offering by the aspirant of his life and love in service to the God in all.

Also worth mentioning is *svadyaya*, here meaning "Self-introspection." Svadyaya is often translated as "study of the scriptures," but the deeper meaning is "study of the spiritual Self." Scriptures and the teachings of the yogis are utilized as a means of Self-reflection. Peering into the mirror of the great teachings allows an aspirant to accurately view the relationship of his personal self to the spiritual Self.

Verse 4

dambho darpo 'bhimānaśca krodhaḥ pāruṣyameva ca
ajñānam cābhijātasya pārtha saṁpadamāsurīm (4)

4. Pride, arrogance and self-conceit, anger and aggressiveness as well as ignorance are the constitutional endowments of darkness, O Partha.

Krishna gives a brief summary of the main characteristics of the constitution of darkness. Understanding the nature of one's darkness is extremely crucial on the spiritual path. After the following verse, the remainder of the chapter examines this issue, its ramifications, and how to rise above its influence. The reason for spending so much time on darkness is that many aspirants fail to appreciate how important it is to deal with the fear, anger, and selfishness that lives buried in the recesses of the psyche.

Many aspirants hear the teachings of the sages about peace, love, and beauty, and they imagine their journey into these realms as one of direct ascendance. The truth of the matter, however, is that the path to the light of love is through the heart of darkness. No one rises to spiritual heights without first clearing the selfishness from their consciousness. A desire for illumination prior to eradicating selfish egoism is a hallmark of premature transcendence.

When many aspirants first begin spiritual practice they are thrilled to enjoy a degree of peace and satisfaction which they had never before experienced. This is a "honeymoon" stage prior to the hard work which they will next undergo. After the initial infatuation with spiritual life has worn off, the aspirant may well become overwhelmed to discover the depths of pain residing within. It is at this stage that many aspirants stop their spiritual practices, as confronting oneself can be such a difficult and laborious experience. But the only way out is through, and the sincere aspirant must proceed into this formidable stage of the journey. In fact, it is often the aspirants with the greatest darkness who eventually achieve success. Perhaps it is a case of the darkest night revealing the brightest stars.

Verse 5

daivī saṁpadvimokṣāya nibandhāyāsurī matā
mā śucaḥ saṁpadaṁ daivīmabhijāto 'si pāṇḍava (5)

5. The endowments of illumination lead one to liberation; the endowments of darkness lead to bondage. Do not worry, O Arjuna. You have the constitution of illumination.

The law is precise: selfishness leads to the pain of bondage, and selflessness leads to the peace of freedom. This is an unambiguous statement that the aspirant can carry with him to keep his path clear. Arjuna is assured by Krishna that his doubts about his own stage of development are unnecessary. Arjuna is worthy of receiving the teachings and, if he applies himself, capable of acting according to his teacher's instructions. Similarly, dear reader, your qualification to learn the Bhagavad Gita and implement the noble teachings of the sages is evidenced by your reading this text. If you were not ready, if you were not worthy, if you were not endowed with sufficient qualities of illumination, you would not be here contemplating this teaching.

Verses 6–20

dvau bhūtasargau loke 'smindaiva āsura eva ca
daivo vistaraśaḥ prokta āsuraṁ pārtha me śṛṇu (6)

pravṛttiṁ ca nivṛttiṁ ca janā na vidurāsurāḥ
na śaucaṁ nāpi cācāro na satyaṁ teṣu vidyate (7)

asatyamapratiṣṭhaṁ te jagadāhuranīśvaram
aparasparasaṁbhūtaṁ kimanyatkāmahaitukam (8)

etāṁ dṛṣṭimavaṣṭabhya naṣṭātmāno 'lpabuddhayaḥ
prabhavantyugrakarmāṇaḥ kṣayāya jagato 'hitāḥ (9)

kāmamāśritya duṣpūraṁ dambhamānamadānvitāḥ
mohādgṛhītvāsadgrāhānpravartante 'śucivratāḥ (10)

cintāmaparimeyāṁ ca pralayāntāmupāśritāḥ
kāmopabhogaparamā etāvaditi niścitāḥ (11)

āśāpāśaśatairbaddhāḥ kāmakrodhaparāyaṇāḥ
īhante kāmabhogārthamanyāyenārthasaṁcayān (12)

idamadya mayā labdhamimaṁ prāpsye manoratham
idamastīdamapi me bhaviṣyati punardhanam (13)

asau mayā hataḥ śatrurhaniṣye cāparānapi
iśvaro 'hamahaṁ bhogī siddho 'haṁ balavānsukhī (14)

āḍhyo 'bhijanavānasmi ko 'nyo 'sti sadṛśo mayā
yakṣye dāsyāmi modiṣya ityajñānavimohitāḥ (15)

anekacittavibhrāntā mohajālasamāvṛtāḥ
prasaktāḥ kāmabhogeṣu patanti narake 'śucau (16)

ātmasaṁbhāvitāḥ stabdhā dhanamānamadānvitāḥ
yajante nāmayajñaiste dambhenāvidhipūrvakam (17)

ahaṅkāraṁ balaṁ darpaṁ kāmaṁ krodhaṁ ca saṁśritāḥ
māmātmaparadeheṣu pradviṣanto 'bhyasūyakāḥ (18)

tānahaṁ dviṣataḥ krūrānsaṁsāreṣu narādhamān
kṣipāmyajasramaśubhānāsurīṣveva yoniṣu (19)

āsurīṁ yonimāpannā mūḍhā janmani janmani
māmaprāpyaiva kaunteya tato yāntyadhamāṁ gatim (20)

6. There are two orders of beings in this world: the illuminating and the darkening. The illuminating have been described at some length. Hear from me now, O Partha, of the darkening.

7. The dark ones do not understand the path of evolutionary activities nor the path of internal integration. In them is not found purity, righteous conduct, nor truthfulness.

8. They claim the world is just a temporal illusion, without a spiritual foundation, without divine guidance, without patterns of causation, believing selfish desire is the sole cause.

9. Stubbornly maintaining this perspective, these lost souls of minute intelligence and cruel activities arise as detrimental forces influencing the world's spiritual decline.

10. Clutching insatiable selfish desires, possessed of hypocrisy, arrogance, and pride, clinging to their false values, in delusion they act with impure resolve.

11. Engrossed with innumerable anxieties lasting until death, arrogantly believing that selfish desires and enjoyments are the supreme objective,

12. Bound by a hundred cords of hope, indulging in selfish desires and righteous anger, they strive without a sense of justice to hoard wealth in order to increase the gratification of their selfishness.

13. Deluded by ignorance, they think, "Today I have gained this and that, and tomorrow I will get more. I have such wealth and more is to come."

14. They ponder, "That enemy I have destroyed and others I will also destroy. I am the actual lord of all things. The world is for my enjoyment. I am perfect, powerful, and happy."

15. They continue, "I am rich and well-born. Who else can be comparable to me? I will publicly demonstrate my religiosity; I will act charitably; I will celebrate my faith."

16. Bewildered by incessant mental agitation, trapped in the net of delusion, addicted to selfish gratification, they fall into a foul, hellish state.

17. Self-righteous, stubborn, intoxicated by pride in wealth, they perform religious rites pompously without caring for the spirit of the law.

18. Egotistical, aggressive, insolent, lusty, full of anger; in their envy they are in opposition to me, the In-dweller within themselves and others.

19. Cruel and hateful, the worst of humanity, I repeatedly cast them into low births in environments of darkness.

20. Entering these low births, they remain deluded throughout cycles of rebirth. Not reaching me, O Kaunteya, they sink to the lowest state.

In the center of life is a cave, within which dwells divine consciousness: love, harmony, and beauty. To reach this cave, one must cross rivers of selfishness, climb mountains of obstacles, and fight beasts of distraction. These rivers, mountains, and beasts are the obstructions described above. Every aspirant would do well to deeply contemplate this description of the darkening influence, for he must become profoundly aware of what lurks in the recesses of his mind.

Verse 21

trividhaṁ narakasyedaṁ dvāraṁ nāśanamātmanaḥ
kāmaḥ krodhastathā lobhastasmādetattrayaṁ tyajet (21)

21. Threefold is the gate of hell, destructive of the Self: selfish desire, hate, and greed. These three should be abandoned.

Spiritual development is simple to evaluate. All one need do is examine to what he extent he has, and to what extent he has not, eradicated selfish desire, hate, and greed. To experience divine love one need not cultivate love, as it exists eternally within the Self. The aspirant must, however, eliminate the three obstacles that cover the awareness of the love.

Although development is simple to evaluate, it is not so easy to accomplish. The threefold gate and the various endowments of darkness do not easily relinquish their grasp. The strength of negative habits is nothing compared to the power within the aspirant. The aspirant must make a bold gesture to abandon these negativities. There is no room for compromise, and there are no reasonable exceptions. Negativities must be completely relinquished. To jump off the cliff of fear and fly into the sky of freedom, one must be without any weight dragging him down.

Verses 22–24

etairvimuktaḥ kaunteya tamodvāraistribhirnaraḥ
ācaratyāmanaḥ śreyastato yāti parāṁ gatim (22)

yaḥ śāstravidhimutsṛjya vartate kāmakārataḥ
na sa siddhimavāpnoti na sukhaṁ na parāṁ gatim (23)

tasmācchāstraṁ pramāṇaṁ te kāryākāryavyavasthitau
jñātvā śāstravidhānokraṁ karma kartumihārhasi (24)

22. One who is liberated from these three gates of darkness, O Kaunteya, abides by behavior which is conducive to Self-expression and travels forward toward the supreme goal.

23. One who disregards the principles of authentic teachings and acts under the promptings of selfish desire cannot attain perfection, nor happiness, nor the supreme goal.

24. Therefore, let the authentic teachings be your authority in determining what is to be done and what is to be avoided. Understanding these teachings, you should undertake your rightful work.

It may seem to the young aspirant that liberation is impossible. Finding his mind filled with the endowments of darkness, plagued by the threefold negativities, he may ponder if he will ever reach his goal. This doubt, though, is just another expression of darkness. Happily, the young aspirant is seen and protected by mighty beings. The sages of the yoga tradition, dwelling in the higher planes of consciousness, are the presenters and protectors of the authentic path. They are aware of each aspirant, and they work tirelessly to help speed him along the path.

The aspirant must do his very best to abide by the teachings. He must put forth every ounce of strength. Then he must rest assured that he is not forsaken by those great souls who love him. As long as the aspirant sincerely abides by the dharma of selflessness, treading the path of the universal yoga, his progress is certain. He need not be perfect; he need but be walking on the path.

Chapter 17

Shraddhatraya Vibhaga Yoga
The Yoga of the Three Patterns of Faith

Verse 1

arjuna uvāca
yeśātravidhimutsṛjya yajante śraddhayānvitāḥ
teṣāṁ niṣṭhā tu kā kṛṣṇa sattvamāho rajastamaḥ (1)

1. Arjuna said: What is the status, O Krishna, of those who disregard the authentic teachings and act from a faith based on inner-prompting? Is this based on balance, activation, or inertia?

At the conclusion of the previous chapter, Krishna instructed Arjuna in the importance of following an authentic spiritual path. Here, Arjuna wonders whether traditional teachings and inner-prompted devotion can be harmonious.

To what extent should one rely on external authorities? To what extent should one rely on internal intuition? He also inquires as to the influence of the three qualities of nature in faith and devotional behavior.

This is the beginning of an important set of teachings, as Krishna speaks on a very practical level. The dialogue is no longer metaphysical; rather the guru instructs the disciple specifically in how to conduct himself.

This chapter will examine how the three qualities of nature influence a person in areas of worship, diet, spiritual offerings, austerities, discipline, and charity. (See Appendix 2.) Most of the commentary in this chapter will be brief, as the teachings contained in the verses speak for themselves.

Verses 2–4

śrībhagavānuvāca
trividhā bhavati śraddhā dehināṁ sā svabhāvajā
sāttvikī rājasī caiva tāmasī ceti tāṁ śṛṇu (2)

sattvānurūpā sarvasya śraddhā bhavati bhārata
śraddhāmayo 'yaṁ puruṣo yo yacchraddhaḥ sa eva saḥ (3)

yajante sāttvikā devānyakṣarakṣāṁsi rājasāḥ
pretānbhūtagaṇāṁścānye yajante tāmasā janāḥ (4)

2. Shri Bhagavan said: The faith of the embodied is of three kinds, arising from their level of development, based on balance, activation, or inertia.

3. The faith of everyone is shaped by their current nature, O Bharata; the being is made of faith. As is his faith, so is he.

4. The balanced worship the divine energies, those influenced by activation worship the energies of acquisition and conquest, and those of inertia worship ghosts and elemental powers.

Simply stated, those of a balanced energy (sattva) are drawn to worship which will enhance their wisdom and compassion. Those influenced by the energy of activation (rajas) will be attracted to those religious paths which promise earthly power and heavenly reward. Those prone to inertia (tamas) will find appealing ancestor worship and psychic phenomena such as séances.

Verses 5–6

aśātravihitaṁ ghoraṁ tapyante ye tapo janāḥ
dambhāhaṅkārsaṁyuktāḥ kāmarāgabalānvitāḥ (5)

karṣayantaḥ śarīrasthaṁ bhūtagrāmamacetasaḥ
māṁ caivāntaḥśarīrasthaṁ tānviddhyāsuraniścayān (6)

5. Practicing terrible austerities not harmonious with authentic teachings, prone to hypocrisy and egoism, accompanied by selfish desire, passion and aggression,

6. Unthinkingly torturing the organs of the body and thus, the In-dweller, know this to be of darkening influence.

Every authentic spiritual path will involve some degree of austerity as the aspirant practices reducing his selfishness and increasing his service. Legitimate austerities will be discussed in the verses below. Here, the guru warns the student against what amounts to a strong temptation for many on the yogic path: engaging in fierce austerities which produce pain in the body.

The reason this is a temptation is that these types of austerities can bring about siddhis, occult powers. The yogic literature is filled with stories about yogis who obtained siddhis, became sidetracked from the spiritual goal by indulging in these powers, and then came to ruin. Krishna warns Arjuna to keep his "eye on the prize" and not be distracted by powers and glamour.

Verses 7–10

āhārastvapi sarvasya trividho bhavati priyaḥ
yajñastapastathā dānaṁ teṣāṁ bhedamimaṁ śṛṇu (7)

āyuḥ sattvabalārogyasukhaprītivivardhanāḥ
rasyāḥ snigdhāḥ sthirā hṛdyā āhārāḥ sāttvikapriyāḥ (8)

kaṭvamlalavaṇātyuṣṇatīkṣṇarūkṣavidāhinaḥ
āhārā rājasasyeṣṭā duḥkhaśokāmayapradāḥ (9)

yātayāmaṁ gatarasaṁ pūti paryuṣitaṁ ca yat
ucchiṣṭamapi cāmedhyaṁ bhojanaṁ tāmasapriyam (10)

7. Even the food enjoyed is of three kinds, as are offerings, austerities, and gifts. Hear from me the distinctions among them.

8. Foods which promote longevity, strength, health, happiness, and cheerfulness, which are sweet, gentle, satisfying, nourishing, and naturally appealing are dear to those living in balance.

9. Foods that are bitter, sour, salty, too hot, pungent, burnt, and burning are liked by those living in activation. Foods which produce pain, unhappiness, and toxicity,

10. Which are nutritionally empty, tasteless, putrid, stale, refuse, and impure are enjoyed by those living in inertia.

The old saying, "you are what you eat" is quite accurate, at least on physical, emotional, and mental levels. The food we eat has a vast impact on our individual consciousness. The foods we find attractive are also a strong indicator as to which of the qualities of nature is predominant. The aspirant eats sattvic foods which bring him into increasing balance, for balance is the platform from which one can ascend to spiritual consciousness. A diet too rich in foods of rajasic (activation) and/or tamasic (inertia) qualities lead to the imbalanced states of aggression and passivity.

Sattvic foods include whole grains, fresh fruits and vegetables, nuts, seeds, dairy products, and other fresh vegetarian foods. Rajasic foods include sharp spices and herbs, stimulants, fish, and excess sugar and salt. Tamasic foods include meat, alcohol, and fermented and stale foods.

While diet is considered a fairly significant influence on spiritual development, it is also worth noting that spiritual growth can take place anywhere, regardless of access to beneficial foods. A healthy, sattvic diet is a great help on the yogic path, but the path remains open for those whose circumstances do not allow for such an aid.

Verses 11–13

aphalākāṅkṣibhiryajño vidhidṛṣṭo ya ijyate
yaṣṭavyameveti manaḥ samādhāya sa sāttvikaḥ (11)

abhisaṁdhāya tu phalaṁ dambhārthamapi caiva yat
ijyate bharataśreṣṭha taṁ yajñaṁ viddhi rājasam (12)

vidhuhīnamasṛṣṭānnaṁ mantrahīnamadakṣiṇam
śraddhāvirahitaṁ yajñaṁ tāmasaṁ paricakṣate (13)

11. The offering which is in balance is offered without concern for reward, in harmony with authentic spirituality, and because one simply understands that such an offering is proper.

12. That which is offered with expectation of reward or public recognition, O Bharatarshabha, is an offering made under the influence of activation.

13. The offering which is inharmonious with authentic spirituality, in which nothing of nourishment is provided, without spiritual expression and no support of spiritual elders, and lacking in real faith is declared to be made with inertia.

This section of verses deals with the influence of the three qualities of nature upon religious offerings. Such offerings include gifts of time or money to a religious organization, participation in rites and rituals, and acting in a leadership fashion in a religious sect. Sattvic offerings are peaceful in spirit, rajasic offerings are self-serving, and tamasic offerings are almost entirely selfish, being offerings in name only.

Verses 14–19

devadvijaguruprājñapūjanaṁ śaucamārjavam
brahmacaryamahiṁsā ca śārīraṁ tapa ucyate (14)

anudvegakaraṁ vākyaṁ satyaṁ priyahitaṁ ca yat
svādhyāyābhyasanaṁ caiva vāṅmayaṁ tapa ucyate (15)

manaḥ prasādaḥ saumyatvaṁ maunamātmavinigrahaḥ
bhāvasaṁśuddhirityetattapo mānasamucyate (16)

śraddhayā parayā taptaṁ tapastattrividhaṁ naraiḥ
aphalākāṅkṣibhiryuktaiḥ sāttvikaṁ paricakṣate (17)

satkāramānapūjārthaṁ tapo dambhena caiva yat
kriyate tadiha proktaṁ rājasaṁ calamadhruvam (18)

mūḍhagrāheṇātmano yatpīḍayā kriyate tapaḥ
parasyotsādanārthaṁ vā tattāmasamudāhṛtam (19)

14. Worship offered to the illumined ones, initiates, spiritual teachers, and other nobles who are wise, which is pure, direct, energy efficient, and does no harm is the austerity of the body.

15. Inoffensive speech which is truthful, pleasant, and helpful and the recitation of spiritual writings is the austerity of speech.

16. Serenity, gentleness, silence, orienting toward the Self, and a mood of purity are the austerity of mind.

17. This threefold austerity practiced with high faith and sincere aspiration and without thought of personal reward is called balanced.

18. Austerity which is unstable and inconsistent and performed to gain respect, honor, and reverence and for the sake of public display is deemed from activation.

19. That austerity which is performed out of foolish ignorance by self-torture or to harm another is from inertia.

Here we have a practical guide to the practice of the threefold austerity of body, of speech, and of mind. We can see that a sattvic, balanced approach is recommended. Rajas drives a person toward "too much;" tamas toward "too little." Rajas brings about self-conceit; tamas brings self-deprecation. Sattva is the yogic balance that integrates the different levels of an individual's psyche.

Verses 20–22

dātavyamiti yaddānaṁ dīyate 'nupakāriṇe
deśe kāle ca pātre ca taddānaṁ sāttvikaṁ smṛtam (20)

yattu pratyupakārārthaṁ phalamuddiśya vā punaḥ
dīyate ca prikliṣṭaṁ taddānaṁ rājasaṁ smṛtam (21)

adeśakale yaddānamapātrebhyaśca dīyate
asatkṛtamavajñātaṁ tattāmasamudāhṛtam (22)

20. Generosity demonstrated without expectation, in the proper place and time, and to an appropriate party is a gift held to be balanced.

21. What is given with the hope of exchanging gifts or personal return or reluctantly given is held as activation.

22. Generosity demonstrated at the wrong time or place, with disdain or patronizingly, or to inappropriate parties is from inertia.

Generosity is one of the greatest expressions of the dignity of humanity. Generosity, however, must be sincere if it is to be noble. Sattvic generosity is venerable because it is based on equality and respect. Rajasic and tamasic generosity may appear to be charitable, but the giver's underlying motives pervert the true spirit of the term. Rajasic generosity is selfish at root, often a passive-aggressive act, and tamasic generosity is proudly or foolishly giving to the wrong party.

Verses 23–27

oṁ tatsaditi nirdeśo brahmaṇastrividhaḥ smṛtaḥ
brāhmaṇāstena vedāśca yajñāśca vihitāḥ purā (23)

tasmādomityudāhṛtya yajñadānatapaḥ kriyāḥ
pravartante vidhānoktāḥ satataṁ brahmavādinām (24)

tadityanabhisaṁdhāya phalaṁ yajñatapaḥkriyāḥ
dānakriyāśca vividhāḥ kriyante mokṣakāṅkṣibhiḥ (25)

sadbhāve sādhubhāve ca sadityetatprayujyate
praśaste karmaṇi tathā sacchabdaḥ pārtha yujyate (26)

yajñe tapasi dāne ca sthitiḥ saditi cocyate
karma caiva tadarthīyaṁ sadityevābhidhīyate (27)

23. *Aum tat sat* is the threefold designation of Infinite Consciousness, the ancient indicator of sages, wisdom texts, and divine offerings.

24. Avow aum as an offering. Be generous, practice balanced austerities, live a life of authentic spirituality, and in all your undertakings act as a vessel for Infinite Consciousness.

25. Avow tat as an offering. Undertake spiritual ceremonies, austerities, and activities as acts of generosity. By performing these you demonstrate you are among those who desire liberation.

26. Avow sat as an offering. Indicate that your existence is one of a spiritual aspirant. O Partha, sat applies to all noble activities.

27. Sat is also represented by an offering spirit, illumined by austerities and generosity in all efforts to mature spiritually.

Aum-tat-sat is a traditional threefold designation of Brahman, Infinite Consciousness. Aum is the pure Self. Tat is the essence of All. Sat represents the eternal truth.

Verse 28

aśraddhayā hutaṁ dattaṁ tapastaptaṁ kṛtaṁ ca yat
asadityucyate pārtha na ca tatpretya no iha (28)

28. Whatever is offered or given as a gift, whatever austerity is undertaken, whatever activity is performed, if it is engaged without proper faith, O Partha, it is based on temporal illusion and holds no value for the present or for future spiritual development.

Krishna answers Arjuna's question from the beginning of this chapter in a conclusive manner. The issue is not as Arjuna originally framed it, a matter of tradition or intuition. Rather, the issue is one of proper faith. Proper faith is sattvic, balanced. It is the harmony between the extremes of too much and too little, aggressiveness and passivity, labor and laziness. Sattva provides a clear channel for the Infinite Consciousness to be expressed through a human being.

Chapter 18

Sannyasa Yoga
The Yoga of Spiritual Renunciation

Verse 1

arjuna uvāca
saṁnyāsya mahābāho tattvamicchāmi veditum
tyāgasya ca hṛṣīkeśa pṛthakkeśiniṣūdana (1)

1. Arjuna said, I desire to know, O Mahabaho, the essential truth of the relationship and difference between renunciation and relinquishing activities, O Hrishikesh, O Keshisudhana (Krishna as Slayer of Non-Necessity).

Throughout the Bhagavad Gita, Krishna has spoken about renunciation and relinquishment. The entire text revolves around Arjuna's initial confusion over whether he should fight or not on the battlefield of Kurukshetra. Arjuna's questions are becoming increasingly relevant and refined. He has contemplated the wisdom in Krishna's answers and is near finishing his queries, preparing to make a decision. In Arjuna's mind, the distinction between renunciation and relinquishment must still be somewhat unclear. It may appear to be a fine point of distinction, but, as Krishna will now make clear, it is very important that these two pillars of proper conduct be correctly understood.

Verses 2–3

śrībhagavānuvāca
kāmyānāṁ karmaṇāṁ nyāsaṁ saṁnyāsaṁ kavayo viduḥ
sarvakarmaphalatyāgaṁ prāhustyāgaṁ vicakṣaṇāḥ (2)

tyājaṁ doṣavadityeke karma prāhurmanīṣiṇaḥ
yajñadanatapaḥ karma na tyājyamiti cāpare (3)

2. Sri Bhagavan said: The traditional understanding of the wise is that renunciation means the renunciation of selfishly motivated activities. Relinquishing the rewards of one's actions is known as relinquishment.

3. Some think that all activity should be relinquished as an obstruction; others say that acts of spiritual offering, generosity, and spiritual austerities should not be relinquished.

When people first hear of the need for renunciation and relinquishment, they are apt to become confused and frightened, for everyone has a sense that certain activities in his life are important and valuable. If God-realization requires the cessation of what brings meaning to life, there is bound to be a hesitancy to begin the practice of karma yoga.

Krishna immediately addresses this concern in verse 2. Renunciation is not the cessation of all activities, just those that are selfishly motivated. Relinquishment is not the cessation of external behavior; it is a mental release of concern with rewards and punishments.

Perhaps the teaching in verse 2 will be sufficient for those who have time to contemplate its profundity and implications, for the entire teaching of proper behavior is to be found here. On the field of Kurukshetra, however, Arjuna did not have such leisure. The battle was painfully imminent, and Krishna needed him to immediately grasp the teaching and apply it to his situation.

So Krishna continued, pointing out in verse 3 the most common confusion question of spiritual conduct. Should one avoid, as completely as possible, activity and relationships in order to avoid complications and karma or are noble activities to be engaged? Next, he provides the answer.

Verses 4–6

niścayaṁ śṛṇu me tatra tyāge bharatasattama
tyāgo hi puruṣavyāghra trividhaḥ saṁprakīrtitaḥ (4)

yajñadānatapaḥ karma na tyājyaṁ kāryameva tat
yajño dānaṁ tapaścaiva pāvanāni manīṣiṇām (5)

etānyapi tu karmāṇi saṅgaṁ tyaktvā phalāni ca
kartavyānīti me pārtha niścitaṁ matamuttamam (6)

4. Hear from me, O Bharatasattama (Arjuna as Truest of the Bharatas), the conclusive statement about relinquishment. Relinquishment, O Purushavyagrah (Arjuna as Tiger among Beings), is threefold.

5. Acts of spiritual offering, generosity, and spiritual austerities should not be relinquished but should be undertaken, for these three are purifiers of the mind.

6. But even these beneficial activities must be undertaken without attachment and relinquishing concern for reward, O Partha. This is my conclusive and highest conviction.

Relinquishment of activities which are conducive to spiritual growth and beneficial for others are not to be eliminated. Rather, they are to be engaged in with the spirit of karma yoga. This is the penultimate teaching for guiding aspirants on the path of wisdom-based behavior.

Verses 7–10

niyatasya tu saṁnyāsaḥ karmaṇo nopapadyate
mohāttasya parityāgastāmasaḥ parikīrtitaḥ (7)

duḥkhamityeva yatkarma kāyakleśabhayāttyajet
sa kṛtvā rājasaṁ tyāgam naiva tyāgaphalaṁ labhet (8)

kāryamityeva yatkarma niyataṁ kriyate 'rjuna
saṅgaṁ tyaktvā phalaṁ caiva sa tyāgaḥ sāttviko mataḥ (9)

na dveṣṭyakuśalaṁ karma kuśale nānuṣajjate
tyāgī sattvasamāviṣṭo medhāvī chinnasaṁśayaḥ (10)

7. The renunciation of necessary and appropriate activities is not proper. Such relinquishment is due to delusion and is declared to be from the quality of inertia.

8. One who relinquishes an activity because it is physically uncomfortable or unpleasant is relinquishing under the influence of the quality of activation. This does not give the spiritual result of authentic relinquishment.

9. One who performs a necessary and appropriate activity, while relinquishing attachment and hope for reward, is undertaking balanced relinquishment.

10. The relinquisher who is fully balanced, in wisdom, with doubts renounced, does not avoid unpleasant activities nor is he attached to pleasant activities.

Here we find a guide to proper behavior in relationship to the three gunas, the qualities of nature. Relinquishment influenced by tamas guna, inertia, is described as delusory. Relinquishment influenced by rajas guna, activation, is inauthentic. Relinquishment influenced by sattva guna, balance, is the path of true karma yoga.

Verses 11–12

na hi dehabhṛtā śakyaṁ tyaktuṁ karmāṇyaśeṣataḥ
yastu karmaphalatyāgī sa tyāgītyabhidhīyate (11)

aniṣṭamiṣṭaṁ miśraṁ ca trividhaṁ karmaṇaḥ phalam
bhavatyatyāgināṁ pretya na tu saṁnyāsināṁ kvacit (12)

11. Never is it possible for a being in incarnation to completely relinquish all activities. One who relinquishes seeking rewards for his actions is rightly called a relinquisher.

12. Pleasant, unpleasant, and mixed are the three types of results arising from actions. These are experienced even after death by those who do not practice relinquishment. There is nothing to be reaped by those who practice true renunciation.

The attempt to achieve some sort of pure relinquishment of all activity is a fantasy. No one alive can completely relinquish all activities. He must, by necessity, at least eat, breathe, and have blood coursing through his veins. What is not a fantasy but an attainable goal, at least by those who live in the karma yoga spirit, is peace. Such a being is the true renunciate, not the one who starves or tries to hold his breath.

In order to experience peace, one must transcend being motivated by seeking pleasant activities, avoiding the unpleasant, and grudgingly accepting the mixed nature of most experiences in this world. Pursuing what one finds attractive and attempting to avoid the unattractive is what produces karma. Karmic results are held to be positive, negative, and mixed. These can be experienced during one's lifetime, during the afterlife experience, or in the next incarnation. All karma, however, is considered bondage because it keeps one tied to the wheel of cause and effect. The goal of the yogic path is not pleasant karma, but freedom.

Verses 13–17

pañcaitāni mahābāho kāraṇāni nibodha me
sāṁkhye kṛtānte proktāni siddhaye sarvakarmaṇām (13)

adhiṣṭānaṁ tathā kartā karaṇaṁ ca pṛthagvidham
vividhāśca pṛthakceṣṭā daivaṁ caivātra pañcamam (14)

śarīravāṅmanobhiryatkarma pārabhate naraḥ
nyāyyaṁ vā viparītaṁ vā pañcaite tasya hetavaḥ (15)

tatraivaṁ sati kartāramātmānaṁ kevalaṁ tu yaḥ
paśyatyakṛtabuddhitvānna sa paśyati durmatiḥ (16)

yasya nāhaṁkṛto bhāvo buddhiryasya na lipyate
hatvāpi sa imaṁllokānna hanti na nibadhyate (17)

13. O Mahabaho, learn from me the five causes for the accomplishment of all actions as presented in the philosophy of essential principles.

14. These are: the body, the agent of action, the subtle instruments, the various energies of effort, and divine providence.

15. Whatever activity one undertakes, whether by body, speech, or mind, whether productive or unproductive, these five are its factors.

16. Since this is the actual situation, only a person of distorted mind resulting from immature intelligence perceives himself as an isolated agent of action. He has no vision.

17. One who is free from the feeling of being the sole influence and whose intelligence is untainted, even though he slays these people, he neither slays nor is he bound by his actions.

This is a very significant set of verses as they outline a holistic, interdependent vision of action. This is the conclusion of samkhya yoga, the philosophy of essential principles, which was previously discussed (2.12–38, 13.5–6). What is being taught here is that the notion of an independent agent of activity is a false notion. There is no separate individual who expresses himself in an external world. Rather, the individual agent is part of an integral process of nature which produces activity. It is simply an interface of body and environment which produces the feeling of individual agency.

The myth of the separate self is simply a culturally accepted belief; it has no foundation in truth. The violin may claim it is the source of beautiful music, but it is actually a piece of wood being played by the musician. The microphone does not speak; it is spoken through. The wave is not the ocean and has no power to produce itself. One who can understand how all beings and all actions interface truly understands. Everything is causing everything; everything is interacting; everything is connected.

Verses 18–22

jñānaṁ jñeyaṁ parijñātā trividhā karmacodanā
karaṇaṁ karma karteti trividhaḥ karmasaṁgrahaḥ (18)

jñānaṁ karma ca kartā ca tridaiva guṇabhedataḥ
procyate guṇasaṁkhyāne yathāvacchṛṇu tānyapi (19)

sarvabhūteṣu yenaikaṁ bhāvamavyayamīkṣate
avibhaktaṁ vibhakteṣu tajjñānaṁ viddhi sāttvikam (20)

pṛthaktvena tu yajjñānaṁ nānābhāvānpṛthagvidhān
vetti sarveṣu bhūteṣu tajjñānaṁ viddhi rājasam (21)

yattu kṛtsnavadekasminkārye saktamahaitukam
atattvārthavadalpaṁ ca tattāmasamudāhṛtam (22)

18. Knowledge, the knowable, and the knower are the threefold incentive to action. The instrument, the action, and the actor are the threefold composite means of action.

19. Knowledge, action, and the actor are recognized as being of three kinds, based on a relationship to the three qualities of nature.

20. Knowledge is in balance when one sees the One ever-existing Being in all beings as undivided in the apparently divided.

21. Knowledge is in activation when one sees a seemingly real separateness among a multiplicity of beings.

22. Knowledge is in inertia when one sees a single effect as if it were the entirety, without relation to cause, and without any association to spiritual principles.

That which is to be known, the psychological knowing, and the knower himself are three factors which are found in all activity. All three of these are profoundly affected by the gunas, the qualities of nature. These verses review how the quality of balance produces advaita, non-dual vision; the quality of activation produces the vision of multiplicity; and the quality of inertia brings forth a confused perception which fails to see the spiritual underpinning of reality.

Verses 23–28

niyataṁ saṅgarahitamarāgadveṣataḥ kṛtam
aphalaprepsunā karma yattatsāttvikamucyate (23)

yattu kāmepsunā karma sāhaṅkāreṇa vā punaḥ
kriyate bahulāyāsaṁ tadrājasamudāhṛtam (24)

anubandhaṁ kṣayaṁ hiṁsāmanavekṣya ca pauruṣam
mohādārabhyate karma yattattāmasamucyate (25)

muktasaṅgo 'nahaṁvādī dhṛtyutsāhasamanvitaḥ
siddhyasiddhyornirvikāraḥ kartā sāttvika ucyate (26)

rāgī karmaphalaprepsurlubdho hiṁsātmako 'śuciḥ
harṣaśokānvitaḥ kartā rājasaḥ parikīrtitaḥ (27)

ayuktaḥ prākṛtaḥ stabdaḥ śaṭho naiṣkṛtiko 'lasaḥ
viṣādī dīrghasūtrī ca kartā tāmasa ucyate (28)

23. Activity which is necessary, performed without selfish attachment, without concern for one's personal attraction or repulsion, without motivation for reward, is called balanced.

24. Activity which is done with great strain, inspired by selfish desire or personal aggrandizement, arises from activation.

25. That activity undertaken in confusion, without regard for consequences, to cause destruction or harm, and without considering one's capacity, results from inertia.

26. The actor who is free from attachment and egoism, full of resolution and enthusiasm, unmoved in success or failure, is called sattvic.

27. The actor swayed by passion, desiring rewards from his actions, greedy, prone to violence, impure, prone to excessive exaltation and depression, is under the influence of activation.

28. The actor who is not seeking yoga, crude, stubborn, deceitful, malicious, lazy, despondent, and procrastinating, has succumbed to inertia.

The influence of the three gunas on activity is described in verses 23–25 and on the notion of oneself as the actor in verses 26–28. The verses speak for themselves; no additional commentary is necessary.

Verses 29–35

buddherbhedaṁ dhṛteścaiva guṇatastrividhaṁ śṛṇu
procyamānamaśeṣeṇa pṛthaktvena dhanaṁjaya (29)

pravṛttiṁ ca nivṛttiṁ ca kāryākārye bhayābhaye
bandhaṁ mokṣaṁ ca yā vetti buddhiḥ sā pārtha sāttvikī (30)

yayā dharmamadharmaṁ ca kāryaṁ cākāryameva ca
ayathāvatprajānāti buddhiḥ sā pārtha rājasī (31)

adharmaṁ dharmamiti yā manyate tamasāvṛtā
sarvārthānviparītāṁśca buddhiḥ sā pārtha tāmasī (32)

dhṛtyā yayā dhārayate manaḥ prāṇendriyakriyāḥ
yogenāvyabhicāriṇyā dhṛtiḥ sā pārtha sāttvikī (33)

yayā tu dharmakāmārthāndhṛtyā dhārayate 'rjuna
prasaṅgena phalākāṅkṣī dhṛtiḥ sā pārtha rājasī (34)

yayā svapnaṁ bhayaṁ śokaṁ viṣādaṁ madameva ca
na vimuñcati durmedhā dhṛtiḥ sā pārtha tāmasī (35)

29. Hear about the threefold distinction in intelligence and commitment as related to the qualities of nature, O Dhananjaya, to be described comprehensively and individually.

30. O Partha, the intelligence which understands the harmony of evolutionary activities and internal integration, proper actions and improper actions, fear and fearlessness, what is binding and what is liberating, is balanced.

31. O Partha, the intelligence which understands spiritual harmony and disharmony, proper and improper actions, but is incomplete and not implemented, is influenced by activation.

32. The intelligence which regards disharmony as harmony and views all things in a distorted manner is from inertia.

33. The commitment which is steadfast in controlling the movements of the mind, vital energies, and senses by yogic steadiness is called balanced.

34. The commitment which is steadfast in pursuing spiritual harmony, healthy enjoyment, and properly obtained wealth, but contains attachments and desire for rewards, O Partha, is from activation.

35. The commitment by which a fool does not seek to overcome sleep, fear, grief, depression, and arrogance, O Partha, is from inertia.

The influence of the three gunas on intelligence is described in verses 29–32 and on commitment in verses 33–35. The verses again speak for themselves. No additional commentary is required for understanding if the student takes the time to study and contemplate the text.

Verses 36–39

sukhaṁ tvidānīṁ trividaṁ śṛṇu me bharatarṣabha
abhyāsādramte yatra duḥkhāntaṁ ca nigacchati (36)

yattadagre viṣamiva patiṇāme 'mṛtopamam
tatsukhaṁ sāttvikaṁ proktamātmabuddhiprasādajam (37)

viṣayendriyasaṁyogādyattadagre 'mṛtopamam
pariṇāme viṣamiva tatsukhaṁ rājasaṁ smṛtam (38)

yadagre cānubandhe ca sukhaṁ mohanamātamanaḥ
nidrālasyapramādotthaṁ tattāmasamudāhṛtam (39)

36. Hear from me now, O Bharatarshabha, the three kinds of happiness. One type, with practice, leads to rejoicing and the end of sorrow.

37. The happiness which may seem bitter at first but is like nectar in the end, which springs from clear insight into the Self, is called balanced.

38. The happiness which arises as a result of the engagement of the senses with their objects, which is like nectar at first but bitter in the end, is the happiness of activation.

39. The happiness which is Self-delusory from the beginning to the end, which arises from sleep, laziness, and negligence, is from inertia.

Every sentient being innately seeks for happiness. Most people fail to find the happiness they want because they do not proceed toward this goal in the proper manner. People are not bad or malevolent when they act in selfish ways; they are simply misguided in their attempts to secure happiness.

Happiness is found in clear insight of the Self. It may be difficult to practice spiritual disciplines in the beginning, but the path becomes increasingly joyous and comfortable as one progresses. This is the balanced happiness which produces lasting results. The happiness of activation is short-lived as it is based on interacting with externals. Since the world is ever-changing, likewise happiness gathered through the world will also change into something else before terribly long. The happiness of inertia hardly resembles any real happiness. It is the stupor of blocking out pain found in numbing activities such as drinking too much alcohol, overeating, and excessive sleep.

Verse 40

na tadasti pṛthivyāṁ vā divi deveṣu vā punaḥ
sattvaṁ prakṛtijairmuktaṁ yadebhiḥ syāttribhirguṇaiḥ (40)

40. There is no sentient being on this earth or among the gods in heaven who is free from the three qualities of nature.

The three qualities of nature—the gunas of sattva (balance), rajas (activation), and tamas (inertia)—are the forces behind all that exists in the realms of temporal creation. The body/mind complex—the physical form, senses, and mental apparatus—are powered by the three gunas. As the gunas revolve in progression, beings change and grow. No one is immune from the power of nature playing through his life.

Verses 41–44

brāhmaṇakṣatriyaviśāṁ śūdrāṇāṁ ca paraṁtapa
karmāṇi pravibhaktāni svabhāvaprabhavairguṇaiḥ (41)

śamo damastapaḥ śaucaṁ kṣāntirārjavameva ca
jñānaṁ vijñānamāstikyaṁ brahmakarma svabhāvajam (42)

śauryaṁ tejo dhṛtirdākṣyaṁ yuddhe cāpyapalāyanam
dānamīśvarabhāvaśca kṣātraṁ karma svabhāvajam (43)

kṛṣigaurakṣyavāṇijyaṁ vaiśyakarma svabhāvajam
paricaryātmakaṁ karma śūdrasyāpi svabhāvajam (44)

41. Philosophers, leaders, businessmen, and manual laborers are vocations reflective of the three qualities of nature and an individual's unique constitution.

42. Serenity, self-restraint, austerity, purity, forgiveness, straightforwardness, wisdom, knowledge, and faith are the activities of a philosopher, born of his nature.

43. Heroism, vitality, steadfastness, resourcefulness, never avoiding a conflict, generosity, and leadership are the activities of a leader, born of his nature.

44. Farming, raising livestock, and business dealings are the duties of a businessman. Manual labor is the duty born of a laborer's nature.

This set of verses presents the *varnashram dharma,* the yogic prescription for social organization. Ancient Indian civilization was built around this organic arrangement that ensured each individual was able to live a fulfilling life based on his inherent passions and skills. This resulted in a peaceful and prosperous society that was the jewel of its time.

Varnashram dharma has been criticized by modern Westerners as being an oppressive and unsympathetic caste system. This criticism is unwarranted and fails to appreciate the organic nature of this social organization. There have certainly been abuses of the varnashram dharma in contemporary India, including rigid caste distinctions and the creation of an "untouchables" class. The causes of these abuses are not the domain of this book, but suffice it to say they are an abomination of the original healthy social system supported by the great yogic sages.

This subject of social organization is vast and not central to the Bhagavad Gita. The notion of a holistic society based on mutual support among social strata is important, however, and the student would do well to ponder these verses and amplify the implications of these basic teachings. (See also 4.13.)

Verses 45–48

sve sve karmaṇyabhirataḥ saṁsiddhiṁ labhate naraḥ
svakarmanirataḥ siddhiṁ yathā vindati tacchṛṇu (45)

yataḥ pravṛttirbhūtānāṁ yena sarvamidaṁ tatam
svakarmaṇā tamabhyarcya siddhiṁ vindati mānavaḥ (46)

śreyānsvadharmo viguṇaḥ paradharmātsvanuṣṭhitāt
svabhāvaniyataṁ karma kurvannāpnoti kilbiṣam (47)

sahajaṁ karma kaunteya sadoṣamapi na tyajet
sarvārambhā hi doṣeṇa dhūmenāgnirivāvṛtāḥ (48)

45. Each devoted to his constitutional duty will attain perfection. Hear from me now how one attains perfection through devotion to duty.

46. Attain perfection through the performance of your duty by worshipping Him from whom all beings arise and who pervades all.

47. Better is one's own duty performed imperfectly than that of another performed perfectly. Performing the activities suited to one's constitutional nature creates no karmic consequence.

48. One should not relinquish the duty which is inherently his, O Arjuna, even if it is less than ideal. For all undertakings are clouded with defects as fire by smoke.

The path to spiritual accomplishment is unique for each aspirant. There are certain broad outlines of proper conduct, attitude, and practice, but every soul must walk on a path that is for his steps alone. Just as each snowflake is unique, so each individuated being is a matchless expression of the one Self.

Each being must find his own path and walk it with enthusiasm. All paths are just paths, leading back toward the Self. But a path with heart, a path that honors the dharma, the inner call, is a way that can rightly be called a spiritual path. Nothing in the world is pure, so an individual should not waste his time seeking some imaginary perfection which does not exist. Peace, however, is a reality that does exist. Let us, then, not so much seek some illusory perfection but find and walk upon the actual and practical path of peace.

Verses 49–53

asaktabuddhiḥ sarvatra jitātmā vigataspṛhaḥ
naiṣkarmyasiddhiṁ paramāṁ saṁnyāsenādhigacchati (49)

siddhiṁ prāpto yathā brahma tathāpnoti nibodha me
samāsenaiva kaunteya niṣṭhā jñānasya yā parā (50)

buddhyā viśuddhayā yukto dhṛtyātmānaṁ niyamya ca
śabdādīnviṣayāṁstyaktvā rāgadveṣau vyudasya ca (51)

viviktasevī laghvāśī yatavākkāyamānasaḥ
dyānayogaparo nityaṁ vairāgyaṁ samupāśritaḥ (52)

ahaṅkāraṁ balaṁ darpaṁ kāmaṁ krodhaṁ parigraham
vimucya nirmamaḥ śānto brahmabhūyāya kalpate (53)

49. One whose intelligence is unattached regardless of circumstances, who is a victor in the Self, whose selfish desires have fled, by renunciation he reaches the supreme perfection of transcendent activity.

50. Hear from me, O Kaunteya, a brief explanation of how one who has attained this perfection attains Infinite Consciousness, that supreme culmination of wisdom.

51. Endowed with pure intuitive intelligence and firm restraint in the Self, relinquishing the influences of sense objects and casting aside attractions and aversions,

52. Maintaining an inner solitude, modest in diet, controlling speech, body, and mind, ever engaged in sublime yogic contemplation, resorting to dispassion,

53. Abandoning egoism, aggression, arrogance, selfish desire, anger, possessions, and possessiveness, and peaceful, such a one is worthy of entering into Infinite Consciousness.

This set of verses is a practical compendium of different teachings that have been presented throughout the text. Krishna's dialogue with Arjuna is near conclusion, and the teacher is summarizing for his student. These concluding verses are a synopsis of all that has been taught, after which the teacher must take his silence and allow the student to think and act for himself.

Verses 54–56

brahmabhūtaḥ prasannātmā naśocati na kāṅkṣati
samaḥ sarvaṣu bhūteṣu madbhaktiṁ labhate parām (54)

bhaktyā māmabhijānāti yāvānyaścāsmi tattvataḥ
tato māṁ tattvato jñātvā viśate tadanantaram (55)

sarvakarmāṇyapi sadā kurvāṇo madvyapāśrayaḥ
matprasādādvāpnoti śāśvataṁ padamavyayam (56)

54. Engrossed in Infinite Consciousness, serene in the Self, one neither grieves nor has egoic needs. Equal-minded toward all beings, one attains a supreme devotion to me.

55. Through devotion one comes to know me, the essential nature of who and what I am. Then, having the wisdom of my essence, he forthwith enters into me.

56. Although still continuing to remain active, taking refuge in me, by my grace he obtains the everlasting, ever-existing state.

The culmination of the spiritual path is presented to the aspirant that his eyes may glimpse the glory that awaits him. This inspiration is essential. The aspirant will need this as food for his journey, to keep him fortified as he passes through the challenges of the spiritual path. Periods of discipline, longing, loneliness, joy, confusion, and all the emotions of an average person await him.

These feelings, moreover, are heightened for the sensitive aspirant. His joy is the joy of the gods, and his pain is that of those in hell. It is an Olympian task placed before the aspirant, with no guarantee of success or promise of support along the way. The heart, however, has a clarion call that must be answered. The aspirant is among those who have answered.

Verses 57–58

cetasā sarvakarmāṇi mayi saṁnyasya matparaḥ
buddhiyogamupāśritya maccittaḥ satataṁ bhava (57)

maccittaḥ sarvadurgāṇi matprasādāttariṣyasi
atha cettvamahaṅkārānna śroṣyasi vinaṅkṣyasi (58)

57. Internally renounce all activities to me, hold me as the supreme, and resort to the yoga of intuitive intelligence while having my state of being wholly fill your individual consciousness.

58. Fill your consciousness with me, and you will overcome all obstacles by my grace. If from egoism you will not listen, you will come to ruin.

The path from the individuated consciousness of the aspirant to that of the supreme is an inner journey. As discussed before, external behaviors are not to be relinquished. It is a renunciation of selfish self-importance that is required. The manas, or cognitive mind, acts in the world, but the buddhi, the intuitive intelligence, guides one's behavior.

When in communion with the Self, the transparent buddhi enables the graceful light of the Self to stream into manifestation as enlightened activity. The aspirant who comes this far in his relationship with his own Self, who has engaged in dialogue with his own inner guru, must follow the inner promptings. If he fails to do so, he will experience acute discomfort as a result of a disharmony within himself.

Verses 59–61

yadahaṅkāramāsitya na yotsya iti manyase
mithyaiṣa vyavasāyaste prakṛtistvāṁ niyokṣyati (59)

svabhāvajena kaunteya nibaddhaḥ svena karmaṇā
kartuṁ necchasi yanmohātkariṣyasyavaśo 'pi tat (60)

īśvaraḥ sarvabhūtānāṁ hṛddeśe 'rjuna tiṣṭhati
bhrāmayansarvabhūtāni yantrārūḍhāni māyayā (61)

59. If you resort to egoism and think, "I will not fight," your resolution is irrelevant as nature will impel you.

60. Through confusion you do not feel like acting, O Kaunteya, but you will act, even helplessly, bound by your own constitutional nature.

61. The Lord dwells in the spiritual heart of all beings, O Arjuna, causing all beings to revolve by his energy of divine magic, as if they were cogs in a machine.

As we saw in verses 13–15, individual prerogative is only one of five components involved in action. In this set of verses, the guru clearly sees the disciple fooling himself with his own fantasies of who he is and how he should behave. Arjuna has come far enough on his spiritual path that he can no longer ignore the inner promptings of his true nature, echoed by the external guru, Krishna. The shakti, the divine energy of the Lord, is the strongest impulse for action. Krishna can see that Arjuna can no more ignore this impulse than an eagle can decide not to fly.

Verse 62

tameva śaraṇaṁ gaccha sarvabhāvena bhārata
tatprasādātparāṁ śāntiṁ sthānaṁ prāpsyasi śāśvatam (62)

62. Seek refuge in Him alone in all ways, O Bharata. By grace you will attain the state of supreme, everlasting peace.

All people are searching for a safe harbor, a place of rest and safety where they are free of fear. Materialistic people seek this refuge in worldly success, attempting in vain to make their homes and lifestyle "pain-proof" by gorging themselves on pleasures and apparent security. Alas, change occurs. Sickness and death show their face; the mansion becomes nothing more than an expensive coffin.

Empires rise and fall, nations are torn asunder, family members die, relationships dissolve; the world is a place of temporary interactions which cease when the karmic energy has expired. Events and relationships are like leaves floating together down a stream. The leaves have no control over the duration of their time together; the force of the current dictates their conjunction and separation.

The only refuge is in the heart of the divine consciousness, which can never forget, never forsake, never betray. Love, eternal love, is ever-present, ripe for the asking. The sage is called a jnani, a person of wisdom, because he is wise enough to take his refuge in love.

Verses 63–66

iti te jñānamākhyātaṁ guhyādguhyataraṁ mayā
vimṛśyaitadaśeṣeṇa yathecchasi tathā kuru (63)

sarvaguhyatamaṁ bhūyaḥ śṛṇu me paramaṁ vacaḥ
iṣṭo 'si me dṛḍhamiti tato vakṣyāmi te hitam (64)

manmanā bhava madbhakto madyājī māṁ namaskuru
māmevaiṣyasi satyaṁ te pratijāne priyo 'si me (65)

sarvadharmānparityajya māmekaṁ śaraṇaṁ vraja
ahaṁ tvā sarvapāpebhyo mokṣayiṣyāmi mā śucaḥ (66)

63. This wisdom, more secret than the greatest secret, has been declared by me to you. Reflect upon these teachings fully, and making your choice, do as you wish.

64. Listen once more to my supreme word, the most cherished secret. Because you are greatly beloved by me, I will tell you what is for your own good.

65. Absorb your mind in me, direct your devotion to me, sacrifice for me, and offer respect to me. You will come to me, I promise you truly; you are so very dear to me.

66. Abandoning all sense of extraneous duties, take your refuge in me, the One. I will remove your egoic self-centeredness. Have no doubt.

Verse 63 seems to be the culmination of the dialogue. Krishna has instructed Arjuna in every conceivable aspect of spirituality. He has answered all of Arjuna's personal and philosophical questions. Every rock has been upturned; every secret revealed. Certainly the guru has completed his task and can now leave the aspirant to make a wise decision.

Yet the dialogue continues. Perhaps we can envision Krishna pausing between verses 63 and 64, seeing something subtle in Arjuna's face which reveals his student still had some small doubt, some creeping fear lingering in his mind. So Krishna continues in verses 64–66 encouraging Arjuna, pleading with him, promising him everything he could possibly want. The guru is more kindly than an aged grandmother doting on her grandchild. Krishna fills Arjuna with spirit, trying his very best to elevate Arjuna to a level where he can receive Krishna's benediction, working his hardest to help Arjuna understand this is the truth which will set him free.

Verses 67–69

idaṁ te nātapaskāya nābhaktāya kadācana
na cāśuśrūṣave vācyaṁ na ca māṁ yo 'bhyasūyati (67)

ya imaṁ paramaṁ guhyaṁ madbhakteṣvabhidhāsyati
bhaktiṁ mayi parāṁ kṛtvā māmevaiṣyatyasaṁśayaḥ (68)

na ca tatmānmanuṣyeṣu kaścinme priyakṛttamaḥ
bhavitā na ca me tasmādanyaḥ priyataro bhuvi (69)

67. This teaching is not to be spoken to one who is spiritually undisciplined, nor to one without devotion or not truly interested, nor to one who is antagonistic to me.

68. One who teaches this supreme secret to my devotees demonstrates the highest devotion to me and shall doubtless come to me.

69. There is no one whose service is more dear to me, nor could there be another dearer on the entire earth.

Teachings about spirituality are not kept secret. Rather, all are called to God's love. Alas, however, few choose to answer. Those who lack devotion, interest, or integrity will simply not be drawn to spiritual life. Their lessons remain still in the lower realms of fear and selfishness. For those who are ripe, there is no greater service to render than to share authentic spiritual dharma, such as this Bhagavad Gita.

Service to others is the expression of spiritual development. When one attains, there arises a natural, spontaneous desire to share. As a generous wealthy man will enjoy sharing his riches, so does the sage enjoy passing on what has been given him. Social service—feeding the hungry, clothing the needy, educating children, and so on—are worthy and noble objectives and should be undertaken if one is so motivated. The supreme service, though, is that which will eradicate suffering forever.

Christ said, "Drink of this water and you will never thirst again." The teachings of the mahatmas, the great souls, are for the purpose of the complete elimination of the consciousness of suffering. The individual who can accept such a benediction enters into Krishna's realm, a consciousness of wonder and beauty. Here all is joy. There may be some human suffering for such a being, but it is not experienced in the same way as an ordinary mortal.

The suffering of the sages is felt by them to be part of the lila, God's divine play. It is like spice in a good soup. Sri Ramakrishna, the great Bengali sage was once asked, "Why does suffering exist in God's creation?" The sage paused and contemplated, then responded, "To enhance the drama." The one who takes his part in the drama of God's love and who shares with the other actors the essence of love performs the greatest possible service and becomes an intimate of the Divine Being.

Verses 70–71

adhyeṣyate ca ya imaṁ dharmyaṁ saṁvādamāvayoḥ
jñānayajñena tenāhamiṣṭaḥ syāmiti me matiḥ (70)

śraddhāvānanasūyaśca śṛṇuyādapi yo naraḥ
so 'pi muktaḥ śubhāṁllokānprāyātpuṇyakarmaṇām (71)

70. I consider one who contemplates this dialogue in a spirit of spiritual harmony to be offering his worship to me through his wisdom.

71. And one who listens with faith and without negativity shall also be liberated and attain the pure worlds of those of meritorious karma.

An important yoga practice is svadhyaya with two equally profound meanings. The first, relevant to verse 70, is reflection upon sva, the true Self. This is primarily an introspective undertaking, whereby an aspirant openly and honestly contemplates his inner dialogue. It is a weighing by the individual of the relative value of different energies in his consciousness in an attempt to access the wisdom of the inner guru. It is also an energetic struggle to determine which of the two opposing forces—the negative Kauravas or the positive values of the Pandavas—will direct his life. The aspirant seeks to internally sense the guidance of God and act in harmony with this divine will.

Verse 71 describes the second, more exoteric practice of svadhyaya as the study of yogic scriptures. In this practice, the aspirant contemplates the teachings of the great sages. He challenges himself to determine whether his consciousness is in harmony with his spiritual ancestors. He uses the authentic spiritual writings as a touchstone to gauge his own progress and priorities. A humble aspirant can learn from spiritual writings regardless of the proximity or lifetime of the author. The sincere aspirant can download, in the terminology of computers, the teachings of the sages and receive their wisdom and blessings.

Verses 72–73

kaccidetacchrutaṁ pārtha tvayaikāgreṇa cetasā
kaccidajñānasaṁmohaḥ pranaṣṭaste dhanaṁjaya (72)

arjuna uvāca
naṣṭo mohaḥ smṛtirlabdhā tvatprasādānmayācyuta
sthito 'smi gatasaṁdehaḥ kariṣye vacanaṁ tava (73)

72. Have these teachings been heard deeply by you, O Partha? With one-pointed attention, O Dhananjaya? Has your delusion of ignorance been dispelled?

73. Arjuna said: Vanished is my delusion; remembrance of the Self I have gained through your grace, O Achutya. I stand firm now, with my doubts gone. I will act according to your word.

The teachings have been delivered. The guru has blessed the disciple with every possible expression of love, wisdom, compassion, and grace. Now the guru must step aside, as a parent must step aside and allow the child to grow. The disciple must take up his own torch and proceed forward, lighting up the darkness as he ventures forth.

The guru and disciple, the soul and God, remain in a dualistic loving relationship within the world of form. Beneath the surface, however, in the oceanic depths of the Self, the two are one in the One. Knowing the drama of the One expressing itself as many, the guru and disciple play their respective roles to perfection.

Verses 74–78

saṁjaya uvaca
ityahaṁ vāsudevasya pārthasya ca mahātmanaḥ
saṁvādamimamaśrauṣamadbhutaṁ romaharṣaṇam (74)

vyāsaprasādācchrutavānetadguhyamahaṁ param
yogaṁ yogeśvarātkṛṣṇātsākṣātkathayataḥ svayam (75)

rājanasaṁsmṛtya saṁsmṛtya saṁvādamimamadbhutam
keśavārjunayoḥ puṇyaṁ hṛṣyāmi ca muhurmuhuḥ (76)

tacca saṁsmṛtya saṁsmṛtya rūpamatyadbhutaṁ hareḥ
vismayo me mahānrājanhṛṣyāmi ca punaḥ punaḥ (77)

yatra yogeśvaraḥ kṛṣṇo yatra pārtho dhanurdharaḥ
tatra śrīvijayo bhūtirdhruvā nītirmatirmama (78)

74. Sanjaya said: Thus I have heard this wonderful dialogue between Vasudeva and the great-souled Partha, causing my hairs to stand on end.

75. By the grace of Vyasa, I personally heard this supreme secret of yoga discussed by Sri Krishna himself, Lord of Yoga.

76. O King Dhritarashtra, as I repeatedly recollect this wondrous and meritorious dialogue of Keshava and Arjuna, I repeatedly rejoice.

77. And as I repeatedly recollect that wondrous form of Krishna, I am greatly astonished, O King, and I repeatedly thrill.

78. Where there is Krishna, Lord of Yoga, and Partha, The Archer, there will be prosperity, victory, spiritual power, and stable morality. This I proclaim with faith!

The dialogue is complete; we return to the opening scene where Sanjaya is reporting to blind King Dhritarashtra events unfolding on the battlefield of Kurukshetra. Arjuna's path is finally clear. His future, however, must still unfold. Perhaps we students of the Bhagavad Gita might pause here to consider that, like Arjuna, we are also at the precipice of what life is to bring.

The remainder of our lives lies ahead of us. Whether this be on a battlefield or in an ashram, home, or office, the teachings remain consistent. God and guru are ever with the individual, but the aspirant himself, by himself, must perform his own dharma. This dharma, which has astonished Arjuna and Sanjaya, may well also inspire us. Distilled to its essence, this teaching of Sri Krishna to Arjuna is "Engage!"

Engage in life! Run not from challenges. Fear not change, sorrow, even death. All existence is sacred. Every event, every relationship, every moment is profound and luscious with divine consequence. Participate fully in all that is your life in this cosmic drama. Make the mundane sacred by your sincerity, transmute the ordinary into the holy by your passion, bring to life the fire of love burning in your being.

O aspirant, drink in these teachings of Sri Krishna, and quaff the nectar of immortality. Take the reins of your chariot, and engage with all that comes to you on the path of life. Love the entire world, and participate fully in the divine play of the sacred universe. Your guide is ever with you. Be with him, and proclaim with faith your rightful prize of prosperity, victory, spiritual power, and stable morality.

Appendix 1
Names and Their Symbolism

Name	Meaning, Chapter. Verse	Also Known As, Chapter. Verse	Conch–Meaning, Chapter. Verse
Dhritarashtra	Blind Mind, 1.1	Bharata – From the Land Dedicated to Light, 1.12	
Sanjaya	Objectivity, 1.1		
Kauravas – Foolish Actions			
Ashvatthama	Stubbornness, 1.8		
Bhishma	Fear, 1.8		
Bhurishravas	Negative Patterns, 1.8	Saumadatti – Son of Somadatta, 1.8	
Drona	Habits, 1.2		
Duryodhana	Selfish Desire, 1.2		
Karna	Isolation, 1.8		
Kripa	Giving to Get, 1.8		
Somadatta	Poisonous Nectar, 1.8		
Vikarna	Insincerity, 1.8		
Pandavas – Intelligent Actions			
Abhimanyu	Mental Focus, 1.6	Saubadra – Son of Subhadra, 1.6	
Arjuna	Pure Aspiration, 1.4	Anagha – Innocent One, 3.3 Bharatarshabha – Best of the Bharatas, 3.41 Bharatasattama – Truest of the Bharatas, 18.4 Dehabhritam Vara – Supreme among the Embodied, 8.4 Dhananjaya – Winner of Wealth, 1.15 Gudakesha – Conqueror of Sleep, 1.2	Devadatta – Gift of Gods, 1.15

Bhima	Steady Breath, 1.4
Chekitana	Immortality Remembrance, 1.5
Dhrishtadyumna	Lucid Intuition, 1.3
Dhrishtaketu	Penetrating Insight, 1.5
Drupada	Dispassion, 1.3
Draupadi	Divine Energy, 1.6
Kashiraja	Noble Radiance, 1.5
Krishna	Who is Truth & Bliss, 1.14

Kaunteya – Son of Divine Actions, 1.27
Kiriti – Crowned One, 11.35
Kurunandana – Delight of the Kauravas, 2.41
Kurusattama – Truest of Kauravas, 4.31
Kurushreshtha – Grandest of Kauravas, 10.19
Pandava – Son of Intelligent Actions, 1.14
Parantapa – Slayer of Foes, 2.3
Partha – Son of Excellent Actions, 1.25
Purushavyagrah – Tiger among Beings, 18.4
Savyasacin – Ambidextrous, 11.33
Vikrodara – He of Awesome Deeds, 1.15

Drupadaputrena – Son of Drupada, 1.3

Achutya – Without Lapse, 11.42
Adyam – Primal One, 11.31
Aprameyam – Immeasureable, 11.42
Apratimaprahbava – Incomparable Greatness, 11.43
Arisudana – Slayer of Enemies, 2.4
Bhagavan – The Divine Being, 2.2
Devara – Great God, 11.31
Devesha – Lord of Gods, 11.25
Govinda – Caretaker of the Senses, 1.32
Hari – Remover of Ignorance, 11.9
Hrishikesh – Master of Senses, 1.15

Paundra – Causes Dissolution, 1.15

Panchajanya – Cause of Elements, 1.15

Kuntibhoja	Divine Invocation, 1.5
Nakula	Without Pain, 1.16
Purujit	One-Pointedness, 1.5
Sahadeva	Godlike, 1.16
Satyaki	Truthful Nature, 1.17
Subhadra	Splendor, 1.6
Shaibya	Unselfish Will, 1.5
Shikhanda	Residing at the Peak, 1.17
Uttamaujas	Peak Virility, 1.6
Virata	Illuminating Meditation, 1.4
Yudhamanyu	Conquering the Mind, 1.6
Yudhishthira	Commitment, 1.16
Yuyudhana	Spiritual Practices, 1.4

Idyam Isham – Adorable Lord, 11.44
Jagannivasa – Abode of the Worlds, 11.25
Janardana – The Answer to Prayers, 1.36
Kamalapattraksha – Lotus-Eyed, 11.2
Keshava - With Beautiful Hair, 1.31
Keshisudhana – Slayer of Non-Necessity, 18.1
Madhava – The Sweet One, 1.14
Madhusudhana – Slayer of Excess, 1.35
Mahabaho – Mighty-Armed, 11.23
Mahatma – Great Soul, 11.20
Prabho – Master, 11.3
Purushottama – Supreme Spiritual Being, 8.1
Sahasrabaho – Thousand-Armed One, 11.46
Varshneya – Scion of Power, 1.41
Vasudeva – God Within, 11.50
Vishnu – Preserver of Life, 11.17
Yogeshvara – Lord of Yogis, 11.3

Kuntiputro – Son of Divine Actions, 1.16

Sughosha – Clear Sound, 1.16

Manipushka – Vessel of Jewels, 1.16

Anantavijaya – Infinite Victory, 1.16

Appendix 2
The Gunas (Qualities of Nature)

Subject	Verses	Sattva (Balance)	Rajas (Activation)	Tamas (Inertia)
Activity	18.23-25	necessary	strained	confused
Actor	18.26-28	without egoism	desirous	stubborn
Arising From	14.17	wisdom	greed	infatuation
Austerity	14-19. 17.5-6	pure	unstable	harmful
Bondage	14.6-9	attachment to happiness	attachment to activity	attachment to negligence
Commitment	18.33-35	steadfast	attached	foolish
Dominant Quality	14.10-13	light of wisdom	greed	dullness
Food	17.7-10	nourishing	spicy/bitter	impure
Generosity	17.20-22	without expectation	for return	patronizing
Happiness	18.37-39	insightful	worldly	delusory
Intelligence	18.30-32	integrated	unimplemented	disharmonious
Knowledge	18.20-22	one undivided Being	multiplicity of beings	effects unrelated to causes
Movement	14.18	progression	stationary	digression
Offering	17.11-13	harmonious	for reward	faithless
Rebirth	14.14-15	pure worlds	worlds of selfish activities	among the deluded
Renunciation/Relinquishment	18.7-9	without attachment	when pleasant	inappropriate
Results	14.16	purity	pain	ignorance
Worship	17.4	divinity	power	elementals

The Author

Yogiraj Prem Prakash is an American-born yogi who spent his formative years thinking mostly about sports, girls, and rock 'n' roll! Thanks to the guidance of his gurus, he has bumbled blindly backward into a spiritual life. Neem Karoli Baba placed him on the yoga path, Baba Hari Dass taught him authentic ashtanga yoga, Shree Maa and Swami Satyananda Saraswati instructed him in vedic and tantric systems of worship, Sri Karunamayi blessed him in the path of grace and liberation, and Baba Ramakrishna Das gave him mantra initiation.

Prem Prakash was presented with the 2007 Annual Service Award by the Institute of the Himalayan Tradition and in 2008 was honored by the Institute as Yogiraj, "an accomplished yogi."

He is the author of *The Yoga of Spiritual Devotion, Three Paths of Devotion, Yoga American Style,* and *The Universal Yoga.* His articles have appeared in many yoga magazines, including *Yoga Journal, Light of Consciousness, Mother Jones, Yoga International, Yoga Aktuell* (Germany), and *Himalayan Path.*

He lives at Kailash Ashram in Middlebury, Vermont, with his wife and son. Prem Prakash is co-director of the Green Mountain School of Yoga:

607 Burnham Drive
Middlebury, VT 05753
803-388-3754
www.gmsy.org

YES INTERNATIONAL PUBLISHERS

Award-winning books for personal self-transformation

Prem Prakash
- *Yoga American Style*
- *Universal Yoga: The Bhagavad Gita for Modern Times*
- *Three Paths of Devotion: Goddess, God, Guru*

Justin O'Brien, Ph.D. (Swami Jaidev Bharati)
- *Walking with a Himalayan Master: An American's Odyssey*
- *Superconscious Meditation*
- *A Meeting of Mystic Paths: Christianity and Yoga*
- *The Wellness Tree: Dynamic Six-Step Program for Optimal Wellness*
- *Running and Breathing*
- *Mirrors for Men: A Journal for Reflection*

Linda Johnsen
- *Kirtan: Chanting as a Spiritual Path* (with Maggie Jacobus)
- *The Living Goddess: Reclaiming the Tradition of the Mother of the Universe*
- *Daughters of the Goddess: The Women Saints of India*
- *A Thousand Suns: Designing Your Future with Vedic Astrology*

Swami Veda Bharati
- *The Light of Ten Thousand Suns*
- *Subtler than the Subtle: The Upanishad of the White Horse*

Theresa King
- *The Spiral Path: Explorations into Women's Spirituality*
- *The Divine Mosaic: Women's Images of the Sacred Other*

Phil Nuernberger, Ph.D.
- *The Warrior Sage: Life as Spirit*
- *Strong and Fearless: The Quest for Personal Power*

Charles Bates
- *Pigs Eat Wolves: Going into Partnership with your Dark Side*
- *Ransoming the Mind: Integration of Yoga and Modern Therapy*

Swami Hariharananda Bharati
- *The Laughing Swami: Teachings of Swami Hariharananda*

Christin Lore Weber
- *Circle of Mysteries: The Woman's Rosary Book*
- *Circle of Mysteries CD Set*

Ron Valle and Mary Mohs
Opening to Dying and Grieving: A Sacred Journey

Alla Renee Bozarth
Soulfire: Love Poems in Black and Gold

Gopala Krishna
The Yogi: Portraits of Swami Vishnu-devananda

Cheryl Wall
Mirrors for Women: A Journal for Reflection

Mary Pinney Erickson and Betty Kling
Streams from the Sacred River: Women's Spiritual Wisdom

The Quarterly Journal of the Institute of the Himalyan Tradition
Himalyan Path: Journal of Yoga, Spirituality, and Wellness